Histor Bike

In the Footsteps of Meriwether Lewis and William Clark

Sheila Ruckley

IndePenPress

First published in Great Britain by IndePenPress

All paper used in the printing of this book has been made from wood grown in managed, sustainable forests.

ISBN13: 978-1-78003-329-7

Printed and bound in the UK
Indepenpress Publishing Limited
25 Eastern Place
Brighton
BN2 1GJ

A catalogue record of this book is available from the British Library

Cover design by Jacqueline Abromeit
Illustrations ©2012 June Coveney
Map illustrations ©2012 Sheila Ruckley

This book is dedicated to my grandson, Douglas

Acknowledgements

My thanks must go first to Tom Armstrong of *Historical Trails Cycling* and all those who took part in the 2010 Lewis and Clark Tour of Discovery. They were the most interesting, helpful, optimistic and positive people I have ever come across and they made the trip for me. I am fortunate indeed to have done the journey across America with them. 2010 was a good year to go. The Missouri flooded badly in 2011, with devastation greater than that suffered in the 1993 floods, referred to in this book. Several campsites we used in 2010 were washed out in 2011 and many of the roads we cycled along were rendered impassable by water. I had been frightened enough in the storms we experienced in 2010. I count myself lucky I was many miles away in 2011.

Tom Armstrong's website is www.historicaltrailscycling.com

Secondly, thanks go to Lesley Knox who gave me a kick to finish writing this account of my cycle ride to the Pacific when I was suffering from post-expedition ennui and could not settle down to putting my thoughts in order. Meriwether Lewis, who co-commanded the Corps of Discovery on its journey across the continental United States between 1804 and 1806, suffered similar indecision on his return and it was years before the journals of the expedition were made public. Indeed, as you will find out, Lewis did not live to see them published and, when they were eventually made available in 1814, no one bothered to send a copy to his co-commander, William Clark.

Thirdly, thanks to all those who read a draft of the book and told me what was good and what was bad. Thanks must go especially to Diana Wright, who wielded her pencil to what I hope is good effect.

I should also like to thank Kathleen Norris for permission to quote from her book, *Dakota: A Spiritual Geography* published by Houghton Mifflin Company (ISBN 0-395-71091-X). I found a second-hand copy of this book in a bakery in Lewiston, Idaho. It gave meaning to the landscape I was cycling through and comforted me on the journey west.

June Coveney, whom I met on Papa Westray when I was on a bike trip in the Orkney Islands, has done a marvellous job with the illustrations. Thanks are due to her for capturing the atmosphere of the journey, even though she was not there.

Finally, thank you to Nigel, Dan and Esme for being supportive of my adventures and to my sister, Alison, for looking after my copy of *People in History* so well for all these years.

About the author

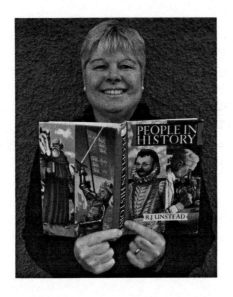

Sheila Ruckley's first love was history. Since retiring from the investment trust industry, she has rekindled this love by exploring the world on her bicycle. She lives in Angus.

Author's note

Although throughout this book the British English spelling variant has been employed, there are some exceptions for which the American English has been retained in the interests of complete accuracy. These include place names and titles (along with their shortened form) e.g. the National Guard Armory and the Armory (not Armoury), and notable events e.g. the Whiskey Rebellion (not Whisky) etc.

Contents

MILEAGE AND ALTITUDE TABLES

St. Charles, Missouri to Nebraska City, Nebraska

Day	Start	Finish	Pop.	Destination altitude (feet)	Miles
		St. Charles		554	
1	St Charles, MO	Hermann, MO	2,689	614	70
2	Herman, MO	Hartsburg, MO	105	561	59
3	Hartsburg, MO	Arrow Rock, MO	76	725	61
4	Arrow Rock State Park, MO	Lexington, MO	4,481	810	61
5	Lexington, MO	Independence, MO	121,180	860	46
6	Independence, MO	Atchison, KS	10,432	866	63
7	Atchison, KS	Falls City, NE	3,933	1004	60
8	Falls City, NE	Nebraska City, NE	6,869	1043	63
9	Day off				483

Nebraska City, Nebraska to Pierre, South Dakota

Day	Start	Finish	Pop.	Destination altitude (feet)	Miles
10	Nebraska City, NE	Fort Calhoun, NE	904	1099	67
11	Fort Calhoun, NE	So. Sioux City, NE	12,213	1102	86
12	So. Sioux City, NE	Yankton, SD	13,866	1247	70
13	Yankton, SD	Lake Andes, SD	760	1467	89
14	Lake Andes, SD	Chamberlain, SD	2,292	1460	86
15	Chamberlain, SD	Pierre, SD	14,072	1696	81
16	Day off				479

Pierre, South Dakota to Williston, North Dakota

Day	Start	Finish	Pop.	Destination altitude (feet)	Miles
17	Pierre, SD	Gettysburg, SD	1,020	2064	74
18	Gettysburg, SD	Mobridge, SD	3,142	1663	62
19	Mobridge, SD	Fort Abraham Lincoln, ND	n/a	1722	96
20	Fort Abraham Lincoln, ND	Stanton, ND	306	1703	72
21	Stanton, ND	Killdeer, ND	681	2247	72
22	Killdeer, ND	Watford City, ND	1,399	2083	65
23	Watford City, ND	Williston, ND	13,014	1890	47*
24	Day off				488

*Too dangerous to cycle. Bikes and cyclists moved in the van

Williston, North Dakota to Great Falls, Montana

Day	Start	Finish	Pop.	Destination altitude (feet)	Miles
25	Williston, ND	Poplar, MT	883	1988	77
26	Poplar, MT	Glasgow, MT	2,870	2116	72
27	Glasgow, MT	Malta, MT	1,816	2257	70
28	Malta, MT	Chinook, MT	1,272	2425	70
29	Chinook, MT	Loma, MT	92	2575	60
30	Loma, MT	Great Falls, MT	59,366	3330	65
31	Day off				414

Great Falls, Montana to Lewiston, Idaho

Day	Start	Finish	Pop.	Destination altitude (feet)	Miles
32	Great Falls, MT	Lincoln, MT	1,100	4760	92
33	Lincoln, MT	Missoula, MT	68,876	3182	79
34	Missoula, MT	Powell Junction, ID	n/a	1916*	58
35	Powell Junction, ID	Kooskia, ID	654	1654	89
36	Kooskia, ID	Lewiston, ID	31,887	745 **	70
37	Day off				388

* At Highway 12
** At confluence of the Snake and Clearwater Rivers

Lewiston, Idaho to Seaside, Oregon

Day	Start	Finish	Pop.	Destination altitude (feet)	Miles
38	Lewiston, ID	Waitsburg, WA	1,262	1266	79
39	Waitsburg, WA	Umatilla, OR	6,302	331	77
40	Umatilla, OR	Rufus, OR	225	213	77
41	Rufus, OR	Viento State Park, OR	n/a	112	60
42	Viento State Park, OR	Portland, OR	566,143	23*	63
43	Portland, OR	Clatskanie, OR	1,621	62	60
44	Clatskanie, OR	Seaside, OR	6,817	7	62
	O the Joy! Seaside, OR.				478
		Total			2730

* At railroad

Altitude information is taken from the United States Geological Survey Geographic Names Information System. For each destination, I have taken the applicable height of the place under the "Civil" category, except where this results in an elevation far different from the location of our campsite (e.g. up a nearby mountain, rather than where we camped) or no such data set exists under that category. In this case, I have taken the available data set. All elevations correspond to those ascertained by a rule of thumb check on Google Earth.

Population statistics are generally taken from the last census information available on the internet (usually the 2000 census). The tables give population at the destination for the day. In the text of this book the population of towns is given in brackets after the name of the town. This is to give the reader an idea of how small many American towns are.

Lewis (right) and Clark (left)

CHAPTER ONE: PEOPLE IN HISTORY

A Sure Cure for All Diseases

Many years ago, I was given a book which was to set the course of my life. It was called *People in History* and it was written by a school master called by R. J. Unstead whose mission was to make history accessible to children. As far as I was concerned, he succeeded. Unstead went on to publish over 40 books, with titles ranging from *Looking at Ancient History* to *Life in a Medieval Village* and from *Life in Aztec Times* to *Queen Anne and Queen Victoria*, but my favourite was *People in History*.[1]

This book now sits on a bookshelf in my sister's house in Sussex. On the front cover, which is made of easy to hold textured board, there is a picture of Sir Walter Raleigh, holding a map and staring into space with a slightly enigmatic look. Perhaps he is thinking of the Orinoco River and his search for El Dorado and untold wealth. He does not yet know that he will meet his end at the hand of James I of England (James VI to the Scots) and that, before he puts his head on the block, he will run his thumb along the edge of the axe and smile as he observes, "It is a sure cure for all diseases".[2]

Next to him, Sir Alexander Fleming, wearing a white coat, sits at his work bench, peering into his microscope, intent on the discovery of penicillin. He has already seen some greenish mould on a shallow glass dish and has remarked "Hm, this is very interesting".[3]

On the left side of the back cover, St Columba, who brought Christianity to Scotland, stands in his brown habit and his leather sandals, clutching his Bible. Looking over his right shoulder is his friend, the old white horse, who laid his head in

Columba's lap, "whinnying sadly"[4] the night before the monk died. Next to Columba, Henry V, resplendent in his armour and his loose coat emblazoned with the "leopards of England and the lilies of France",[5] raises his sword. He is at Agincourt and is about to shout "Today, England shall pay no ransom for me!"[6]

People in History is divided in four parts. Part 1 is 'From Caractacus to Alfred'. When it was published everyone knew who Caractacus was and no one would have said "Alfred who?" Part 2 is 'From William the Conqueror to William Caxton' and part 3 is 'Great Tudors and Stuarts'. The final part is 'Great People of Modern Times'. It begins with Charles Edward Stuart and it ends with Florence Nightingale, Captain Scott, Lawrence of Arabia and, finally, Sir Alexander Fleming himself. Now I find it hard to believe that, in my lifetime, Florence Nightingale was considered part of the modern age, let alone Bonnie Prince Charlie. All in all there are over 40 stories about individuals whose ideals, setbacks and achievements helped to shape British history. The stories are beautifully illustrated, with line drawings by J. C. B. Knight and vivid colour plates by Faith Jaques, who went on to do the first illustrations for Roald Dahl's *Charlie and the Chocolate Factory*. The size of the font used in the book decreases as the reader progresses through each part, perhaps in recognition that reading skills will progress as the book is read.

On the loose endpaper of *People in History* are the words: 'To Sheila, with love from Mummy and Daddy, Christmas 1957'. They are written in my father's hand. Five years later, on the paste endpaper, I wrote my name in capital letters, with a pencil, and added my form number, II26. In 1971, and for the benefit of my sister, not me, my mother wrote this list underneath my name:

Divorced
Beheaded
Died
Divorced
Beheaded
Survived

Next to each word on the list is the name of the wife of Henry VIII whose fate is thus described. The aide-memoire is stated, in pen, to be 'per A. M. Hubbell', the headmistress for whom our mother worked. When Aileen Hubbell retired, she added to her usefulness by presenting to our mother her Merriam Webster Dictionary, with the inscription 'I bequeath to you this valuable property'.

Inside the pages of *People in History*, there is a folded, yellowed page from the *Daily Mail* dated Saturday, January 30th 1971 with the headline, 'Which of Henry's Wives Are You?' It features a photograph of the actresses who played the six wives of Henry VIII in the television series of the same name. It was this series which inspired my sister to memorise how each wife died and have the same recorded courtesy of Aileen Hubbell.

Mother receiving wisdom from Mrs Hubbell

Finally, and also in pencil and in capital letters, the name of my niece appears on the loose endpaper, above the original inscription to me. There is no date next to her name, but it is written in a childish hand, when she was perhaps ten or thereabouts. By this fashion, each one of us has laid claim to this masterpiece which we have treasured.

I have no need to turn the pages of the book to remember its contents. I read it so many times that, even now, I can recall almost every detail of all the stories. Or so I thought. Until I checked, I was certain that Gregory's response, on being told that the fair-haired children in the slave market were Angles from Britain, was "Non angli sed angeli". I was wrong. *People in History* anglicises it to "They look more like angels from Heaven to me".[7] Gregory later became Pope and sent Augustine to Britain, where he landed, foreseeing the high-speed train link, at Ebbsfleet in Kent. For a long time after reading this story, I was worried about being captured and ending up in a market in Rome.

I had also only imagined the illustration of Richard the Lionheart shut up in the castle at Dürnstein by the dastardly Leopold, Duke of Austria. The actual drawing by J.C.B. Knight shows Richard lying on the ground before the castle of Chalus-Charbrol, having been wounded in the left shoulder by an arrow from a crossbow. This might have been avoided had Richard put on his chain mail, but neither the circumstances of the injury nor his forgiveness of the archer just before he died are explained in *People in History*. We are just told that Richard was killed by an arrow when besieging a castle and that "John, the worst of men, became King of England".[8] This description of John has always leapt to my mind whenever I have been introduced to someone of that name.

In Part III (and now in a smaller font), the story that I loved the most was that of the Mayflower, the little ship which set out from Plymouth on 6th September, 1620 for "the new land of America".[9] I was not that keen on the heroine of the chapter, Priscilla Mullins, as the illustration showed a demure young woman at her spinning wheel. I was not interested in that or her courtship with John Alden, who was too shy to ask her to marry him. Instead I liked the fact that one day, while out collecting berries, she had turned round and come face to face with an Indian who had smiled and said, "Welcome! Me Samoset".[10] I wanted to meet that Indian, who is shown, in Faith Jaques' colour illustration, standing with his arms folded, with his bow, a quiver of arrows and golden bands on his ankles.

The best story in Part IV was how James Wolfe captured Quebec. Recently I saw Dan Snow explain this in a television documentary, but he could not create the suspense of the *People in History* account or the heart thumping that occurred when its narrative got to the French sentry's challenge "Que vive?"[11] I still think the line drawing in the book of the British boats going down the St Lawrence River at night by the cliffs below the Plains of Abraham captures the drama more perfectly than any graphic or visual aid on television.

Later, at my grammar school in Sussex, the Tudors and Stuarts were the ones to inspire me, thanks to the teaching of Miss M. Packham. There were only five of us in the class so we had near individual attention. I owe my ability to pass exams solely to Miss Packham's insistence that for the first 45 minutes of a three-hour essay examination, we were not to start writing. Instead we had to plan our answers on a piece of rough paper. Mollie Packham marked essay plans, not essays. Only when she considered our plans to be up to the required standard did she let us loose with prose. In between standing over our desks analysing our plans she took us to places such as Parham Park, where in the Long Gallery of that Elizabethan house, she would stride up and down giving impromptu lectures on Tudor politics.

My favourite book, having moved on from *People in History*, became *Reformation Europe* by G. R. Elton, a historian born as Gottfried Rudolf Ehrenberg in Tübingen, Germany in 1921. His family moved to Prague in 1929 and then fled to Wales in 1939 to escape persecution. Within four years, and despite not having spoken English when he arrived, he graduated with a degree in history from the University of London which he obtained by correspondence course. Elton's writing exhibits the sheer erudition and exuberance of his scholarship. On top of all that, he is a cracking good storyteller. I was gripped as soon as I read that the Reformation "lay under the often brooding presence of Charles V".[12] The Holy Roman Emperor was, according to Elton, proof that "an unprepossessing exterior and absence of a great intellect were no bar to eminence if a reasonable intelligence was allied with a sense of purpose and a dedication to work."[13] Elton did not approve of the trend to make history fit into any ideological stance. He still believed in individuals. His approach, like that in *People in History* became unfashionable. The fact that there is now a G. R. Elton Appreciation Society on Facebook may indicate a revival of interest, but he probably would not be pleased that on the website devoted to him "Appreciation" is spelt "Appriciation".

The Yearning to Escape

I had always wanted to see the places which were part of the narrative of the history books I enjoyed so much. When I was young, though, there was little opportunity to travel. Going abroad was something I never thought I would do. It was unthinkable that it might one day be within my reach. As we would say now, it was not even on my radar. I made up for the lack of ability to travel, which I longed to do, by listening to *Desert Island Discs*. This fed my yearning to escape from these shores. Now I can see that it was a very odd thing for a young child to do. I listened to it intently, taking particular note of the book the castaway wanted on the island along with his or her chosen luxury. Isobel Barnett's (29th October 1956) was a hot water bottle. This was a very sensible choice. I made note of it and have never regretted taking one with me every time I travel. Once, camping in Iceland, I could have sold my hot water bottle for a kingdom to any one of my fellow travellers. In the United States, where such things are unknown, those who have never seen one look on in amazement when one is produced. Those who know what it is make pitiful sounds, suggesting that you might like to leave it behind when you leave. When I was about eight, the realisation dawned that the guests on *Desert Island Discs* did not, in fact, go to a desert island. I was outraged at the deception. Somehow it meant that I too would never escape.

I also cycled, what I thought at the time was all over south east England, but which was actually only perhaps a ten-mile radius from home, looking at whatever I came across in my adventures. In those days it was possible, from the age of eight or nine, to go off on one's bike. No one considered it neglect to allow a child a do that. I did not realise at the time that I would have to wait until I retired to rediscover the same freedom. Only then did I see Passau and Regensburg, two great cities of the Reformation and the castle at Dürnstein on the Danube where Richard the Lionheart had been imprisoned. Only then did I follow the river to Vienna, where Charles V had pushed Suleiman's army back towards Constantinople in 1529. And I cycled all the way there to do so.

After *Reformation Europe*, it was American history that captivated me. I came to it by accident, not design, despite my earlier encounter with the voyage of the Mayflower in the pages of *People in History*, because I had originally decided to study British history at university. However, two terms of British history at the University of East Anglia was enough for me. I jumped at the chance to change to study American history in the exciting American Studies department which had been set up by Malcolm Bradbury, the novelist, now sadly dead. He was generous with his knowledge and accessible with his time, holding once a week, I seem to remember, an open seminar at which anything relevant to American Studies could be discussed. Like most seminars at UEA it often migrated to the bar. Everyone smoked Players Number Six. During my second year at UEA, I went to a party every single night. I did as much as I could to disguise the fact that I was a swot. It was all so much more exciting and fun than the Whigs and the Tories.

The opportunity to spend time in America came up. I was desperate to go. The thought that I would be able to fly across the Atlantic to New York was like a miracle. The first time I went to the United States, I had first to meet a bus at Victoria Bus Station. All the passengers destined for the USA were weighed, along with our luggage. We were then taken to a runway in Essex, which had a hut by it. That was Stansted Airport. We landed in Bangor, Maine, before flying onto New

York. I am sure we landed in a freight terminal, but I did not care. I had seen Manhattan from the air and my heart was thumping.

I was very fortunate to be able to go to Wellesley College, just outside Boston, for a year. Then, and perhaps now, Wellesley had a reputation for being a highly academic college for the female children of the rich and well connected. Most students then were moneyed, upper class and white but many, like me, were on scholarships. One girl on my floor in the dorm mentioned darkly to me that Wellesley had had a quota. I had no idea what she meant. She told me she was Jewish and she meant for people like her. Nowadays, Wellesley is more diversified and ranks in the top four for ethnic diversity among private liberal arts colleges in the USA.[14]

It was said that even the cockroaches at Wellesley wore Gucci. It was certainly a place of great privilege, set in 500-acre grounds with a private lake and a world-class arboretum. The student facilities had the atmosphere of a comfortable country club. Afternoon tea was served. Madame Chiang Kai-shek (or Soong May-ling as she then was) had been a student there and had, it was rumoured, arrived with her own maid and silk sheets. Hilary Rodham, who graduated in 1969, was the first student ever to be chosen to address the staff and student body at Commencement (graduation). She was already marked out for fame and that was before she married Bill Clinton. Madeleine Albright, the first female US Secretary of State was educated there, like me, on a full scholarship. The teaching was superb. There was an honour code. At the library, you were trusted to check out books yourself and return them. Exams were run on the same basis. You were on your honour to write your answers in your own room in the time allotted without looking at your notes. I spent a lot of time shaking my head with disbelief and saying to myself, "This would not work in England".

It seemed to work there. I would rather have died than not live up to the standard expected of a Wellesley girl. But the biggest shock was that Americans worked hard and turned up for classes at 8am, an hour which at UEA would have guaranteed nil attendance. A bell sounded the hour and if the tutor had not turned up to teach by the time it ceased ringing, students could walk out of the class. No one was ever late. It was an ordered, cultivated and civilised environment. I loved it. Wellesley was probably the nearest I will ever get to heaven. I thought the rest of America might be same.

The City upon a Hill

My time at Wellesley gave me the opportunity to see what the people on the Mayflower had started when they arrived in the New World further down the coast at a spot they named Plimouth, spelling it with an 'i'. Ten years later, in 1630, the Puritans of the Massachusetts Bay Company arrived. Eleven ships, known as the Winthrop Fleet, arrived full of people who wanted to escape from the antics of Archbishop Laud. He thought they should buckle down and accept his view of Church of England doctrine. He might have been better throwing in the towel and going to America with them, as he was beheaded fifteen years later. The first Governor of the colony, John Winthrop, was an English lawyer from Groton in Suffolk. He was the first person to document the notion, prevalent even today, that the people of America live in a chosen land and have a specific destiny to fulfil. In a sermon preached on board the *Arbella* on the journey out he said the eyes of the world would be upon them in their new lives. The colony would be a "City upon a Hill". Having experienced life in and around Boston, I could see what he meant. I thought there was probably no better place to be on earth. Of course, Winthrop was an Englishman, and not an American. He did not know that 140 years later British redcoats would shoot dead five of their own citizens in the colony which he had founded and thereby provoke a rebellion. This would turn into a Revolutionary War and result in the citizens of the colonies discarding their British nationality and becoming Americans.[15]

Democracy in America

Two years after arriving at Wellesley, and after a year back at UEA, I found myself at the University of Pennsylvania in Philadelphia. I soon discovered that graduate school in America was a tough, exhausting and sometimes brutalising environment. On arrival, someone took me aside and said, "When you are an undergraduate, people want you to pass. Here, we do everything we can to fail you".

It was true. I spent most of my time in a state of high terror and worked relentlessly. The bucolic surroundings to which I had become accustomed in Norfolk and at Wellesley had been replaced by an inner city campus on the fringes of a very run-down part of town. There was no afternoon tea. I was told you could buy a house down the road for $1 provided you lived in it. Who would want to? It was considered too dangerous to go the library at night, which was a shame as it was open 24 hours a day.

I followed a rigorous study timetable, much of which was devoted to passing the obligatory foreign language exam, which must rank alongside the driving test as one of the most anxiety creating experiences in life. The difference is that if you fail your driving test, you can take it again. If you failed the foreign language exam, you could not be awarded a post-graduate qualification. All you were required to do in the examination was translate some text from De Tocqueville's *Democracy in America*. It had to be completely correct. I had not done French since O level and was frightened. Religiously, I attended the class, commonly known as 'French for Dummies', with frequent petitions to God to look down kindly upon me. At night the French books came out and I swotted with my friend, Sue, who also had to sit the exam. We tested each other until we were bleary eyed with tiredness. My knees buckled with relief when I found out that I had passed. I still can't speak French.

My love affair with American history took a bashing in Philadelphia. I had loved being near Boston where I had soaked up all the history of the Boston Massacre, the Tea Party and the Battle of Bunker Hill. I had been fascinated by the history of immigration to the city, much of which was from Ireland. Massachusetts was Kennedy country. Not everyone liked them. One girl at Wellesley had said to me, only half ironically, "I am so glad my great-granddaddy made his money honourably in slavery and not in liquor like those jumped-up Kennedys". Political correctness was still to come, and not before time.

I pondered over the fate of Sacco and Vanzetti, two Italian immigrants. They were anarchists who the police thought had committed murder in Braintree while carrying out robberies. Naturally, it was said, the purpose of the robberies was to finance their radical activities. They were tried, twice, in the court house in Dedham. The names of both these places in Massachusetts reflect, of course, its origin as an overseas East Anglian settlement, as do many of the other towns in that State. Boston is in Suffolk County.

The names of the defendants still touch a raw nerve in Massachusetts. The judge, William Thayer, was not exactly impartial, referring to Sacco and Vanzetti outside the court as "anarchist bastards". Sacco and Vanzetti were found guilty and all appeals failed. It is clear they were entirely innocent. After their execution in the electric chair, Thayer's house was bombed and he had to live in his club in Boston, for the rest of his life, with personal bodyguards.[16]

It was all a bit different in Philadelphia. There I was a short bus journey away from the site of some of the most momentous happenings in the history of the world, namely those that took place in the United States Continental Congress when the theories of American democracy were first enunciated, and I could hardly take time out to explore the city where it took place. I was, indeed, at an institution founded in 1749 by one of the Founding Fathers of the United States, Benjamin Franklin, and I could not enjoy his achievements. I could not even get excited about William Penn, born in London in 1644, who had founded the colony (hence Pennsylvania) and I was sick of being enclosed in a room, wading through records of the early Quakers in Philadelphia.[17] I did not have a car and it was too difficult to find time to visit Valley Forge, the camp of the American

Continental Army or Gettysburg, where the Confederate Army under Robert E. Lee had been defeated in 1863.

It was, of course, always possible to find time to sit in Cy's Penn Luncheonette. A crowd of us used to gather there to calm our minds playing pinball before suffering the sarcasm of one particularly unpleasant professor. Cy (Sam Braverman) was a Philadelphia institution and his bar a solace for the soul. Where Cy's once stood, there is now a Starbucks coffee shop, proof indeed that things seldom get better. I realised that I was not cut out to do historical research. I could study and pass exams, but the academic life was not for me. Eventually, I found the last refuge of the arts' graduate and became a lawyer.

CHAPTER TWO: MERIWETHER LEWIS AND WILLIAM CLARK

The Journals

Before I left Philadelphia, I went down to Baltimore in Maryland to visit an English friend from UEA who was studying at Johns Hopkins. It had amused me no end to hear that someone had come up to her in the library and had said, "Are you really English or just some snob from Wellesley?"

Out of the blue, she presented me with a gift. It was of such generosity that I am still taken aback. She gave me the two, beautifully bound volumes which I have next to me now as I write:

> *The Journals of the Expedition under the Command of Capts. Lewis and Clark to the sources of the Missouri, thence across the Rocky Mountains and down the river Columbia to the Pacific Ocean, performed during the years 1804-5-6 by Order of the Government of the United States.*[18]

My enthusiasm might have been dulled by the minutiae of research in Philadelphia, but my eyes were now opened again to the joy of that great story which is America. I was to discover in these journals two individuals who would inspire me as much as anyone I had read about in *People in History*. They were Meriwether Lewis and William Clark, two army officers who were commissioned by President Thomas Jefferson to find a navigable route across America to the Pacific. As I looked through the journals of the expedition and at the colour plates showing, for example, an Iowa Warrior, an Osage Chief, the Interior of a Mandan Hut and a Buffalo Dance, I thought of Faith Jaques' colour plates in my childhood book. I examined the line drawings by Lewis and Clark of the birds and boats, and the fish and plants they had seen on the expedition. I studied the sketch maps they had drawn. They brought to mind the illustrations of J. C. B. Knight. I determined to see the country that Lewis and Clark had explored when they left St. Louis in 1804. I would have to wait many years to do it.

A Big Country

As anyone who has been to the United States soon realises, it is an immense country, more than twice the size of the whole European Union. Today, including Alaska and Hawaii, it is either the third or fourth largest country in the world, depending on what waters are included, how the USA calculates its own area and who owns other areas in the world, for example those that are disputed between China and India. The United Kingdom, which is roughly the size of the State of Oregon, comes in at 79th place in the world land mass stakes, between Guinea and Uganda. Give or take a few hundred thousand square miles, the United States is over 3.7 million square miles. Its border with Canada is 5,526 miles long, that with Mexico 2,067 miles and it has over 12,000 miles of coastline. Excluding Alaska and Hawaii, which have their own time zones, the continental United States has four time zones, Eastern Standard Time, Central Standard Time, Mountain Standard Time and Pacific Standard Time. On the east coast you are five hours behind Greenwich Mean Time and standing on the beach at the Pacific you are eight hours behind.

The United States was not always as large as it is today. In 1800, just before Jefferson became President and only a few years after the end of the Revolutionary War (more commonly referred to in the UK as the American War of Independence; that term being perhaps less painful to the defeated side) there were already 16 states. These consisted of the original 13 British colonies along the Atlantic coastline being, in the order that they ratified the US Constitution: Delaware, Pennsylvania, New Jersey, Georgia, Connecticut, Massachusetts, Maryland, South Carolina, New Hampshire, Virginia, New York, North Carolina and Rhode Island.

In addition there was Vermont, an area which had been claimed both by the states of New York and New Hampshire and then admitted as a state in its own right in 1791. Vermont was landlocked, with British North America (present day Canada) at its northern border. Next there was Kentucky, which became a state in 1792 and had, originally, been part of Virginia. Kentucky was similarly landlocked and was east of the Appalachian Mountains, the first large range of mountains you find as you travel west across the continent from the Atlantic. These mountains extend 1,500 miles or so from the south to the north at the western edge of the coastal plain and run parallel to the coastline. And finally, there was Tennessee, admitted in 1796, also east of the mountains and south of Kentucky. It had previously been part of the Southwest Territory. That is, it had been under the jurisdiction of the federal government and considered an area which might, one day, become a state (such as Puerto Rico today).

Under the United States Constitution, once a territory becomes a state, the main power source should be the state government. The states (i.e. the people) hold all the powers not delegated to the United States by the Constitution nor prohibited by it. That is one of the reasons Americans get so het up about big government. The encroachment of centralised power emanating from Washington is seen by many to be unconstitutional. The federal government only has the powers expressly granted to it by the Constitution, namely to collect taxes, govern interstate commerce and coin money, regulate currency, set weights and measures, declare war, and raise and maintain an army and navy.

The federal government also has the implied power to do anything deemed necessary and proper in the exercise of its express powers. Therein lies the rub. Many say that Washington relies on this catch-all to infringe on the powers of the states and the liberty of the individual. For example, what gives Congress the power to legislate in favour of Obama's health care reforms and require Americans to have health insurance? ("The interstate commerce clause" say the federal lawyers. "Rubbish!" say the opponents). The health care row in America is not about health. It is about the Constitution.

Some powers are shared or concurrent so that, for example, both the states and the federal government can levy taxes. Accordingly, becoming a state is a momentous event. It signifies that the area has grown up and can effectively govern itself, save in those areas in which the federal government has powers under the Constitution.

Back to the United States in 1800: Vermont, Kentucky and Tennessee were the 14th, 15th and 16th states. There were also three territories of the United States making up the gap between the 16 states and the Mississippi River which was further west still from the Appalachian Mountains. These territories extended from just above what we now call the Gulf of Mexico as far north as the Great Lakes and the border with British North America. The first territory was the Northwest Territory, part of which would become Ohio, state number 17, in 1803. The second was the Indiana Territory which would, together with the rump of the Northwest Territory, become the state of Indiana, the 19th state, in 1816. The third territory was the Mississippi Territory which became the 20th state in 1817. What became the 18th state, we shall discover soon. Significantly, the Mississippi Territory did not extend south to the waters of the Gulf of Mexico.

The area to the south of it was controlled by Spain and was known as West Florida. Spain also owned what is now modern Florida, then referred to as East Florida.

Finally, to complete the map of the United States in 1800, there was an area of land north of the Mississippi Territory over which Georgia and the United States argued. Georgia gave up its claim in 1804 and the area became part of the Mississippi Territory and thus part of the 20th state.

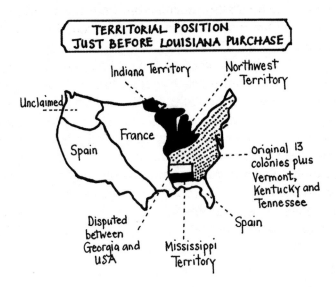

TERRITORIAL POSITION
JUST BEFORE LOUISIANA PURCHASE

Indiana Territory

Northwest Territory

Unclaimed

Spain

France

Original 13 colonies plus Vermont, Kentucky and Tennessee

Disputed between Georgia and USA

Mississippi Territory

Spain

Beyond and to the west of the United States and its territories (which stopped right in the middle of the continent at the Mississippi River) there was a vast area of land known as Louisiana. It was settled and controlled by the Spanish, who had obtained it from the French in 1763. Spain also owned an equally large area to the west of Louisiana including what is modern-day Texas, California, Arizona and Nevada. North of the Spanish possessions, and also bordering the Pacific, was an area including present day Oregon and Washington which was, as yet, unclaimed. The Russians occupied what is modern-day Alaska.[19]

That all these areas were occupied by Native American tribes did not cut any ice when it came to the scramble for land.

Jefferson Attains Office

In 1801, Thomas Jefferson, a Virginian born into a plantation family in 1743, became the third President of the United States and then only by the skin of his teeth. He had tied for the Presidency with Aaron Burr in the Electoral College, the body which still officially decides the outcome of presidential elections. Under the rules, the vote then went to the House of Representatives where, no doubt exhausted by a failure to come to a conclusion after 35 ballots, the members decided to heed the advice of Alexander Hamilton, who had been the first US Secretary to the Treasury. He did not like Burr. In fact, he detested him. Hamilton persuaded the Representatives to choose Jefferson on the 36th ballot, even though the two men had very different views on the future of the new country, Jefferson being someone who might today belong to the Green Party and Hamilton a big state centralist. As convention had it then, Jefferson became President and Burr Vice-President, a simple form of deciding office which might well be emulated successfully in modern times and save a lot of horse trading for office. [20]

Thomas Jefferson

It is probably unthinkable to suggest that Hamilton's motive had anything to do with the fact that he had been embroiled in a rather nasty little sex scandal involving a Maria Reynolds. Hamilton had paid to her husband, albeit unwillingly, what might be described as a retainer in exchange for the privilege of sleeping with his wife. Not content with blackmail, the husband, James Reynolds, tried to implicate Hamilton in a financial scandal. He did not realise that Hamilton, foreseeing the modern trend to come clean in the press by pre-emptive strike, would tell all in a pamphlet written in his own hand. In this, he suitably and predictably made clear that he was very sorry for what we would now call lapses of judgement. Meanwhile, Maria had taken James to the divorce court, employing, as her attorney, Aaron Burr. [21]

Alexander Hamilton

There was to be no happy ending. Hamilton, somewhat obsessive about Burr – to be fair, on account of Burr's political principles as well as his connections with Maria – could not keep his mouth shut. Perhaps having had too much to drink, he more than hinted, at a public dinner, that he had a lot up his sleeve about Burr which he might reveal at a later date.

This was a step too far for Burr who called upon Hamilton to recant and when he did not, challenged him to a duel. Following the family tradition of losing in a duel, his own son having died in such fashion, Hamilton was mortally wounded in the duel with Burr and died on 12th July 1804.[22] It was a sad end to the man who was responsible for the world's first modern financial system and whose portrait now appears on the back of the current US $10 bill. He is the only person featured on United States paper currency not to have been born in the US, hailing as he did from Nevis in the West Indies, and only one of two such persons featured not to have attained office as President (Benjamin Franklin, who appears on the $100 bill, being the other one).[23]

Aaron Burr

The Louisiana Purchase

As we have discovered, the United States did not have the continent to itself when Jefferson became President. Its immediate neighbour west of the Mississippi was a European power. On the face of it, this was Spain, who had obtained the whole of Louisiana from France in 1763. In October 1800, however, Spain and France came to a secret agreement whereby Spain agreed to transfer the land back to France.

The circumstances under which they came to this agreement at the Third Treaty of Ildefonso are too complex to explain here but, suffice it to say, they were all to do with the Pyrenees, and wars against Britain by France and Spain. During one of these, Britain lost Menorca to Spain, an event which makes one wonder what the island would be like today for a holiday had it remained British. The terms of the treaty included provision for Spanish citizens in Louisiana to keep their properties, the right of the clergy to remain unmolested, the transfer of six battleships to France and a pledge by France to honour Spain's right of pre-emption over Louisiana should the French decide to get rid of it for the second time. In addition the French gave the Spanish a kingdom in Italy, the Kingdom of Etruria, which only lasted until 1807. So all of Louisiana reverted to France, even though the inhabitants were Spanish speaking and Spanish troops were garrisoned there.

In the way of relationships between great powers, no sooner had the ink dried on the paper which had solemnised this transaction, than Napoleon agreed to sell Louisiana to the United States, reneging on his promise to the Spanish to give them first refusal on the land. Given that Louisiana comprised 828,000 square miles of territory and extended north from the Gulf of Mexico to present day Canada, and west from the Mississippi to the Rockies, this was a pretty shoddy thing to do to the Spanish. It did, however, result in an excellent deal for the Americans, as Jefferson was only asked to pay $15 million for Louisiana. A down-payment was made in gold, with the balance agreed to be paid in United States bonds. An English banker called Alexander Baring travelled to the United States to collect these personally. Napoleon, desperate for cash, discounted some of the bonds with Barings, receiving 87.5% of their face value. In this way, Barings financed the war by the French against the British. It was not the last time that Barings would be in the news. A severe financial recession, which came to be known as the Baring Crisis, or the Panic of 1890, was caused when Barings made some injudicious investments in South America and had to be rescued from bankruptcy; so, too, many of us remember when it went bust in 1995 as a result of the activities of infamous trader Nick Leeson.

The Louisiana Purchase was such an enormous land deal that the area obtained would eventually become: Arkansas, Missouri, Iowa, Oklahoma, Kansas and Nebraska, portions of modern-day Colorado, Wyoming, Montana, Texas, New Mexico, South Dakota, North Dakota and Minnesota, and even part of modern Canada. All this was purchased for less than 3 cents an acre. Part of this area was admitted to the United States as the 18th state, Louisiana, in 1812.[24]

Control of the Continent

What prompted Napoleon to get rid of Louisiana and why on earth did he sell it to the United States? Why did Jefferson want it? The answer to this last question lies in who was ultimately going to call the shots on the North American continent.

If you remember, in 1800, Spain owned West and East Florida, so, prior to the secret deal with France to transfer ownership of Louisiana, Spain had actual control of the whole of the lower Mississippi River down to the Gulf of Mexico. Spain thus controlled the Port of Orleans, near the mouth of the Mississippi, and accordingly the destiny of the continent.

The easiest way for the American settlers west of the Appalachians (i.e. those in Indiana Territory, Kentucky and Tennessee) to get their goods to market was to put them on barges and float them down the Ohio and Mississippi Rivers to New Orleans. This avoided the immense difficulties of getting cargo upstream and hauling it east over the mountains. Then, at New Orleans, the goods would be put onto ocean-going vessels to the Gulf of Mexico and shipped out.

This ability to ship goods out was crucial to the development of the territories west of the Appalachians, as without access to an ocean port, development could not progress effectively.

All worked well while New Orleans remained in Spanish hands, even though the United States had to tread carefully with Spain to ensure it could get its goods out of the country. It successfully negotiated an agreement whereby the Spanish would permit the Americans the right of deposit in New Orleans. In this way, goods sent down the river could be warehoused, without payment of duty, until they could be loaded onto bigger vessels for export.

But Thomas Jefferson reacted with alarm when he discovered that the Spanish had agreed to transfer Louisiana back to France. Spain was a relatively exhausted empire and had posed little threat to the United States, but France was a different kettle of fish – or rather bowl of sugar, as the French had designs on creating an empire from the Caribbean sugar trade and serving it with produce from Louisiana.

Jefferson's alarm intensified when the right of deposit was revoked in New Orleans in 1802 by the Spanish administration which was still in place. This constituted a direct threat to the United States. Jefferson decided he had to stand up to the French who were obviously behind this dastardly act. He sent a delegate to Paris to negotiate the purchase of New Orleans and the right of free navigation of the Mississippi. To everyone's astonishment Napoleon agreed to the sale of New Orleans, and threw in the rest of Louisiana along the way.

Why did Napoleon do this? Was he mad? Not really. He was trying to manage his risk. He got nervous when Jefferson let it be known that the United States would ally with the British in North America against the French if Napoleon got out of line. The last thing Napoleon wanted was the Americans chumming up with their former masters on the American continent. He had enough on his hands dealing with the British in Europe.

Secondly, Napoleon was piqued because the Spanish had decided not to play ball with his ambitions and had refused to sell Florida to France. This was instrumental in thwarting Napoleon's aspirations for an empire in the south of the continent and in the Caribbean. If he could not get his hands on Florida, did he really need Louisiana?

Thirdly, the French realised that, occupied as they were in fighting wars on the European continent, they simply did not have the infrastructure, or the manpower, to cope with Louisiana as well. They rationalised that if the Americans took control over this vast tract of land, it would alarm the British, who, despite having lost the Revolutionary War, still had designs elsewhere on the continent, in British North America and on the Pacific Coast.

Finally, a sale of Louisiana would ensure that Napoleon had some cash to pay for the costs of continued war against the British in Europe.

So the deal was done and Louisiana became a territory of the United States of America. The deal instantly doubled the size of the nation, and ensured free passage along the Mississippi. It was a triumph for Jefferson, even though some curmudgeonly old politicians sniffed and thought it a waste of time. They moaned that anything west of the Mississippi was a useless desert, forgetting perhaps that the land was peopled by Indians, who would scarcely have agreed with this assessment. Beneath their vocal complaints was the fear that the vested interests of the east might be threatened by people moving west. God forbid that these people might create new states and show some independence of thought and mind against the original states. Despite the reservations, Jefferson got his way and the United States Senate ratified the purchase.[25]

And as to the French? Well, within a year or so of the Louisiana Purchase, Nelson had defeated them at the Battle of Trafalgar.

Expansion West

The Louisiana Purchase also achieved something close to Thomas Jefferson's heart. It allowed the new republic room for expansion and provided territory that would take it nearer to the Pacific Ocean. Jefferson had long envisioned that the United States would be a nation from sea to sea. The deal brought his dream closer.

For many years, the Spanish, British, Russians and Americans had all been exploring the Pacific coast of the continent by sail. The Spanish had established a naval base in Mexico and used it to explore northwards. The Russians had established fur trading posts in Alaska. A Scot, Alexander Mackenzie, had reached the Pacific at Bella Coola in modern British Columbia in July 1793, travelling overland across Canada. He had scratched his name on a rock to prove it, and also produced a map, of which Jefferson was to receive a copy in 1802.

James Cook and George Vancouver had sailed up the Pacific coast exploring that area for the British. In common with an American sea captain, Robert Gray, they had looked for a substantial river which would empty into the Pacific Ocean, as this would offer a gateway to the North American continent from the west. Gray had noticed some sandbars at latitude 47° 17' north but had not been able to cross them as the currents were too strong. He had a suspicion that they might mark the mouth of a great river but was scoffed at by Vancouver, whose ship he had come across. Vancouver tried to convince Gray that no great river could exist at that latitude.

Fortunately for his reputation in history, in May 1792, Gray tried again. He crossed the sandbars and, indeed, found his great river. For nine days he explored upriver, taking longitudinal measurements. He named the river, Columbia, after his ship, the *Columbia Rediviva* ('Columbus Revived').[26]

Jefferson knew that the Columbia was an essential artery for the health of America's prospects as a nation. He had to find a way to get to it from the populated states and territories of the east.

The first expeditions to get to the Pacific had come to nothing. They were plagued by confusion as to whether the best way to find the route to the Pacific was to go via Siberia, an attempt which ended with Catherine the Great deporting the enthusiastic explorer to Poland; the treachery of another expedition leader who turned out to be a spy for the French; and the incompetence of yet another whose resolve failed him before he had even crossed the Mississippi. Helpfully though, he left words of wisdom for his successors. These included the observation that it is easier to plan than to execute and the suggestion that being equipped with a tent might not be a bad idea. Jefferson knew that the new nation needed to up its game. He took it upon himself to hand pick someone with the skill and tenacity to get to the Pacific and back and whom he could trust implicitly.

The man he chose was Meriwether Lewis.

Meriwether Lewis Joins Jefferson

Meriwether Lewis was only 27 when Thomas Jefferson invited him to the White House to be his private secretary and then commissioned him to organise and lead an expedition to the Pacific. Jefferson played safe. He knew Lewis' family, and its estate, Locust Hill, neighboured Jefferson's own in Virginia. Lewis was the archetypal all-American boy. He could shoot, hunt, trap, fight Indians, find his way around in the wilderness and stay out all night in the snow on his own, barefoot. This was all before he was 10. By his teens he knew how to run an estate. He came from good stock honed on the frontier, was committed to the land, patriotic and brave. He was just the kind of person you could rely on.

By the time he joined Jefferson, Meriwether Lewis had lost both his father, William Lewis, and the man his mother then married, John Marks. William Lewis died from chills a few days after coming off his horse while crossing an icy stream. Lewis was only five. When his mother remarried six months later, the family decamped to Georgia to the Marks' estates, but Lewis returned to Virginia when he was 13 to go to school. John Marks died when Lewis was 18 and Lewis went back to Locust Hill with his widowed mother. Lucy Meriwether Lewis Marks was a formidable and talented woman. Amongst her many accomplishments was smoking her own hams for dispatch to the White House while her son was in residence.

Thomas Jefferson needed one of his own kind to help him and Meriwether Lewis was just the kind of self-reliant self-starter he was looking for. As a widower with no sons, Jefferson was also happy to have the company of a personable young man who was inquisitive and intelligent. He gave Lewis bed and board in the White House. There Lewis slept in the dank bedroom in the east wing of that uncomfortable building, where Abigail Adams had hung her washing. Lewis got on well with Thomas Jefferson. He took most of his meals with him and was at his table when Jefferson entertained the important people of his time.[27]

And what a table it was! Jefferson was one of the most charismatic, cultured, well-travelled and erudite men of his age. He was definitely someone who would have featured in an American *People in History*. Born in Virginia and educated there, he had lived in France whilst negotiating the future of his country after the Revolutionary War. The civilising aspects of his time there had had an effect on his receptive mind. In common with many of his gender and class, he had been absorbed as a child by the computer games of his day, namely primers, which had instructed him in Latin, Greek and French. A fun time for Jefferson at the College of William and Mary in Williamsburg, which he entered when he was 16, was to read the works of the British Empiricist philosophers such as John Locke. He did this under the instruction of Professor William Small, a Scotsman born in Carmyllie in Angus, just down the road from where I am now writing this account, and who, Jefferson said, probably fixed the destinies of his life.[28]

However, Jefferson was not just industrious at his books. His energies also translated into architecture, including the building of his beloved house, Monticello, for which he cleared and levelled a mountaintop before beginning construction in 1769. He had a huge vegetable garden at Monticello and, probably uncommonly for his time, explained that his diet consisted primarily of vegetables. He was very keen on manure and its benefits to the soil. No wonder people flocked to his table. He was the first (and perhaps the last) 'foodie' President, employing a French chef, and keeping his own records of when fresh vegetables appeared in the markets. He published his own book on the kitchen garden in the odd moments he had away from his vineyards, whose produce complemented his love of good food.[29] Not that Jefferson was parochial in his tastes; he was a lover of European wines and brought them over by the shipload, preferring to deal directly with the owners of the vineyards rather than their middlemen.

The author of a recent book on Jefferson and wine, John Hailman, points out that Jefferson was one of the most knowledgeable wine amateurs of his age, even going to the lengths of trying to establish cork-oak orchards at Monticello to provide a solution to the problems of bottling wine. However, Jefferson dismissed sparkling champagne, which had only recently been introduced, as a passing fad.[30] Above all, Jefferson was the kind of person who lit up a room and for engaging company he was without peer. His White House was a Camelot long before that of the Kennedy era, a fact recognised by Jack Kennedy himself when, having assembled every living American Nobel laureate in the White House for a dinner in April 1962, he opened his remarks to them by saying:

> *I think this is the most extraordinary collection of talent, of human knowledge, that has ever been gathered together at the White House – with the possible exception of when Thomas Jefferson dined alone.[31]*

Preparations for the Expedition

Lewis was rather more organised in his planning for the expedition than those who had preceded him in the challenge, no doubt in part because he spent many an evening talking with Jefferson and poring over the President's map collection, which was the most comprehensive in the United States. One of these was the Mackenzie map. It was instrumental in Lewis setting off under the misapprehension that crossing the Continental Divide and reaching the Pacific would be easy. After all, if Mackenzie's map showed that he crossed the mountains through an easy pass, with a portage of only 700 yards to the other side, (i.e. where the boats had to be carried overland), what reason was there to assume that it would be any different further south? Lewis was to be severely disappointed on finding his own crossing far more arduous than Mackenzie's.

Meriwether Lewis

Lewis' natural organisational skills, mastered on the family estates in Virginia and Georgia, were enhanced by lessons in such subjects as botany, geography and surveying, all of which would be useful on an expedition. How to look after the men in the event of illness or accident was also included, thanks to the efforts of Dr Benjamin Rush of Philadelphia, one of the founding fathers of the new republic, who had studied medicine at the University of Edinburgh. Dr Rush not only taught Lewis what he thought he might need on the expedition but also furnished him with a supply of his eponymous 'Bilious Pills'. These pills, referred to on the expedition as 'Thunderclappers', a description that needs no further explanation, were to be well used. The members of the expedition, collectively known as the Corps of Discovery, would self-administer them liberally, with predictable results. Along with the Thunderclappers, Lewis assembled a range of equipment consistent with Dr Rush's view that illness was due to excesses which needed to be purged. This included tools for poking and extracting, binding, cutting and draining, as well as some items which would not be out of place in a modern health-food shop; cloves, nutmeg, camphor and ipecacuanha. All this was packed in a medicine chest which, given the contents, many members of the expedition no doubt hoped would not be opened for them.

Lewis' Companion and Soul Mate

Having been entrusted with the task of leading an expedition to the Pacific, Lewis was astute enough to realise that the journey might be a lonely one for its leader. He knew he would benefit from the company of an individual whom he trusted completely. He chose a man called William Clark, who had retired from the US Army in 1796, perhaps after a bout of malaria, and had gone back to his estate, Mulberry Hill, near Louisville in Kentucky, to recover. The call from Meriwether Lewis may have been a welcome relief to Clark. Back at Mulberry Hill, he was trying to deal with a mess caused by his older brother who had left the army after being accused of being drunk on duty. The feckless sibling had left a trail of debt in his wake. Clark sold the farm at Mulberry Hill to his younger brother and agreed to join Meriwether Lewis. The expedition to the Pacific was to be a military one and Clark re-enlisted, accepting co-command of the expedition.

The men had met in the Army. Lewis had obtained a taste for military life when, in 1794, he had joined a militia organised by President George Washington to suppress an uprising on the frontier against the Federal Government. This came to be known as the Whiskey Rebellion. As the name suggests, it was a protest against a tax on whiskey which had been imposed by our unsuccessful dueller, Alexander Hamilton, when he was Treasury Secretary. It is not hard to imagine the reaction of the enterprising folk on the frontier to this bright idea of Hamilton's. Some of them were paid in whiskey and many of them turned their hard-earned crops into the liquor, which was easier to move east over the mountains to market than grain. Their opinion of Hamilton was not helped by the fact that Hamilton also had the audacity to refer to the water of life as a luxury. This whiskey tax, which came into force in March 1791, was the first duty ever levied on a product produced in the USA. Crucially, those in favour of it conveniently forgot that the principle of no taxation without representation should apply as much to the backwoodsmen as it had to the Bostonians who had chucked tea into the harbour of their city. The lands which the rebels occupied west of the Appalachian Mountains were the non-voting territories. The people who lived there had no say in presidential elections or in what taxes they should pay. It was no wonder they felt aggrieved.

William Clark

Nonetheless, things escalated, as they usually do; intimidation of excise men took place, the tax went uncollected, calls to arms were made and answered, people were arrested, bystanders were shot and everyone got on their high horse. The matter came down to a simple question: "Hey! Who is in charge here? Is it the federal government or a bunch of rebels?"

Lewis's home was on the other side of the mountains from the rebels, and he helped to ensure that the answer was the government. Things dragged on. Nothing was achieved. And after all this fuss and a good deal of needless bloodshed, Jefferson repealed the whiskey tax when he became President.[32]

Meriwether Lewis had enjoyed the militia life during the Whiskey Rebellion and decided to join a volunteer army which led him to service under one of the most famous generals in United States history, General "Mad" Anthony Wayne. This colourful figure, who suffered from gout, had distinguished himself in the Revolutionary War, and had earned the name "Mad" after refusing to come to the assistance of a patriotic soul who spied for him against the British. The spy, "Jemmy the Rover" had been imprisoned for disorderly conduct and naively thought that Wayne would get him out of jail. Wayne refused and urged his captors to give him 29 lashes. This, according to Jemmy, was madness. The name stuck.[33]

Lewis would have stayed with Mad Anthony had he not blotted his copybook by having a spat with a fellow officer. Mad Anthony did the decent thing by transferring Lewis, out of sight and further trouble, to the Chosen Rifle Company, an elite bunch of sharp shooters. There he was under the command of William Clark. No doubt Lewis was grateful to Mad Anthony for getting him out of a hole of his own making. As for Mad Anthony himself, he was the inspiration, many years later, for a would-be film star's change of name. Marion Morrison changed his name to John Wayne, after the general, at the instigation of his director at the Fox Film Corporation, Raoul Walsh.

Meanwhile, Lewis never forgot his commanding officer in the Chosen Rifle Company and it was Clark who came to mind when he and Jefferson were planning the expedition to the Pacific.

The Great Wilderness

From Gray's observations of the Columbia River and their own knowledge of the country between the Atlantic and the Mississippi, Lewis and Clark were certain, before they set off for the Pacific, that the continent was about 3,000 miles wide. From the fur traders who had gone west and north up the Missouri River, Lewis and Clark understood the Missouri extended up to and beyond the Mandan Indian Villages, near present day Bismarck, North Dakota. Further west than that was a bit of a mystery, but they did know that the land was peopled by Indian tribes and that a mountain range had to be crossed before they would find the Columbia River. In short, Jefferson had purchased Louisiana without knowing what the terrain was like and what the expedition members would encounter as they crossed it. That did not stop him from having an opinion as to what Lewis and Clark might find.

In common with others of his day, Jefferson referred to the land Lewis and Clark would cross as a great wilderness. Jefferson surmised they might find mammoths there and no doubt looked forward to hearing an account of them when the expedition returned. His directions to Lewis included the requirement to make and record, with "great pains and accuracy"[34] observations about the geography and terrain, the minerals, the flora and fauna and the indigenous people whom they were to treat with respect, provided it was reciprocated. Armed with this knowledge and relevant specimens, they were to return by whatever means expedient. This gave them the option to get passage on one of the ships going up and down the Oregon coast and return by way of Cape Horn.

In the event, Lewis and Clark returned by land, having overwintered on the Pacific coast at Fort Clatsop, a rudimentary fort which they built near present-day Astoria and named after the most agreeable of the local Indian tribes. They reached St. Louis on 23rd September, 1806 to a warm welcome. By then they had been away for nearly 29 months and everyone had given them up for dead, supposing that they had been killed by Indians.

As for a navigable route – even though they got to the Pacific and back – it simply did not exist, as the journey undertaken by the Corps of Discovery, with all its many difficulties, was to prove.

CHAPTER THREE: THE LEWIS AND CLARK TRAIL

The Modern Trail

For periods during the two hundred years or so after Lewis and Clark and the Corps of Discovery returned from the Pacific, the expedition was largely forgotten by the American public or dismissed as not having achieved much.

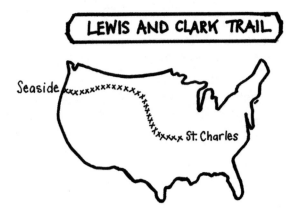

Its significance was underestimated and the wealth of information in the journals kept by Lewis and Clark was unappreciated.[35] In a sense it was like the indifference to space exploration which manifested soon after Neil Armstrong went to the moon. When anyone could get to the Pacific, especially after the completion of the transcontinental railroad, what was the big deal about Lewis and Clark? Some, however, kept the flame alight.

In 1978, the federal government established a series of National Historic Trails across America, one of which is the Lewis and Clark Trail. Lewis and Clark travelled by boat up the Missouri, by horse and foot across the mountains, and by canoe down the Columbia River. The modern trail follows their route as closely as possible but uses the highways and, in some places, smaller roads. It is designed for the traveller in a car.

In 1996, Stephen Ambrose's book about the expedition, *Undaunted Courage,* was published. It is a gripping account of the expedition and must be the first next stop for anyone whose appetite for Lewis and Clark is whetted by this account of my journey along the trail. In 1997, Ken Burns, the American film producer, made a film about Lewis and Clark. In 2002, National Geographic followed suit with *Lewis and Clark: Great Journey West.* 2003 was the bicentennial of Jefferson's commission to Meriwether Lewis to find a route to the Pacific. All these things marked a resurgence of interest in the Lewis and Clark expedition.

Today there are countless books and websites devoted to Lewis and Clark. In fact, there is so much information available on the expedition, it is impossible to take it all in. Many people follow the trail in their cars or mobile homes ('RVs') each year. A few people cycle it, mostly in groups, as it is an arduous ride

From St. Louis to the North Dakota/Montana border

and extremely difficult without support; even so, people do sometimes cycle it alone.

A few years before I retired, I came across information on the internet about bicycle tours which follow historical trails in America. I kept a watch on this website for several years until, to my surprise, I saw that there was a tour scheduled for 2010 which would follow the Lewis and Clark Trail. Numbers were limited. I dithered about joining up. Having always wanted to travel along the Lewis and Clark Trail, when the opportunity was there before me, I was suddenly uncertain as to whether I

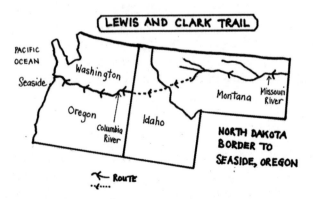

From the North Dakota/Montana border to Seaside, Oregon

had the bottle to do it. I am glad I put aside my fears and signed up. I am also glad I joined a group. I would not have the ability or courage to do it on my own. It was thought that a side effect of the expedition's bicentennial would be an economic boost to communities along the trail. I think it is fair to say that this did not happen. The self-sufficiency of the RV community has ensured that many of the old-fashioned highway motels along the route have closed. Small shops are not viable when RVs can stock up at supermarkets in big towns. The cyclist has to survive on what facilities are open along the way – and there are not many. The trail is a long journey through run-down America.

Lewis and Clark were away for nearly two and a half years. Most of that time was spent getting to the Pacific. The journey back to St. Louis took only six months. There and back, they travelled nearly 8,000 miles.

Following the Lewis and Clark Trail on a bicycle, I would be away for 44 days and I would cover just under 3,000 miles. The journey would give me plenty of time to follow the account of Lewis and Clark's expedition as told through their journals, which I had been given so many years before.

My application to join the expedition to the Pacific was accepted. I received instructions to meet up with the Lewis and Clark Tour of Discovery on the evening of 7th June 2010 at the Jean Baptiste du Sable Park in St. Charles, Missouri, with a well-tuned bicycle and my camping and travelling kit. This was to be packed in no more than two small, soft bags and weigh no more than 50 lbs. The next morning we would set off for the Pacific. Our journey would take us through Missouri, Kansas, Nebraska, Iowa (briefly), South Dakota, North Dakota, Montana, Idaho, Washington and Oregon. Our destination was Seaside, Oregon.

Ulterior Motives

I had another reason for wanting to cross America to the Pacific. I'd had the good fortune to work for a company which had had long associations with the American West. The Alliance Trust, one of the UK's largest investment companies, had started its life off in Dundee in 1888 as the amalgamation of several mortgage companies that lent money to Oregon farmers. Improbable as it may sound now, the distance between Dundee and Oregon posed no object to the entrepreneurial men who saw that opportunity was to be made by borrowing cheap at home and lending it abroad at higher rates. When the transcontinental railroad was completed in 1869, travel across America became more feasible than in the days when a journey involved sailing round Cape Horn, or travelling across the Panama Isthmus, or, painfully and slowly, making one's way across the continent by wagon train.[36] It was possible to run businesses on the west coast of America from Dundee and invest to make returns for those at home, whilst fulfilling the needs of the Oregon settlers who were crying out for capital.

And there was plenty of money in Dundee. A good few people had got rich on the back of jute, not least because the manufactured product in the form of sacks and tent material was sold to both sides in the American Civil War and had then provided the covers for the 'prairie schooners' or wagons which had forged their way west over the Oregon Trail.[37]

Oregon had always had close links with Britain. In fact, Britain and the United States had both claimed the area and had argued about it until, in 1818, they signed a treaty in London agreeing to occupy Oregon jointly. What we call Oregon today is the area which stretches south from the Columbia River to California. In the early nineteenth century, it covered a much larger area and included what is modern-day Washington State and parts of Canada.

The whole of Oregon was called the Columbia District by the British. It was managed and administered by the great Hudson's Bay Company, which had been established in 1670 under a Royal Charter granted by Charles II. The HBC was an enormous undertaking. Its charter gave it the right over all the lands and waters which drained into Hudson's Bay, an area of 1.5 million square miles. It controlled the fur trade and, with it, the native peoples who supplied furs to the company, long before white fur traders began to establish themselves. Without a shadow of a doubt, the HBC was a mega-brand, long before anyone had thought of the term.

When I was 19, I decided that I wanted to work for the HBC and walked into their London headquarters, Beaver House, to enquire about job prospects. Even the name of the building inspired me as I could imagine myself in a log cabin in the snow, with a friendly beaver family building a dam nearby. I did not get beyond the front desk. "We don't take women", I was informed, with complete indifference. I felt certain this wasn't true. Of course they took women, but probably only to do the typing. I wanted something more exciting, such as trapping, or at least running a store in Manitoba. In those days most women accepted such comments without argument, however cross they made us feel. I left the building, plotting revenge. I had to wait a long time for it. A few years ago, an American by the name of Jerry Zucker rescued the HBC from bankruptcy. If that wasn't enough of a bitter pill for it to swallow, on Zucker's death, his wife, Anita, became the Governor of the HBC. She took office 338 years after the date of its founding.

Beaver House is no more, although the façade can still be seen in the atrium of the Royal Bank of Canada offices in London. The HBC is now owned by a private equity firm which also owns the upmarket American department store, Lord & Taylor. This modern venture is not too far from its origins. Fashion was the reason for the fur trade and today, fashion is still central to the business.

When Britain and the United States finally came to an agreement about Oregon, they decided upon the 49th parallel as the northernmost boundary of their joint occupation. The United States relinquished some land north of this, which it had obtained in the Louisiana Purchase. In turn, Britain gave a chunk of land, south of the 49th parallel in present-day North Dakota and Minnesota, to the United States. This state of affairs lasted until 1846. By then the British were beginning to face up to the inevitable. Hordes of American settlers began arriving from the United States. Like King Canute, Britain could not stop the tide. It dropped its claim to land south of the 49th parallel and, accordingly, its joint occupation of Oregon. The 49th parallel became the border between the United States and British North America and still constitutes a lot of, but not the entire, boundary between the United States and Canada, which came into existence in 1867. (Most Canadians actually live south of the 49th parallel.)

When I joined the Alliance Trust in Dundee in 1988, it was a very old-fashioned place. It was not hard to imagine the original directors of the Dundee mortgage companies sitting round the dark oak boardroom table in the dim light, examining reports from their agents in North America, who were, within a few years, based as far as Saskatchewan in the north and Texas in the south, and from the Pacific in the west to South Carolina in the east.

Over a hundred years after the company had been founded a descendant of the first appointed agent in Texas still looked after the interests of the company in that state. The company had been one of the shareholders in the Matador Land and Cattle Company, which owned the vast Matador Ranch in Texas. The purchase involved 100,000 acres of land and 40,000 cattle, with another 203,000 acres and an additional 22,000 cattle being acquired before the ink was dry on the sale papers. By 1910 the Matador Land and Cattle owned 861,000 acres in Texas and leased 650,000 acres in South Dakota and Canada.

In 1951 the shares in the company, which had been run from offices in Panmure Street in Dundee, (although the day-to-day ranch headquarters were in Colorado), were sold to an American syndicate and the land and cattle divided among fifteen corporations.[38] Three of these were bought by Fred Koch who established the enterprises which later became Koch Industries, one of the largest private companies in America. Today guests can stay at the ranch in one of 12 suites named after characters connected with the history of the ranch and hunt for white-tailed bucks and quail.

A director from Dundee sits among the cowhands

Dundee money had also been lent to Charles Goodnight, perhaps the greatest ever Texas cattle rancher, for his properties in the Texan panhandle which were in the Palo Duro Canyon, the second largest canyon in the United States. With John George Adair, he established the JA ranch in 1876, but not before the area was cleared of its native populations, the Comanche and Kiowa Indians, by the US military. The Indians were forcibly moved to Oklahoma and their horses destroyed. The loan to Goodnight defaulted in 1933 and some of the land became a Texan state park, with revenues finally paying the loan off in 1945.

Over the years, the Alliance Trust gradually changed its focus of interest from mortgages to fixed interest securities, equities and mineral rights, mainly in the form of oil and coal. Discovery of oil in 1932 on land owned by the Alliance Trust in Louisiana resulted in a geological formation in southern Louisiana being named the Alliance Sands. To this day, the formation retains the name and has appeared in a recent study on the possibilities of geothermal energy.[39]

American Quarto

So great was the American influence when I joined the Alliance Trust in 1988 that, years after the mortgages had been repaid and most of the land sold off, the company still used American quarto paper for its ordinary correspondence. Its last agent in Idaho retired while I was there and writing to this man, using American quarto of course, in the days before email, I often thought how much I would like to see Idaho. The last thing this agent did when he retired was to send over to Dundee a large box of records, which he had been storing in his basement. In the box was the original certificate of incorporation of one of the Dundee companies, which I had been looking for in the vaults for years without success. It had been in Idaho since the 1920s. Joining the Tour of Discovery and cycling the Lewis and Clark Trail would give me the chance to see some of Idaho and, by way of a bonus, I would end up in Oregon, which I had longed to see since first becoming captivated by the history of the company.

One of the first agents of the Oregon and Washington Trust and Investment Company, an antecedent Dundee mortgage company of the Alliance Trust, had been William Reid, a lawyer who established an extensive legal practice in Scotland acting for American claimants.

In 1868, the widow of Abraham Lincoln actually chose this man in Dundee to help her prepare a book called *Reminiscences of Abraham Lincoln*. President Grant appointed Reid US Consul in Dundee and Reid held that office until he went off to Oregon himself in 1874. Before he left, he wrote a pamphlet called *Oregon and Washington Considered as a Field for Labor and Capital*. This was a bestseller and, according to a document in the Oregon Historical Society Library, exerted an incalculable influence upon that portion of the Union of the United States.[40] I determined that when I got to Oregon I would track Reid down and see if there was any indication there that he had disgraced himself by not understanding conflicts of interest, as this stain had permeated his reputation in Dundee. (There wasn't. In fact, the record I found praised him for his sagacity and honesty.)

William Reid

That people flocked to Oregon may, in no small part, be due to the fact that a Dundee solicitor saw the opportunities it offered and decided to do something about it. Reid's pamphlets, encouraging immigration, were translated into Flemish, German, French and Spanish and were distributed at the Paris and Philadelphia expositions of 1876. Reid himself set up the Oregon State Board of Immigration, established banks, used hydroelectric power to manufacture bricks and organised the Oregon Railway Company. It was perhaps inevitable that he bit off more than he could chew, leading the directors of the original mortgage company in Dundee to complain that he had exceeded his authority. Relationships became acrimonious and he was dismissed.

Where Drought Is Unknown

The first chairman of the Oregon and Washington Investment and Trust Company was the Earl of Airlie. His family seat was

Airlie Castle in the Vale of Strathmore, a wide valley situated just north of Dundee between the Sidlaw Hills and the Grampian Mountains. It is a beautiful area – I can testify to that as I live there. Airlie Castle had, in fact, been burnt down in July 1640 by the Earl of Argyle who arrived at the castle with an army of 5,000 men. The then Earl was abroad (i.e. in England) ardently offering his services to King Charles I and had left his son, Lord Ogilvie, in charge. Ogilvie took one look at Argyle's men and fled. Who can blame him? Not content to leave his men to the destruction, Argyle personally grabbed a hammer and bashed away at the doors until he "did sweat for heat at his work".[41] The family decamped to nearby Cortachy Castle where the present Earl still lives, perhaps still too traumatised with ancestral memories to return to Airlie, which remains the seat of this aristocratic house.

When the early Scottish settlers arrived in Oregon, many of them headed to a valley equally beautiful to that which they had left behind in Strathmore, that of the Willamette River, a tributary of the Columbia. Not only were they struck by its resemblance to their home in Angus, but, as one of the directors of the Oregon and Washington Company remarked, the Willamette too was a place where "Drought is unknown and the harvest never lost"[42].

Beavering away at his mission to criss-cross Oregon with a series of narrow gauge railroads, Reid persuaded the Earl to invest in one which would run from Portland to the southern Willamette Valley on the west bank of the river. The first section was completed in 1881 and terminated at a place appropriately named Airlie; it did not, however, result in much good fortune for the Earl, as he promptly fell ill and died.

Going north towards Portland, the town of Aitken was renamed Dundee, in honour of the majority of investors who were back home by the River Tay. A railroad on the east bank was started. There were plans to bridge the Willamette River at Dundee, obviating the need to use the steamers Salem and City of Salem, which permitted access between the two railroads. All came to nothing due to the fierce rivalry between Reid and another entrepreneur, Henry Villard, who had his own railroad dream in the form of the Oregon Railway and Navigation Company. The crafty Villard sent an agent to Scotland and persuaded the shareholders of Reid's railroad to lease it to his company. Reid withdrew from the management of the railroad, the Oregon Railway and Navigation Company repudiated the lease and the Oregon Railway Company, Reid's baby, went bust. Undaunted, Reid went to court, won, incorporated another company, the Portland and Willamette Valley Railway, and went back to work building the railroad. It was taken over by the Southern Pacific Railroad in 1890 and converted to standard gauge. The branch to Airlie ran until 1928 when it was abandoned.[43]

I had cycled through Airlie in the Vale of Strathmore many times and I also decided that joining the Tour of Discovery to the Pacific Coast in Oregon would give me the opportunity, at the end, to visit the Willamette Valley and have a look at the Oregon Airlie. I hadn't quite realised then that the Oregon Coastal Range of mountains was between the ocean and the Willamette, but bus and train, and the hospitality of two members of the Tour of Discovery, were to come to my rescue. I found Airlie to be very much like its Angus counterpart, absent the castle, but with the more useful addition of a winery producing excellent Pinot Noir.

CHAPTER FOUR : HOPE

Go West

The history of America is a great story and peopled with characters every bit as interesting as those in my childhood book. From those who were caught up in the witchcraft trials in Salem in 1693 to the silversmith who rode through the night to warn the patriots that the British were coming (although Paul Revere never actually shouted those words of warning); from Benjamin Franklin and his lightning rod to Thomas Edison and his light bulb, there is more than enough excitement to keep the student of history entranced. The story of America is one often marred by tragedy and conflict. You do not have to go further than the Civil War or the systematic and almost wholesale destruction of the Indian peoples to see that. Yet it is also a story permeated with hope.

From the beginning of European settlement, millions of people have looked to America in the quest for a better life. Whether that life is realised or not on an individual basis does not matter. What is important is that the promise of it remains intact. Many times during my journey across America, I was struck by how true this is. Our local paper in Angus is full of stories about people raising money for charity, who did what to whom and what punishments they are receiving, and the shortcomings of public services. Go to North Dakota or Montana and you will see that there are fewer articles about what people want government to do and more news about people who have moved to America and how pleased they are to be there. There is a conscious pride in becoming an American and having the opportunity to make a go of it.

For many, the American West is synonymous with that promise of hope. Jefferson's vision of a republic from sea to sea eventually resulted in a collective contagion to get to the other side of the continent. This was encapsulated in the phrase 'Manifest Destiny'. Like John Winthrop, who had visualised a new life in America as akin to being in a "City upon a Hill", the idea of being specially chosen was something that became the birthright of the American people – and not just those born there. Between 1820 and 1890, the United States received approximately 15 million immigrants, many of them answering the call to 'go west'.

I cannot say whether the prospect of driving to the Pacific Ocean in a car brings a tingle of excitement to the driver and passengers, as I have never done it. Setting off for the west coast on a bike, however, is pretty thrilling. It is not just the objective in itself which gives focus. It is what that objective means. The West. Freedom. Open spaces. A more individualistic society. A better life. There was something magical about following the trail west and the path of millions who had gone before us.

The West Wind Doth Blow

There is, however, one disadvantage to cycling west. The prevailing wind blows from the west. The result is many days with it in your face as it slows your progress, sometimes to such a pace that it may be just as quick to walk.

Most of the cyclists we met on our way to the Pacific, perhaps numbering 30 or so in total, were doing what most people would say is the sensible thing. They were cycling the opposite way from us and were heading east towards Missouri, or, in some cases, even to the Atlantic. One solo cyclist I met near Vermillion, South Dakota, told me with great pride that he had managed 152 miles the previous day with a tailwind behind him. When we got into Montana and then into the Columbia Gorge it was torture to be waved at by cyclists coming the other way at a rate of knots with the wind propelling them uphill, when for us, pedalling downhill could only be achieved by keeping the head down and trying to forget about the pain in the legs and in the backside. Cycling west means that you become obsessed with the wind. If it drops at night, it means an anxious night in the tent listening out for any suggestion that it is picking up again. If it does not drop at night, it means an equally anxious night fretting about the relentlessness of the wind and praying for respite and sleep.

Usually the wind would abate at night and there would be an early morning window when we could cycle along blissfully, enjoying the scenery, wondering why it was all such hard work the day before and imagining, falsely, that we would be favoured with a calm day or, as a prize above all, a tailwind. Suddenly and usually before 8am, the first stirrings of the enemy would be felt. Immediately, it became harder to pedal, the saddle felt more uncomfortable (or, for the Americans, the seat, as in America seats are on bicycles and saddles only on horses) and we would have to change down a gear or two (or more).

Our camp routine meant an early start, but the further west we cycled, the earlier we tried to leave to beat the wind. In Chinook, Montana I got up at 3.45am in an effort to sneak as far as I could along the highway before the wind realised that I was trying to fool it. I pedalled out of camp with shouts ringing in my ears:

"Don't you dare go on that highway in the dark!"

"Come back and at least have some coffee."

"Have you got lights?"

"If you go now you'll get too far ahead."

It was to no avail. And there was no chance that I would ever get too far ahead.

Would I choose now to do the trip going east with the wind behind me and perhaps have an easier time of it? Probably not. Despite only being able to make slow progress, going west against the wind was all part of the challenge, although there were times along the way when I would have strongly debated this point. At Rufus, Oregon, it took some of us over an hour to cycle the five miles to the next town, Biggs Junction, with the full force of the wind roaring up the Columbia battering our faces and nearly knocking us off our bikes. That was horrible, but the great thing about cycling east/west, regardless of any sentiment about being a cog in the history of western expansion, is that the most spectacular scenery and the better climate is to be found towards the end of the journey.

Setting off early to beat the wind

Two of our party, Judy and Mike, were on their third Lewis and Clark cycle ride, having done it east-west, west-east and now east-west again. Apart from the fact that their sanity must be in question for subjecting themselves to this gruelling trip three times, Mike pointed out that however bad it was going west against the wind, especially along the Columbia Gorge, it was better than cycling towards the debilitating humidity and heat of Missouri. I soon learnt to appreciate those remarks as our first couple of weeks were spent in the hot sponge-like atmosphere of Missouri, Kansas and Nebraska. The thought of drier days and cooler nights ahead as we moved north following the course of the Missouri was something I clung onto. I soon learnt too that cycling west means you do not have the sun in your eyes all day. The sun was to become my enemy more than the wind.

Lewis and Clark Prepare to Leave St. Louis

The anticipation I felt about going west must have been nothing compared to that of the Corps of Discovery as Lewis and Clark made their preparations to leave for the Pacific by boat up the Missouri River in May 1804. To get to the Missouri from St. Louis, on the Mississippi, Lewis walked overland to a small village on the river called St. Charles, or, as it had been called only a short time before, San Carlos. Clark and the rest of the men went north by boat from St. Louis to the confluence of the Missouri with the Mississippi and then upriver to St. Charles.

St. Charles. (pop. 63,644) is now an upmarket suburb of St. Louis employing people in the financial services, telecoms and aerospace industries, as well as in the hideous super casino which dominates the waterfront and is one of the major employers. In 1804, though, it was a pretty rough fur trading post, described by Clark as having one principal street, a mile in length, running parallel with the river, with about 100 houses. The old town today is just like that, except the rough fur traders have been replaced by people browsing in bijou antique shops and drinking skinny lattes in coffee bars. Clark thought the 450 inhabitants, who were mostly descended from the French, "ill-qualified for the life of the frontier". He said their exertions were "all desultory; their industry is without system, and without perseverance".[44] He noted that they did not cultivate the land but preferred to hunt and trade with the Indians.

After Lewis joined Clark and the rest of the Corps of Discovery, they set off, but they only made three miles before the wind and the rain forced them to camp. This must have been frustrating because they had already delayed their departure long enough. Being prudent men, and sensitive to the fact that many people in the area might have some bruised feelings about the sale of Louisiana to the United States (including the Spanish Governor who was still *in situ*), Lewis and Clark had decided to delay their departure up the Missouri until the formal transfer of the land constituted by the Louisiana Purchase to the United States. They had the wit to see that raising the Stars and Stripes as they set off might be a tad tactless before an official transfer ceremony had taken place. This formal ceremony took place three and a half years after the secret deal of 1800 between the Spanish and the French which had started the whole thing off. It was a momentous occasion. By now the circumstances of the transfer, first to the French and then to the Americans, were, of course, public knowledge and everyone wanted to make sure their part in the transfer progress would be reflected in the official ceremony.

On 9th March 1804, by the banks of the Mississippi river, the Spanish flag was lowered and the French flag was raised to the sound of canons and some of the Spanish no doubt shaking their heads and saying, "Why was I the last to know about this?"

Then in a supremely intelligent PR move, the French flag was permitted to fly over the territory until the morning of 10th March 1804, whereupon it was lowered and the 15 stars and 15 stripes of the American flag were hoisted. After the ceremonies, everyone repaired to a slap up meal in St. Louis.

By this time, spring 1804, there were 17 states as Ohio had been admitted as number 17 on 1st March 1803. How come then there were only 15 stars and 15 stripes on the flag at the transfer ceremony? The reason is that an Act of Congress had provided for a flag with 15 stars and 15 stripes in 1795 after Kentucky became the 15th state. Perhaps it did not realise how the nation would expand. In 1818, when Congress realised adding a stripe for each new state would make the flag a mess, it was decided to go back to square one. Congress decided upon a flag with 13 stripes, representing the original 13 colonies. There was to be a star for each state, with the accession of a new state marked by the addition of a white star on the next 4th July following admission.[45]

The Corps of Discovery had marked time waiting for these ceremonies across the Mississippi River at Camp Dubois on the Wood River in modern-day Illinois. They found waiting around very tiresome. They were safely in United States territory, out of sight of the Spanish Governor, but they were anxious to get going. Winter was, however, no time to start an expedition and they had no choice but to wait for the transfer ceremonies and, more importantly, the arrival of Lewis and the boat which would take them up the Missouri.

While the men waited, Lewis had organised men and supplies along the Ohio River and prayed for the keelboat, which he had ordered in Pittsburgh, to be finished. The boat Lewis had commissioned in Pittsburgh to take them up the Missouri was a 55 foot long craft. It displaced three feet of water, had a large sail and sported 22 oars. It also had a series of lockers in the middle of the craft, going lengthwise. These were cleverly designed, as the lids could be lifted up to act as shields in the event of attack. At the stern there was a small covered area and a cabin.[46] Two smaller, flat-bottomed boats called pirogues were also commissioned to go upriver. Two horses were to be led along the bank and also used for hunting game.

Waiting for the keelboat to be built, Lewis was frustratingly delayed by the drunkenness of the boat builder who was prone to waste the day sleeping off the excesses of the night before. The rogue was unsympathetic to Lewis' entreaties to get the boat ready quickly. He knew Lewis would not be able to get a similar boat built anywhere else and took his time. When it was finally completed, Lewis sailed the boat down the Ohio River, realising at the same time that he had to increase the number of expedition members as it was no easy craft to handle.

Clark, meanwhile, had to deal with the expedition members at Camp Dubois on his own. This was no easy task at times as inactivity led the men to hunt for grog and fight.

Surly Days

I too had kicked my heels for a while before meeting my fellow members of the Tour of Discovery. I had stayed, not like Clark in a tent on the banks of the Wood River, near the confluence of the Mississippi and Missouri Rivers, but in a high-rise hotel near the St. Louis Arch, that great monument to Western Expansion designed by the Finnish architect, Saarinen, who sadly did not live long enough to see it completed. Many of us on the tour had felt the need to see the Arch before setting off, as well as the National Geographic Film of the Lewis and Clark expedition which runs continuously in the museum under the Arch and is a must for any would-be adventurer following their trail.

My New Bike

A good bicycle is the most important piece of equipment for a ride across America and I also needed some time to try out the bicycle I had ordered. This was a midnight blue Surly Long Haul Trucker, a superb machine which had been the recommendation of the bike shop, and which proved to be an ideal bicycle for this tour. I had ordered butterfly handlebars to be fitted, which are extremely uncommon in America and became a talking point every time I stopped.

These Surly LHTs are much admired, and I soon joined a group of people who, having ridden a Surly, would not wish to ride any other kind of bicycle. The first time I took it out, on the riverside cycle trail which goes north along the Mississippi from the Arch, cyclists stopped to talk to me and just about all of them opened the conversation with "Hey! A Surly!". I felt like saying, "Yes. Aren't I wonderful for making such a fantastic choice", but it really had little to do with me and all to do with good advice from the bike shop.[47]

The riverside trail passes Laclade's landing, the restored historical area housing a hideous floating casino (paired by an equally hideous casino on the Illinois side of the Mississippi) and then quickly takes you out into the countryside towards Chain of Rocks Bridge, which is part of the celebrated Route 66 across America. On the way out of town you can see men fishing, Tom Sawyer-like, on the banks of the Mississippi, as well as American gray foxes, wild turkeys and red winged blackbirds. I was convinced the foxes were coyotes, which are common in St. Louis, but another cyclist on the trail was adamant that what we had seen, running along open ground by vegetation next to the river, was a pair of foxes. Coyotes would have to wait.

I had set off on my Surly on my practice ride, before the start of the Tour of Discovery a few days later, well before 6am. My objective was to get as many miles in as possible before the suffocating heat and humidity of a summer's day in St. Louis. I think it was about an hour later that I realised that it was going to be a long, hot day. I cycled up river, waited for the Chain of Rocks Bridge to be opened and then went over into Illinois, just for the hell of it. A policeman in a Granite City Police car told me I could ignore the "Trail closed" signs and cycle up river on the Illinois side of the Mississippi. I tried to do this, but the surface was too rough for my tyres and I had no puncture repair kit with me. Prudence made me turn around. On the way back into the city, and once again on the Missouri side of the Mississippi River, the cycle trail was buzzing and the mercury was rising. Many people, including myself, were grateful for the free iced water handed out by volunteers at a rest stop near the Mary

Meachum Freedom Crossing, which marks the spot where the Underground Railroad crossed the river. This was not a latter day Jubilee line, but the name given to a resistance movement against slavery and a series of cross-country routes used by slaves attempting to flee from their masters to freedom. Like those who many years later sought to escape the draft during the Vietnam War, many of them made for Canada (or British North America as it was then). But here in 1855, by the Mississippi, nine slaves tried to escape by boat to Illinois. No slavery existed in Illinois, but it was an offence to assist a fugitive slave from another area. The police were waiting for them on the banks of the river in Illinois. The runaway slaves had been assisted by Mary Meacham, the wife of a local African American clergyman, who found herself in court in St. Louis for her troubles. There is no record of what happened to her, but St. Louis was where some of the fundamental theories of slavery were soon to be tested in the Court House where she may have appeared herself. This city was the scene of the infamous Dred Scott decision in 1857.

An Infamous Decision

Missouri Territory, which had been part of the Louisiana Purchase, sought admission to the United States as a state in 1819. Its application provoked a tussle between the southern states, where slaves were considered an economic necessity, and the northern states where slavery was prohibited. Missouri was in the south. Its economic viability depended on slaves working the cotton plantations, which were incredibly labour intensive. It was no surprise that it wanted to be admitted to the Union as a slave state. Both sides were anxious to preserve the balance of power (slave states and free states then being equally represented in the Union) so a compromise was reached. A northern, free state was created by carving territory out of Massachusetts, one of the original 13 states, and naming it Maine. Missouri was then admitted to the United States as a slave state. The number of free states and slave states in the Union thus remained equal. A virtual border was created at 36° 30' north to the effect that territory lying north of that would be free. However, any fugitive slaves caught north of the line could still be apprehended and returned south of the line, which is exactly what had happened to those Mary Meachum sought to help. Slaves could be returned to their owners as if they were runaway dogs or horses.

Dred Scott had been born a slave in Virginia in 1795. He was owned by Peter Blow, who then sold him to another slave owner, John Emerson, in 1830. Emerson then moved to Missouri, a slave state by virtue of the eponymous Compromise, and took Scott with him. His travels not yet over, Emerson moved on to Illinois and then to Wisconsin Territory, still accompanied by Scott. Unlike in Missouri, slavery was prohibited in both these areas. Was Scott then a slave or not? He was living in free land, so how could he be a slave? Well, no one asked the question there and then. Scott continued to work for Emerson. In 1836, he married, which slaves were not officially permitted to do, so it appeared as if he must be free. Yet still there was no enquiry regarding his status.

Eventually, after Emerson's death, Scott returned to Missouri with his family to work for Emerson's second wife, Eliza. Back in this slave state, Scott asked Eliza Emerson, in 1843, whether he could purchase his freedom. She refused. If only she had been generous, how different history would have been. She thought of Scott as a chattel. He had been hired out for gain and she did not want to lose her ongoing source of lucrative income. Undaunted, and helped by the abolitionist movement, Scott decided to sue for his freedom, relying on the argument that as he had previously been resident in areas where there was no slavery, he should now be emancipated in this slave state. He lost on a technicality, but was granted a new trial. This time the jury found that Scott and his family were not slaves, but free people.

Eliza Emerson, however, appealed to the Supreme Court of Missouri, handing the case over to her brother, John Sanford, who was the executor of her late husband's estate. Keen as she was to make sure Scott remained a slave, she had by then moved to Massachusetts, a free state, which does seem a trifle hypocritical. The Missouri Supreme Court held that Scott and his family were slaves. Eliza remarried, this time to an abolitionist, and changed her views on slavery.

DRED SCOTT.

Dred Scott

Scott appealed to a federal court which, unhelpfully, directed that the courts of Missouri should decide the issue. As they had already ruled that Scott was a slave, this got no one anywhere. The appeal then went to the United States Supreme Court which found that the whole case had been futile. Scott was a slave. A slave was not a citizen. Only citizens could sue in a federal court. Therefore Scott could not sue in the court. The Supreme Court also gave Congress a slap on the wrist, saying it was beyond its powers to say whether states should be free or not. And as a final blow, it held that territorial legislatures had no power to prohibit slavery and that taking a slave into free territory would not deprive the owner of his right of property in the slave. Nothing had moved on since the days of Mary Meacham and the runaway slaves.

So much for Dred Scott, who was unaware that President-elect Buchanan had exerted political pressure on some of the Supreme Court Justices. He had asked them not to risk rocking the boat by finding in Scott's favour. The decision is remembered, not only for its place in the history of race relations in the United States but also for the Court misspelling Sanford's name in the judgement, adding a "d" where none existed. It also created a panic in the stocks of railroad companies expanding east-west across the continent and the near collapse of several banks, as everyone grew jumpy about whether the west would become a battleground between slavery lovers and those who wanted its abolition. Two months after the decision, the sons of Scott's first owner purchased his emancipation. I like to think that the hard-nosed Eliza Emerson had a pang of conscience about that. Scott worked in a St. Louis hotel and died in 1858.[48]

Hopeville

St. Louis prides itself on being a bicycle city, with 'Bike St. Louis' marked cycle lanes around the city and up to Forest Park, the site of the 1904 World's Fair, which is bordered by mansions built at the same time. These fantastic houses, set in their own grounds, are a far cry from the housing estates north of the downtown football stadium. These areas are so run down that, cycling through them as soon as the sun came up, following a sign to the park marked on the riverside cycle trail, I wondered if I had stumbled across some huge Steven Spielberg film set for a post-apocalyptic world. This was heightened by the fact that the only other vehicle on the road, a gold Bentley, drew up beside me at an intersection. The cool dude in shades, driving it, looked at me as if I were from another planet, which I guess I was. Having watched too many episodes of *The Wire*, I lost my nerve and made my way back to the riverfront trail. Later on I asked someone about the signed cycle route, expressing disbelief that cyclists could be directed through these streets.

"But no one would ever cycle it alone," I was told.

On my way south along the west bank of the Mississippi, I realised I had failed, on the way north, to see a tented community tucked in behind the large concrete wall which lines the Mississippi and forms part of the city flood defences.

Rows of large, new-looking, blue Colman tents were erected in neat rows, with families sitting at picnic tables. It was insufferably hot and there was little or no shade. At the edge of the tented area on a wooden post was a hand-painted sign which read 'Hopeville'. Intrigued, I got talking to a man who emerged from one of the tents, neatly dressed in blue jeans, a plaid shirt and a baseball cap over his long, grey hair. I asked him what the sign was.

"Well, Ma'am," he replied, "Hopeville is a place for those who ain't got no place to live. It's for the homeless."

The tents, he told me, had been donated by a local church.

Later on, I would think a lot about those homeless people living in tents by the Mississippi, so near to the casinos and the luxury downtown hotels. Heat is hard to bear, but while you can go back to your air-conditioned hotel room or car, or even go into a coffee shop for some respite, it is difficult to appreciate how hard. I was to find out. On the trail, no matter how tired you are, you can't go into your tent until the temperature drops sufficiently to make sleep possible and being outside, day after day in relentless heat, saps your energy and resolve. For us on the Tour of Discovery, it was all part of the challenge and we knew we could escape to an air-conditioned motel room when we had a day off. When I did so, I would think of Hopeville and wonder if the hopes of any of the people there had been realised or whether, as they sweated the nights away by the banks of the Mississippi, only the sign comforted them that sometime and somewhere, America would offer them a better life.[49]

CHAPTER FIVE: HARMONY

The Tour Begins

Twenty of us gathered at the campsite by the banks of the Missouri in St. Charles before setting out on the Lewis and Clark Trail. Twelve people had signed up for the whole trip to the Pacific, one rider would cycle only as far as Great Falls, Montana and three were with us for the first week only. There were four members of staff. Yes, this was to be a fully supported cycle trip. Not exactly one for softies, but one where luggage would be carried, campsites organised in advance, route directions given and most meals provided. Lewis and Clark had carried their supplies in the keelboat and the pirogues and had lived off the land. We would have two vans to carry our luggage and to act as 'sag stops' along the way. This is the term Americans use to signify where you can get water and food or decide to rest ('sag') by taking a ride in the van for a few miles.

Age Cannot Wither Them

When Lewis and Clark set off from St. Charles, the Corps of Discovery comprised just over 40 people. Most of them were young volunteer soldiers picked up along the way, especially in Kentucky, and they were joined by French Canadian watermen or 'voyageurs'. One of these men was employed as a hunter and the other, a one-eyed Creole, who the men called St Peter, as an interpreter.[50] Most of the expedition would go all the way to the Pacific and back, but some were only to go as far as the Mandan Indian Villages on the Missouri River. They would then return with news of the expedition's progress. They were called, not unreasonably, the 'Return Party'.

Included also was York, born into slavery, and left to William Clark in his father's will. After the expedition, York asked Clark to grant him his freedom. After all that they had been through together, Clark refused, which is very disappointing to the modern mind. He even beat York when York got sulky as a result of this refusal, and this dents Clark's image further. It is not clear whether Clark finally relented and granted him his freedom, or whether York ran away. We do not know what happened to York, but we can conjecture there was no happy ending, at least not immediately. In January 2001, York was posthumously made a sergeant in the US Army by President Clinton, shortly before he left office.

The expedition's plan was to go upstream against the flow of the Missouri. This would require considerable confidence in the robustness of their boats and those manning them. The Missouri was not to be trifled with. Huge trees and vast amounts of debris would meet them head on, underwater trees would threaten to hole the boats and a course would have to be navigated to avoid sandbanks. To give some idea of the strength of the water they were moving against, it is worth remembering that, on the return journey downstream, they were sometimes able to cover 80 miles a day.

Compared to the rigours of the river, our cycle ride looked easy. For the first few days we would be cycling along the Katy Trail, a traffic-free cycle and walking trail which extends along the river for 225 miles from St. Charles to Clinton, Missouri. We would have two overnight stops on the trail, at Hermann and Hartsburg, and then would leave the trail, cross the Missouri at Boonville and join the highways which would first take us to Arrow Rock State Park and then north and west, following the course of the Missouri into the great wilderness.

Before we had left St. Charles, we had all had time to observe our fellow cyclists and judge what the next 44 days were going to be like with those of them who had signed up for the whole trip across the country. The biggest difference between our group and the Corps of Discovery was age. Lewis and Clark were young men and they took youngsters with them. The average age of the members of the expedition was 27, with the youngest man 17 and the oldest 35. Later on their journey they would travel with a baby, Jean Baptiste Charbonneau, also known affectionately as 'Pomp', the word for 'leader' in the language of his mother, Sacagawea, a Shoshone Indian. She accompanied Lewis and Clark, along with her French-Canadian husband, Charbonneau, who was meant to earn his keep as an interpreter. Pomp isn't counted in establishing the average age of the expedition, but still, the Corps of Discovery was a young man's game. Variously, its members came from Virginia, Connecticut, Kentucky, Maryland, Massachusetts, New Hampshire, North Carolina, Pennsylvania, Tennessee, Virginia and ... Germany. Most of the voyageurs were French Canadians.

Missouri

Lewis was devoted to the last member of the expedition, Seaman, his Newfoundland dog, bought for $20 on the way to St. Louis. Poor Seaman was spooked by bears on the Missouri and suffered horribly from the mosquitoes. Lewis recorded that the dog howled with the torture he experienced with them. The journals do not record if Seaman was also spooked by watching Lewis eating dog. During the course of the journey, the expedition got through over 200 dogs, which they found delectable eating. Clark, however, could not, at first, bring himself to eat dog.

To put it delicately, the Tour of Discovery 2010 was at the other end of the age spectrum. Most of us were retired, some were over 70 and the oldest rider was 77. It was no surprise to me that most of the cyclists doing the journey would be post-paid employment, as not many people can take sufficient time off work to cycle across America, but I did not expect so many septuagenarians on the trip. It was a surprise when I found out the age of some of my fellow riders. I soon noticed that the older the rider, the younger, fitter and more glamorous they looked.

Those members of the tour who had signed up for the whole trip or the greater part of it were first, Wendy and Alcy, who were cycling home to Oregon. Wendy was a physical therapist (what we call a physiotherapist) and Alcy a hugely talented glass maker and designer, not that she had much time for glass production on the trip. Having met them, I soon thought that Wendy would make an ideal President of the United States and wondered why she did not hold that office, for the world would certainly be a better place if she did. Bev, a retired biochemist and the oldest in the group, was from Minnesota. She was always neatly turned out and very fashionable, especially in her mauve sweater which I coveted. Bev had the smallest bag and the greatest amount of useful gear, including a kettle, which I swear she dematerialised each day to get back into the bag. She was probably awarded a gold medal somewhere for sensible packing. She was utterly inspiring on and off the bike.

Mike B., a retired teacher and a perfect gentleman, was from Colorado and Judy and Mike, charming, clever and thoughtful, were from Alaska. Jay, another perfect gentleman with a talent for making friends, came from North Carolina and Larry, who was the tallest in the group, and a superb consistent bike rider, came from Georgia. Larry, like me had a Surly LHT, but his was a trifle bigger than mine. In common with Bev, Larry had a talent for packing. From the smallest of bags, he even produced a camping chair in which he reclined outside his tent, reading a book. I could not believe my eyes when I saw this.

"How do you do it?" I said. "How do you pack?"

"I've been doing this a very, very long time," he drawled. "Let me tell you. You need three pairs of shorts. That's all".

Ken hailed from Connecticut and Gil, who was to leave us after a few days because of an accident, from Alaska. Ayako, who was from New York, but originally from Japan, was one of the oldest riders and followed the rule that glamour went with age. No matter what the conditions, she looked calm and unruffled on the bike and after a long hard day in the saddle still looked elegant and as if she had just freshly showered and dressed.

Hans Ruedi, who left us in Great Falls, Montana, was from Switzerland. I was soon to see that he was the grand old man of cycle touring. The trip staff were Tom from Nebraska, who was running the show, Karl the bike mechanic from Kansas and the cooks, bottle-washers and general factotums, Kit from Maryland and Sue from Washington.

We would not have been complete without a dog, and we had Griffin, a fearsome creature who looked half-wolf, half-husky. This was deceptive as he was a real softy; good tempered, gentle and with pleading eyes that said "Feed me". We were not permitted to do so as this job was only for Tom, his master. Griffin and I were to become good friends in Atchison, Kansas, but how this came about will have to wait until later.

Discipline on the Trail

The enlisted men on the Lewis and Clark expedition were subject to military discipline. One of the privates, John Collins, could not resist tippling whiskey. He was frequently drunk and, worse, when put on guard duty, he decided to steal from the communal supply. That got him 100 lashes. Another enlisted man, Tom Howard, was subjected to court martial for showing a bad example to the Indians. Too lazy to call for the gate to be opened at Fort Mandan, he had climbed over the wall, a feat which was then copied by an Indian looking on, causing the commanders to fear their security would be compromised. Discipline had to be strict when safety was at stake, although some mercy was shown to Alexander Willard, who fell asleep on guard duty. Death could have been his sentence, but instead he too got 100 lashes.

John Newman was one of those people who would try any commander's patience, whinging and muttering and causing dissent. He was packed off to St. Louis with the Return Party, but only after he was put to hard labour for not being able to keep his mouth shut. Sent back with him, also after hard labour, was Moses Reed, who was foolish enough to attempt desertion, a somewhat silly thing to do when survival away from the expedition was precarious. One man who found this out to his cost was George Shannon, because he got lost near present day Yankton, South Dakota. He had been sent out to find two pack horses which had strayed. He stayed out all night and got back to the river, hoping to catch up with the expedition when he reached its next night camp.

Unfortunately, he was ahead, and not behind, Lewis and Clark. It was two weeks before they caught up with him, by which time he was nearly dead from starvation. He had lived on grapes and a rabbit which he had killed with a stick. It was a sobering lesson on having the correct equipment. Clark noted that among all that plenty, Shannon had nearly perished for lack of bullets.

Amazingly, there does not seem to have been any friction between Lewis and Clark. This is a surprise for two reasons. First, Lewis was not an easy character. He was prone to melancholy, which ran in his family. Today we would probably say he suffered from depression. Jefferson had known about this affliction when he appointed him his private secretary, as the family was well known to him, plus he had observed it during the time Lewis had lived in the White House.

Some have asserted that this depressive tendency is the reason why there are long gaps in Lewis' journal of the expedition, but no one really knows for certain. What is clear, though, is that after the expedition finished, Lewis never settled down to normal life. He couldn't discipline himself to write up the journals for publication (a task which eventually fell to Clark, along with Nicholas Biddle, a Philadelphian who was to become President of the Second Bank of the United States – the first having lost its charter); did not live up to the job when he was appointed Governor of Louisiana, couldn't get anyone to marry him, drank too much and was generally a mess.

On 10th October 1809, he stopped at Grinder's Stand, a log cabin which served as an overnight lodging house, situated along Natchez Trace, a trail in Tennessee. Into the cabin with him went an axe, a rifle and some pistols. Mrs Grinder, the wife of the lodging house keeper, heard some gunshots. Lewis died the next day. Theories abound as to whether it was suicide, or whether he was murdered by intruders, or by Mr Grinder in circumstances that need no intelligence to imagine. But the truth may be simple. As anyone who has been on a challenging journey with close companions will understand, life was never as good again for Meriwether Lewis once he arrived back through the wilderness from the Pacific.

The second reason it is remarkable there was no disharmony between Lewis and Clark is that Clark could so easily have borne a grudge against Lewis but did not do so. If you remember, Clark had been Lewis's commanding officer in the Chosen Rifle Company. He had made captain in the Army before Lewis. When he agreed to come out of retirement to co-command the expedition, he re-enlisted. All this was agreed on the basis that he would regain his former rank as captain, so each man would be a co-commander and co-captain.

Eventually, Clark's commission came through, but it was for that of a second lieutenant, not a captain. By this time, Clark was already on site in Illinois, dealing with men and supplies and he would have wrecked all their plans by stomping off back to Mulberry Hill in a huff. His disappointment was real and, to add insult to injury, he did not get paid for all the time he had spent on expedition matters prior to the commission coming through. Lewis was also embarrassed. He told Clark that the difference in military rank would make no difference between them and, as far as he was concerned, Clark would be an equal in co-command. They decided not to say anything to the men and, indeed, this treatment of Clark was not revealed until years after the expedition.

When we visited Fort Clatsop, on the last day of our cycling trip, where the Lewis and Clark expedition overwintered in 1805/1806, I paid special attention to a replica of a list which Lewis had drawn up on 18th March 1806. The purpose of the list was to make known to the informed world that the persons whose names appeared on it had been successful in their mission to reach the Pacific and that, on that day, they were leaving to return to the United States by the same route. The first name on the list is that of Lewis and he states his military rank and regiment. Clark's name is next. He is designated as Captain of the expedition, with no military rank stated.

Surely Clark's disappointment must have rankled? Perhaps not. Clark was, on the whole, a decent person, despite his treatment of York, which could not have been atypical for the time. He was obviously able to rise above a slight, which many would have let fester until sparks flew. After the expedition, Clark married a woman called Julia Hancock and had five children, one of whom he named Meriwether Lewis Clark. After his wife's death, he married her cousin, Harriet Kennerly Radford, and had three more children. He had a successful career and ended up as Governor of Missouri Territory in 1821 and then Superintendent of Indian Affairs. Just before he left office, President Clinton conferred on Clark, posthumously, the rank of Captain in the American Army.[51]

Despite the military discipline, the lashings and the expulsions, the Lewis and Clark expedition, as a whole, must have been a cohesive one. This was in no small part due to the solidarity evidenced by the commanders. The hardships of the journey were so terrible and the physical and psychological demands on each person so great, that any group weakened by bickering and dissent would surely have failed.

An example of solidarity occurred at present day Loma, Montana, when there was doubt about which way to go at a confluence. Which river was the Missouri? Lewis instructed a thorough, 10-day exploration of the area, before making his decision. All the men thought he made the wrong one, but they followed without complaint. Clark, of course, supported Lewis' decision, which turned out to be correct. Had they followed the other river, which Lewis named the Marias after his cousin, Maria Wood, the expedition would have gone too far north and away from the course across the mountains which would lead them to the Pacific.

Fortunately for all on the Tour of Discovery 2010, we were a happy group and we did not need military discipline to keep us in order. That we were to find out within a few days as we all settled happily into the camp and cycling routines. Even so, the tour organiser, Tom, was taking no chances. At the campsite in St. Charles on the first evening, he handed each of us an official-looking document and asked us to sign it. No sign, no tour.

We scrutinised the document closely, and discovered that it asked us to acknowledge that we had signed up for an extreme endurance event. If there was anyone who had not realised that, it was a bit late now to find out. It also asked us to acknowledge that the tour organiser was entitled to order us off the tour if we were a disharmonious influence in the group. He would decide what behaviour was the cause of disharmony and his decision was final.

Before signing, we all looked at each other. Was anyone going to be a whiner or a troublemaker? No. Was anyone going to complain at the first hill? Of course not. We were all up for it. So we all signed happily, but probably all also made a vow to ourselves not to be the one accused of creating 'disharmony'.

CHAPTER SIX : ST. CHARLES, MO TO NEBRASKA CITY, NE

Days 1 to 9
7th June to 16th June 2010
483 miles

Riding on the KT

The Katy Trail, which we joined at its eastern terminus, is named after the railroad along whose bed it now runs: the Missouri-Kansas-Texas Railroad. The railroad was started in the 1860s as part of the Union Pacific, Southern Branch and, after it became a separate company in 1870, it eventually went onto link Kansas City and St. Louis with Galveston in Texas. The name 'Katy' derived from the initials of the last two states in its name, with 'KT' also being the company's ticker symbol on the New York Stock Exchange.

The KT was the only railroad to enter Texas from the north. For most of its life, its engines were painted bright red, which was probably the colour of the face of one of its general managers, William G. Crush, who, living up to his name, deliberately engineered a head-on train collision near Waco, Texas in 1896. For some bizarre reason, he thought this would attract ongoing business to the railroad, perhaps by those who wanted to risk all. Two trains faced each other on a four-mile track. Anyone who wanted to watch the show was charged $2 by Crush to be taken to the scene. So many people took up the offer that the police had to be called to push the crowd back to what was meant to be a safe vantage point. This took some hours, by which time the crowd, as well as the trains, had built up a head of steam. Excitement must have been high when the trains set off, *sans* crew, who had jumped off after tying the throttles open. The trains hit each other at 90 mph; two boilers exploded, three people were killed, more were wounded and the official photographer lost an eye.[52]

The Katy Trail

Our progress down the Katy Trail was less dramatic. The surface of the trail is like white cat litter; fine when it is dry but dirty and cloggy when wet, with an ability to worm its way into every part of a bicycle. Being an old railroad and alongside the Missouri, it is flat and easy riding. Wildlife abounds: wild turkey, deer, snapping turtles, thousands of tiny little frogs (one hitched a ride on the top of my helmet for miles) and the occasional snake. But for several reasons, we were glad to get off it and onto the highway. The trail is like a tunnel through dense undergrowth. After a while, this gets boring and one longs for a vista. More importantly, the creature which has the upper hand on the trail is the mosquito. It is impossible to stop to take a photo without a swarm of them descending so quickly that we were often forced to put our cameras back in our bags and pedal on, priceless shot forgotten. At Hartsburg, Missouri we came across four lads who were camping and who had no repellent with them. Having nothing better to do, they had counted their respective mosquito bites which numbered 525 in total.

For us, bothered to distraction on the Katy Trail, the only thing that made the mosquitoes bearable was the knowledge that, however much we suffered from them, the Corps of Discovery had had it worse. Clark tried to fend them off by spelling 'mosquito' 19 different ways in his journal, perhaps out of distress that their repellent – a mixture of candle grease and bear or hog fat – did not really do the trick. The men had nets and although they did not know what caused malaria, one third of the medicine budget had been spent on Peruvian Bark, which was later found to contain quinine, and was of some relief to those who took it. At least we did not have to cope with malaria, but every time I got a bite I was reminded that mosquitoes here may carry West Nile Disease, a nasty little thing which can kill.

We hadn't been on the Katy Trail for very long when I realised that this whole adventure was going to be rather more difficult than I had expected. Already, we had had our fair share of rain, which at Treloar, a tiny unincorporated community, was torrential enough to send us scurrying for shelter for a couple of hours, under the porch of the disused Treloar Mercantile Company. With a flat, traffic-free, 225-mile bicycle trail near the big city of St. Louis, I had expected the Katy Trail to be served with numerous upmarket, trendy coffee shops, wine bars and restaurants. The abandoned, crumbling buildings were a surprise. I got the impression that the prospective opportunities of such a bike trail had just not caught on.

The First Electric Storms

By the time we crossed the Missouri at Hermann, Missouri (pop. 2,674) the rain had abated long enough for us to pitch our tents at the municipal park at the south end of the town, near the Texaco gas station. Hermann had been established by German settlers in the 1830s with the objective of transporting to Missouri all the traditions of their native land, including wine making. But this industry, which had initially thrived on the banks of the Missouri, had been destroyed by Prohibition and was not revived until the 1960s. Now Hermann is the centre for Missouri viticulture, which sadly we were not to sample. However, had we been offered a glass of the best Chambourcin from the local Hermannhof Winery, we probably would not have been able to summon up the energy to raise it to our lips, so great was the heat and humidity. I found Mike B. from Colorado slumped against the wall of the wash-house in the park, muttering dark thoughts about how he would never, in a million years, be able to live in a climate such as this. Weather records for Hermann for that day show that the maximum temperature was only 80°F.[53] It felt a lot hotter. Breathing felt like sucking air through a hot sponge. It was just too much effort to leave the campground and explore the town.

It wasn't much later that the thunder and lightning started, with a sound and light display that I felt sure must be a recording of the Russians approaching Berlin at the end of World War II. Alone in my tent, I was terrified, with little to occupy my thoughts except how awful this all was and was I the only one not fast asleep? It was a good job I did not know then, as the trees in the park cast shadows on the outside of the tent, that Hermann was home to one of the most notorious murderers in the United States, Richard Honeck, who stabbed his victim to death with an eight-inch Bowie knife. For a time, he held the record for the longest custodial sentence ending in a prisoner's release on parole (rather than execution), having been sent to prison in November 1899 and not released until December

1963. During all that time, he received only one four-line letter and two visitors, the second being a newspaper reporter in 1963, who stumbled across news of Honeck's incarceration in a prison newspaper and was instrumental in him being granted parole. The night in the tent at Hermann seemed almost as long as Honeck's sentence, but unlike Honeck, I did not, on release, receive a proposal of marriage from a German. Having learnt something from being inside for so long, Honeck wisely tuned down the offer of matrimony and moved to Oregon.

The next morning, having survived the storms, we rose and rode on through Boone County, named after the famous pioneer and frontiersman, Daniel Boone. He had moved, at the age of 65, from Kentucky, when he reckoned it was becoming too overcrowded, and had established a homestead near the Missouri in 1799 (when it was Spanish territory). His homestead, which has been renovated and is now open to the public, is owned by Lindenwood University. This institution has its main campus in St. Charles and much admired by the residents of that town, not least of all because it carries no debt. It also lets its students pay its fees in kind. This is good news for the children of farmers who are able to pay for the education of their children in the form of pork which is used in the university canteens.[54]

Flood Warnings

The next night on the Katy Trail, at Hartsburg (pop. 78) it was flood that preoccupied my mind. We had only cycled 59 miles that day, probably not far enough to tire mind and body (although I, for one, was done in). My imagination had run riot when Nancy, the former mayor, had come down to the campsite at the Lions' Club Pavilion, where we were treated to a meal, home cooked by the members, of pulled pork, baked potatoes, salads and pecan pie. It was a delicious spread, overlooked by the beaming faces of those who had done the cooking.

American Pulled Pork

- Chop up some onion and put in a pot with a splodge of tomato ketchup, some vinegar (cider vinegar if you like), brown sugar and tomato paste. Add some hot pepper.
- Experiment, trying some Lee and Perrins Worcestershire Sauce and some dried mustard. Mix it all up.
- Add a pork shoulder and coat the meat with the sauce.
- Cook for hours in the oven until the meat falls away from the bone, making sure that there is enough liquid in the pot so the pork does not dry out.
- Take the pork out, reduce the liquid.
- Pull the pork shoulder apart and put the strings of meat back into the sauce.
- Put on a picnic table with hamburger buns, pickles, salad, crisps and whatever else you fancy.
- Shout "Enjoy"!

The Lions' Club members getting the food ready

Nancy's mission was to tell us about the 1993 floods, when the town had been cut off for weeks and people came from 31 States to help with the flood relief. I had already heard about the 1993 floods when I was in St. Louis, where the discharge from the flooded Mississippi had been 485 million gallons a minute, enough to fill the Busch Baseball Stadium every 65 seconds. Downtown St. Louis had been saved by the flood defence wall which now sheltered the homeless at Hopeville, although the water reached to within two feet of the top of its 52 feet height. I had seen the plaque on the steps up to the Arch from the Mississippi which marked the high water mark. That the water could have been that high was sobering but had not worried me unduly in my room on the 27th floor of my St. Louis hotel. Now, in a tent, near the Missouri at Hartsburg, it was easy to fret.

During the 1993 floods, a man from Quincy, Illinois, James Scott, saw an opportunity of a lifetime. Perhaps tired of the binds of matrimony to Suzie, who worked on the Missouri side of the Mississippi, he realised the floods gave him the chance to make sure she remained there. With Suzie safely across the water, he would have the freedom to booze, fish and have an affair. To achieve this unseemly objective, he breached a levee causing 14,000 acres to flood and washing out all the bridges for 200 miles. The force of the flood was so great that a barge was sucked off course and slammed into a gas station, causing a fire.

Hartsburg camp

Scott, who had burnt down his school as a child, made the mistake of bragging about breaking the levee and was eventually convicted of intentionally causing a catastrophe. A catastrophe was exactly what I was worried about as I lay in my tent. I had pitched it next to the children's slide in the campground and spent the night wishing I had paid more attention in science lessons as wasn't there something about not being near tall, metal objects in a storm?

Fortunately there was no storm that night and we set off cheerfully on our 61-mile ride to Arrow Rock. We all felt a frisson of excitement when Tom told us we could make a stop at Chuck's Bicycle Store in Boonville (pop. 8,282), where Amish horses and buggies were tied up along the main street. It became a rule of the tour to stop at every bike shop as you never knew when you might find the next one. On this occasion, however, and despite being called in advance, Chuck kept us waiting. He found us lined up outside the shop as he drove up in his old car, slowly climbed out of the driver's seat and said, "A've been picking cherries and making mahself a cherry pie".

Cherry Pie? Goodness! Our cherries in Scotland would still have some months to go before picking, I thought, wishing too that Chuck had brought some pie along. There was nothing to entice me to spend money in Chuck's store. It looked like a museum of bicycle parts, whereas, only three days into the trip, I was keen to browse through fashionable bike gear and designer sunglasses, rather than old spokes, chains and hubs. No such luck.

The Pursuit of a New Tent

Arrow Rock, (pop. 79) was aptly named because once upon a time the Indians had made arrowheads there from the local flint. It was also where Lewis and Clark would have lost one of the boats, on 9th June 1804, had some of the men not leapt into the Missouri and pulled it free from drifting logs. For my part, it was the place I decided that I had to do something about my tent.

In the interests of being able to get up and on the trail quickly in the mornings, with a wake up no later than 5am , I had brought a small pop-up tent, of a kind which had been well tested in force 8 storms in the Outer Hebrides. What I had not fully appreciated though, was that cycling through Missouri and into the Typhoon Alley States of Kansas, Nebraska and South Dakota, humidity necessitated a large tent which would allow a through draught of whatever air was available. I had also found that extra space was needed when you were to spend 44 nights in a tent. My tent offered neither of these features. The ability to get it down and packed away within 15 seconds, which was much admired by my fellow campers, paled into insignificance as they expressed alarm that I was spending the nights in a "sweat box". At Arrow Rock State Park, where we had camped, I decided I would buy a new tent at the first opportunity. Thus fortified, I left Arrow Rock full of anticipation about my forthcoming purchase.

Arrow Rock campsite

There were no tents to be had in Lexington, Missouri (pop. 4,453) our next stop after another 61 miles on the road. On the way there, we had rendezvoused in Marshall, Missouri (pop. 12,433) by the statue of Jim the Wonder Dog, who reputedly could understand and carry out commands given to him in any language or in Morse code. The canine antecedent of Paul the Octopus, who correctly predicted results in the 2010 Football World Cup, Jim could choose the winner of the Kentucky Derby, predict whether a pregnant lady would have a boy or a girl and pick out a visitor from Kansas from a crowd of people. The one thing Jim could not do was find us anywhere in Marshall to get anything to eat, so we moved on, leaving the town to ponder on its claim to fame.

At Lexington, incorporated in 1845, we made our camp overlooking the Lions' Club Lake, in an area of parkland, also donated by the Lions' Club, east of the business district. We used the adjacent swimming pool for showers. I was beginning to admire the American skill for joining together for the greater good. The Lions were formed in 1917 by a Chicago businessman who asked the question "What if people put their talents to work to improve their communities?" Within three years the Lions were an international organisation, with an emphasis on improving the lot of the blind and the visually impaired. It's not all about swimming pools and parks; to date, and to quote only one statistic, 137 million doses of Mectizan, to treat and control river blindness have been donated by the Lions in 15 countries.[55]

In common with many towns, Lexington has a Lewis Street and a Clark Street. Passing near the site of the present town on 19th June 1804, the Corps of Discovery had seen pelicans and had found gooseberries and raspberries, which perhaps gave some relief from the boils from which Clark had recently recorded the men suffering. Relief after a day's cycling came to us in the form of a visit from another mayor, this time bringing his tourist trolley with him, a flat-bedded trailer hauled by a tractor. We climbed on board and were treated to a tour of the Civil War sites, Lexington being the home of two important battles, both Confederate victories. In the first Battle of Lexington, in September 1861, the troops of the Missouri State Guard, who were loyal to the Confederate cause, soaked bales of hemp in river water overnight and, using them as cover, rolled them up hill towards the Union garrison which they captured, in no small part because the Unionist fire fizzled out as it struck the wet bales of hemp.[56] The punishment meted out to the captured Unionist soldiers was being required to listen to a lengthy speech by the Missouri Governor, after which they were all permitted to leave, supposedly on parole. It was during this battle that a cannonball lodged in one of the pillars of the courthouse in Lexington, the oldest courthouse still in continuous use west of the Mississippi and still with the cannonball in the pillar for all to see.

Mr Mayor

Our trolley tour also took us through the historical district, where many of the nineteenth century antebellum houses were built with quarters for the slaves who had also dug out the town's goose pond. In a small town, Mr Mayor can tell you who lives in each house and, in many cases, how much they paid for it. Here, in the 'Bible Belt', he told us, the worthy inhabitants attend the Bible classes which are held every evening except Wednesdays. That evening is reserved for baseball.

Lexington was once the biggest and most prosperous city in Missouri, a supply stop for the thousands of people who were to go west on the Santé Fe, California, Oregon and Mormon Trails. It was the headquarters for Russell, Majors and Waddell, the largest trading company in the west. These three men were also to found the Pony Express, which ran from St. Joseph, Missouri to Sacramento, California and allowed a message to be transmitted from coast to coast in 10 days (halfway by telegraph and the remaining journey by horseback riders, with a change of horses roughly every ten miles). The town also flourished because of the steamboat trade, but is now remembered in this regard because it was the location of the Saluda disaster. In April 1852, over 150 Mormon immigrants, mainly from England and Wales, were killed when the boilers of the ship taking them up the Missouri exploded.

The Captain of the Saluda had spent two days trying to get the steamboat round a bend in the river near Lexington, but was unable to make headway because of the currents in the narrow channel. Obviously getting cross and impatient, he ordered an increase in pressure. The boilers of the Saluda exploded and bodies were thrown high into the air. About 50 people survived, not including the Captain. The people of Lexington took any surviving orphans into their homes and brought them up as their own.

Lewis and Clark had their own battles with the Missouri currents. The journals record almost daily struggles against them and the obstacles which made the journey upstream so difficult. On 8th June 1804 for example:

The current was so rapid and the banks on the north falling in so continuously, that we were obliged to approach the sandbanks on the south. These were moving continuously, and formed the worst passage we had seen, and which we surmounted with much difficulty.[57]

A few weeks later on 2nd July 1804, they had to stop and repair their mast, which had been broken when the boat ran into a tree overhanging the water. They must have been pleased to stop as shortly before the current had been so strong, it had taken 20 oars and all the poles they had to stem it. They did their repairs near the site of an abandoned French fort. It was said that the French had all been killed by Indians. Only a few days later, on 6th July, they had to tow the boat along with ropes. They made 14 miles that day on which they saw a rat, killed a wolf, and one poor unfortunate suffering from sunstroke was the recipient of Dr Rush's draining techniques.

The Factory System

At the Second Battle of Lexington, the Unionist troops were pushed back along the Independence Road. It was to present day Independence (pop. 121,180) that we pedalled a mere 46 miles the next day, with me still resolved to purchasing a new tent. The night before, I had tried keeping the tent door open in order to get some air, only to find that, by this act, I had signalled every mosquito in town to come and get me. It had, however, allowed me to see the myriads of lightning bugs or fireflies which hovered around the campsite at night; the fantastic bioluminescence occurring in their bodies filling me with amazement and wonder.

The road to Independence brought another day of terrible rainstorms, but we were able to shelter from the worst of them at Fort Osage. Safely inside the museum there, we put our hands over our ears when a deafening clap of thunder signified a cloudburst outside. We waited and waited. Finally, we decided to set off, preferring to brave the rain rather than sit through a third viewing of a film about prairie grass. Fort Osage is on a bluff overlooking the Missouri which Lewis and Clark had identified as a suitable site for a future fort. Years after the expedition, it was built under Clark's direction, when he was Superintendent of Indian Affairs. It was named after a neighbouring tribe and was part of the US Government's factory system, a chain of 28 forts along the frontier designed to secure peace with the Indians and stability between various tribes. The theory was that if the government controlled the Indian trade, the Indians could not be exploited by individual commercial traders. Naturally, the government wanted a monopoly on supplying the Indians as well, in return for this protection. It also wanted to ensure that any French fur traders dealt only with the trading forts and could not sell their furs privately.

Mosquitoes find a home

Fort Osage only lasted until 1819, when trading moved further west to Council Bluffs, near present day Omaha, in response to increasing numbers of people creeping west. The factory system itself only continued for a further four years until it was abandoned in 1822 under pressure from individual traders who did not think it fair that the government had a monopoly.[58] The fort stands now as a sad reminder that, by 1808, the Osage Indians had ceded much of their land to the United States in return for protection and the right to trade at the fort. That protection was illusory as in 1825, the Osage were forcibly removed to a reservation in present-day Kansas.

Shopping in the Garden of Eden

On the way into Independence through Sibley and the back roads to town, I followed Wendy and Alcy. We were wet and cold, despite the temperature, as after a while, no clothing keeps out the incessant rain and you begin to feel chilled. We were all keen to arrive at our destination, in my case because I was anxious to get to a camping shop to buy my new tent. Our arrival was delayed by coming across one of our number wandering around aimlessly where the railroad tracks cross North Twyman Road. It was Mike B. and he had fallen off his bicycle when crossing the tracks. From his confused state and the enormous crack to be seen in his cycle helmet, he was obviously in need of medical assistance. Wendy telephoned Tom who took about ten minutes to arrive. Mike B., meanwhile, was adamant that the bike which we had picked up off the road was not his, that the water bottles on it were certainly not his and that generally he was on a bike ride but not in Missouri. Tom whisked him off to hospital with Wendy taking care of him, where, after some scans, he was pronounced fit to continue on the journey, provided that he rested up for a day in the van.

Our campsite in Independence was at the RV park near the railway station. There we were to prepare ourselves for the first of many nights listening to the sirens of the freight trains that shape many memories of cycling through the American West. At Independence, they pass through the station every ten minutes or so and the thought of this was too much for Bev, who asked me if I would share an apartment at a local B&B with her that night. Larry, too, jumped ship in favour of the comfort of a real bed. With less than a week on the road, I was surprised at how keen I was to agree to this suggestion to get out of the heat. I was even more delighted to find that the owners of the B&B (who had recorded, in their garden, five inches of rain falling in one hour that day) would take me to an outdoor store to buy a new tent. They were real southern people. Susan wore a long flowery frock and a large, wide-brimmed hat. Her husband spoke with a soft southern drawl and told me all about his job as a medical illustrator as he drove me to the out of town shopping centre. There wasn't much choice of tents there and stupidly, I took what was available, not really stopping to think about whether it would stand up to the rigours of the trip. All I could see was that the tent available offered superior ventilation and was big enough for me to spread out my stuff inside.

Independence, birthplace of the only President of the United States who had to live with his mother-in-law because he could not afford his own home, namely Harry Truman, is now nothing more than a suburb of Kansas City. It was once proclaimed as the site of the Garden of Eden by Joseph Smith, the founder of the Mormon religion, who might have changed his mind had he had to contend with the train sirens. Founded in 1827, it became an important 'jumping off' point for those who wished to journey west by wagon train along the Oregon and Californian Trails, as well as for the Mormons travelling to what became Salt Lake City. The Mormons, who were driven out of the city in 1833, crept back and now the Independence sky-line is dominated by the monstrous spire of the Temple of the Community of Christ, one of the Mormon denominations.

My shopping expedition did not leave much time to explore Independence and our stay in the B&B was a short one. We had to be up by 4.30am to begin the route north towards the Mandan Villages and Bismarck, North Dakota.

Our destination the next day was to be Atchison, Kansas, (pop. 6,430). We were picked up outside the B&B, after a breakfast of blueberry muffins, and taken back to the campsite, so that the whole tour could leave together. Normally, we cycled as we pleased, either alone or with someone else, as pace and inclination suited us, with all the riders strung out along the road (often for many miles as the cycling became more demanding). But today we had to cycle through Kansas City and Tom did not want anyone to get lost. For the first hour or so today we had to stay together, with the slowest riders, such as myself, up front with Tom, who was leading the convoy out of town. Knowing the

American cycling etiquette was essential. "Car up" meant there was a car coming towards you; "Car back" signified a car trying to overtake, and "On your left" meant "I am about to overtake you on your left". Overtaking on the right was *verboten*.

My fellow cyclists had impeccable cycling manners. No one nagged me about my speed ("Hurry up, you can do better than that") or my choice of gear ("You shouldn't be in that gear, you know") which I had come across at home. These people had nothing to prove and were always positive ("Hey, you are doing just great"). Most of all, no one suggested that instead of cycling I should be at home doing the dishes. A cyclist I had never met before greeted me with these words one Sunday morning when I went out with a group at home. After that, I decided to cycle on my own in Scotland. And so we left Independence. I was excited about leaving behind our first state on the ride, Missouri, and getting into Kansas.

"Are we in Kansas yet?" I kept yelling at Tom, who was just ahead of me.

"No, Dorothy," he kept yelling back.

It was then I discovered that the Kansas City we were cycling through is in Missouri, not Kansas. To be fair, there is another Kansas City across the Missouri, which is in Kansas, not Missouri, which makes it all very confusing.

On the way to Atchison, we stopped at Parkville, Missouri (pop. 4,059) where John Collins had received his 100 lashes for stealing whiskey on 29th June 1804. Frank's Italian Restaurant, where we got food, was very near the railroad. Every ten minutes a huge freight train would pass through, with the sirens blasting. Hans Ruedi told us that the trains were carrying coal from the coal fields of Wyoming, which is the number one coal-producing state in the United States, producing one third of the coal used in the nation. Each day, 80 trains, each a mile long with 110 cars, take the coal down the line.[59] By my reckoning that means 40 trains each night and we got used to hearing all of them.

A Night with the Dog

Leaving Parkville, we cycled past wild turkeys on the side of the road and then crossed a river which, according to the sign by the road, was the Platte. Sight of this river filled me with excitement, as I thought at the time it was the famous river, also called the Platte, which is part of the history of the Oregon and Mormon Trails. I found out later that what we had crossed is, indeed, and very confusingly, also called the Platte, but sometimes distinguished from its more famous namesake by adding 'Little' before 'Platte'. I should have known from its small, muddy, miserable-looking appearance that what I was looking at was not the huge Platte river that flows from the far west into the Missouri south of Omaha, but another tributary of the Missouri which joins the river from the east near Farley, south of Fort Leavenworth. Later we would cross the better known Platte and I would think of the days when it was described, by the people in the wagon trains who followed its course, as being a mile wide and six inches deep at its mouth. Exploring its course would have to wait until another trip. We were heading north, not west.

We finally pedalled into the state of Kansas when we crossed the Missouri at Fort Leavenworth, the oldest US Army base west of the Mississippi. Alcy got a puncture right outside the main entrance to the Federal Penitentiary, one of the places in the United States where serious criminals are incarcerated. It was also one of the few places in the United States I was aware that CCTV cameras were in operation. My fellow cyclists were horrified that we in the UK put up with CCTV in our high streets.

After Fort Leavenworth, we had a long slog up and down, up and down, through the Kansas Glacial Hills along Highway 7, and down to the Missouri River at Atchison. These hills caught me by surprise and by early afternoon, when the sun was overhead, I was finding it hard going. I hadn't reckoned on gradients like this so early in the trip, and at one of the sag stops Mike said that I was getting very sunburnt. This was despite having applied maximum factor sunscreen. There was no shade and I was suffering.

Atchison was the birthplace of Amelia Earhart, the first woman to fly across the Atlantic. This caused a media storm in June 1928 even though she did not pilot the aeroplane. As she said of herself, she was just like a sack of potatoes on board. Two months later, she flew solo across the North American continent and back, this time taking the joystick, and in 1932 she made a solo Atlantic crossing from Newfoundland to Northern Ireland. She became a lecturer at Purdue University and a supporter of the rights of women before she disappeared in 1937, near Howard Island in the Pacific, whilst trying to circumvent the globe in her Lockheed Electra 10E.

None of the romanticism that might be associated with early aviators was apparent to me in Atchison. Parts of it were so run down that I refused to believe my route instructions. Surely I was not going to have to ride along there, under the bridges? It all looked so decrepit and dangerous that I phoned Sue in the sag van for reassurance. Sure enough I was on the right road. There was nothing to worry about. All I had to do was follow the road and then turn left along the banks of the Missouri where I would find the campsite. From there we would be bussed to the YMCA, where showers were available.

It was a glorious afternoon when I pitched my new, well-ventilated tent in the park overlooking the Missouri at Atchison. We all hoped there would be no more rain. The river was high, fast flowing and sweeping a lot of debris downstream. We were anxious to ensure that we camped well away from any danger should the river overflow. Two nights before, 19 people had been killed when the Little Missouri had risen dramatically after a flash flood and its waters had devastated a campground in Arkansas.[60] Surely we would have a peaceful night.

That was not to be. Shortly after midnight, the rain started and steadily got harder. The wind increased to over 50 mph (I discovered later). Lightning and thunderstorms soon followed. To my horror, in one corner of my new tent, I found that the floor was wet. I quickly packed all my gear, including my sleeping bag, into my bags and sat in the tent thinking "What the hell do I do now?"

It was clear that I was going to get wet, unless I did something as the water continued to pour into the tent. I put my waterproofs on and went outside, congratulating myself on my foresight in knowing which tent belonged to Tom. Poor Tom was going to have to get up too. I shouted his name. Within seconds he was out of his tent. The rain was so hard we could hardly hear each other speak. He told me I could shelter in the van, which was at least wind and water proof. And so it was that Griffin became my companion for the night. He was a gracious one, allowing me to share his quarters, but he was not sufficient a gentleman as to allow me to stretch out on the bench seat. Instead I had to lie at his feet on a rug between the seat and the cool boxes which held our ice and fizzy drinks. It was hard to sleep. I tried not to think about the tent, the rain and what I was going to do next about my sleeping arrangements. It was hard not to expend energy pondering my incompetence.

It was no comfort to me that, when Lewis and Clark had camped here, one of their number, Joseph Field, had been bitten by a snake. That had been on the 4th July 1804, the 28th birthday of the United States of America. Each man had been given a gill of whiskey in celebration. I had nothing to celebrate. There was no whiskey for me that night and I dared not even look at the dog food, in case Griffin decided that he did not, after all, like me as a van mate.

A night with the dog

But I was lucky I was still on the tour. That afternoon, whilst cycling into Atchison, Gil from Alaska had fallen off his bike and had broken his elbow. That was the end of the cycle ride to the Pacific for him. Karl's daughter and her husband drove over from their home a few hours' drive away, and took him back with them, so that he could recover for a few days before making his plans to get back to Alaska. We all missed Gil. He was great fun and good company. I had also been looking forward to hearing more about Sarah Palin, who lived in the same town. Gil had been the one to tell her that one of her daughters did not meet the required standard on a sports team he was coaching. She was fine about it, he assured us. He obviously liked her a lot. I had hoped he would tell us more about her, but that was not to be.

The next day I felt pretty rough after the traumas of the night. We set off early and made our way to Troy, Kansas (pop. 1,054), which had been a stop on the Oregon Trail and a changing post, or relay station, for the Pony Express.[61] It had also been visited in 1860 by the English explorer Richard Burton, who pronounced it to be comprised of a few "wretched shanties".[62] For us it was the place where we got a good breakfast of eggs, bacon and hash browns to set us up for one of the most beautiful rides of the trip – along the Missouri flood plain, with high bluffs on our left and meadows of wild flowers on our right, over which pale blue and black butterflies fluttered. This road took us into Nebraska, our third state of the ride. At White Cloud we were greeted by an Indian Chief who had come down from the casino on the reservation to see us. How he knew we were coming, no one knew.

In 1985, two bodies had been found on an outlying farm close to Rulo (pop. 226), the next water stop for us down the road from White Cloud. They were the victims of a white supremacist, sadistic cult which had stockpiled weapons in the expectation of a final battle between good and evil. The leader of the cult imprisoned one of the victims in a shed and fed him on chicken feed before torturing him to death. The other victim was a five year old who had somehow fallen out of favour. Rulo seemed such a peaceful little place as we cycled through it, with no hint of its dark past, but knowledge of it stopped us from lingering there. With ten miles to go to Falls City, Nebraska, our destination for the night, I elected to ride the rest of the way in the van. I had had too much sun and knew that if I got sick with sunstroke that would be the end of the trip for me. Tom, fortunately, did not go in for instruments to drain the blood, but there was no cure except to get in out of the sun. Better to ride the last ten miles today than miss the rest of the journey.

Shelter from the Storms

Falls City (pop. 4,671) and 60 miles from Atchison, is on the Nemaha River, another tributary of the Missouri. Like the Meachum Crossing, it was a stop on the Underground Railroad where runaway slaves could find shelter and support. It was also the birthplace of Pee Wee Erwin, who played jazz trumpet with Benny Goodman and Tommy Dorsey. Almost too predictably, Falls City was also the site of an infamous murder; in 1993, a transsexual called Teena Brandon was killed solely because she was discovered to be a woman living as a man. I was beginning to wonder if every town on our way out west would be the site of a notorious murder.

We, however, had rain, not murder, on our minds, as Falls City turned out to be a re-run of Atchison, with a beautiful, clear afternoon turning into a torrential rainstorm after dinner. This time I was more relaxed. I had, for the sake of form, pitched my tent, but I could see that it was not going to stand up to the ferocious winds and the horizontal rain. I had kept the pop-up tent but could not face its confines in the heat. As luck would have it, the town park, where we were based, had a log cabin with a large, screened porch and, luxury of luxuries, an air-conditioned dining room-cum-kitchen. I elected to sleep inside. Ken, who only had a bivvy bag, decided to do the same and we marked out our respective territories on each side of the long, trestle table in the middle of the cabin. Even with my iPod earphones in, with the volume at maximum, and the air-conditioning on, I could still hear Ken snoring and I determined to sleep as far away from him as possible in future. Tents were still on my mind, but Tom had cheered me up immensely by telling me that he had to go home to Lincoln, Nebraska, the next day to get the van serviced. He said he would go to a proper outdoor store and get me a decent tent for the trip.

The rain continued the next morning and we found the minor road to our destination, Nebraska City, 63 miles away, well and truly closed by construction works that we could not get through. We were forced to cycle on Highway 73 and then Highway 75 north, which was a major road, at least to me. I would never have cycled on anything remotely resembling it in the UK. We would become all too familiar with it over the next couple of days. Stopping at Darling's café "just south of the overpass" in Auburn, Nebraska for breakfast, an establishment I voted as serving the best hash browns of the entire trip so far, spirits were high as, in Nebraska City, air conditioning awaited us. We were to spend two nights camping in the National Guard Armory and enjoy our first day off. The sun was still bothering me, but the knowledge that I would soon be inside a cool room made me determined to cycle all the way into Nebraska City. Sue and Kit in the sag van stopped to make sure I was alright and offered me a lift for the last six miles into town, but I turned it down. I was nearly there and I had to keep going.

John Brown's Body

In common with many American towns, Nebraska City (pop. 7,228) is built on a grid system, but instead of having numbered streets, it has numbered Corsos (Corso being the main street through historical Rome). It adds a touch of glamour to this delightful little town on the banks of the Missouri, to which we were welcomed, at 4th Corso, on the way to the Armory, by three children selling homemade lemonade at a stall. Charmingly they were selling it at 50 cents a glass or two glasses for one dollar.

That lemonade certainly tasted good and was as refreshing as the hot, powerful shower in the National Guard building, where we unpacked all our gear and laid out our sleeping bags on the floor of the air-conditioned gymnasium. I felt euphoric at having completed the first tranche of the journey, at the prospect of a day–off and in the knowledge that a big, tall, crew-cutted National Guard Sergeant would be on duty all night, keeping us safe and secure. I wanted to join up there and then.

Two glasses for $1

In 1854, the Missouri Compromise, which had ensured a balance between free and slaves states under the union of the United States, had been overturned by the Kansas-Nebraska Act. This legislation permitted the inhabitants of each territory to decide for themselves whether the land they occupied should approve or prohibit slavery. The Act had caused endless trouble in Kansas when both pro- and anti-slavery supporters had moved into the territory, with both sides determined on making the territory conform to their principles on the subject. Blood had been spilt, some of it by 'Beecher's Bibles', the nickname for the guns supplied from funds raised to support the abolitionists by a Rev. Henry Ward Beecher. The clergyman, however, was safely back east in Brooklyn, New York where he was a well-known activist. Beecher would have been right at home in the age of the internet. Perhaps as a result of not being allowed to celebrate Christmas or his birthdays as a child, he loved the publicity associated with his many causes, which included the rights of women and Darwinism; naturally, he was a superstar preacher. If he were here today, he would be beaming his sermons worldwide from some mega-church complex, complete with a crèche. In common with many of his ilk in modern times, he was even embroiled in a nasty scandal involving the wife of a friend, for which he was put on trial. The husband took the news of Beecher's acquittal hard and moved to Paris, which may have been of some solace.

The cottonwood tree (*Populus deltoids*) lined the banks of the Missouri when Lewis and Clark made their journey to the Pacific and still graced all our campsites. Indeed, next to the Armory there was a cabin which had been built from the wood of this tree in 1855. It had originally been the home of the Mayhew family who had come to Nebraska territory from Ohio to make a better life for themselves. Alan Mayhew had staked a claim for 160 acres, which was possible even before the Homestead Act of 1862 and had built his cabin with the help of Henry Kagi, his brother-in-law. Kagi was an opponent of slavery and it was probably he who persuaded the Mayhews to help runaway slaves. So it was that the cabin became a stop on the Underground Railroad. A tunnel was built from the cabin to a nearby creek. This afforded any slave on the escape route, who had made it to the Mayhew Cabin, the opportunity to move onto open country and then to the next stop on the Underground Railroad. I looked in vain for the creek until I realised that the cabin had been moved, before restoration, from its original site out of town.

Looking at the Mayhew Cabin, I wondered why such a tiny little shack had survived long enough to be restored. Perhaps it would have disappeared into history had Kagi not been associated with one of the most famous events in American history, namely the raid, in 1859, on the US arsenal at Harper's Ferry in Virginia. We usually associate this raid with another name, that of a person whose body lies a-mouldering in his grave – John Brown.

John Brown was one of the countless people back east who had spent years trying to escape the miseries of debt and bankruptcy as their various businesses failed. Unlike the rest of them though, he became the Che Guevara of his time, with revolution on his mind and the abolition of slavery as his cause. He honed his skills by killing five slave owners in Kansas, which he visited when he heard talk of the fierce and bloody debate there on slavery following the Kansas-Nebraska Act. Buoyed by this success, he determined upon Harper's Ferry as his next objective. His plan was to steal arms and munitions from the arsenal and give them to slaves in the area. He felt sure the slaves would immediately answer his call to rise up against their masters. So confident of success was he that he took it as certain that popular revolt would erupt throughout the south and slavery would come to an end.

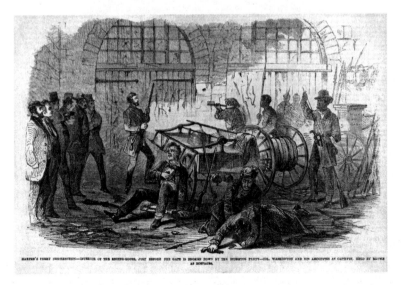

John Brown holds hostages inside the Armory at Harper's Ferry

The raid, however, was a disaster. Kagi was killed along with nine other supporters of Brown. Seven more were captured, including John Brown himself. One insurgent escaped. The US Army contingent, led by Robert E. Lee, lost one man and another was wounded. It was all over in three minutes. John Brown was tried for treason and hanged. Yet the raid itself had a profound effect on the nation, on both sides of the slavery issue, and was not unconnected to the eventual outbreak of the Civil War at Fort Sumter in South Carolina in 1861.

Henry Ward Beecher

As for the Rev. Beecher, as one might expect, he was energised by the Civil War. He raised funds for the Unionist cause by holding mock slave auctions from his pulpit, while on occasion wielding the very chains in which John Brown had been restrained after Harper's Ferry.[63] When the flag of the United States was raised over Fort Sumter on 14th April 1865, towards the end of the war and on the fourth anniversary of its lowering at the beginning of the conflict, our Henry was there to deliver the main speech. On the same day, but a few hours later, a man sat down in his seat in a theatre in Washington, DC to watch a performance of *Our American Cousin*. Minutes later, Abraham Lincoln was dead, assassinated by John Wilkes Booth in order to avenge the cause of the south and the supporters of slavery.

My Beautiful American Laundromat

If there is one thing that can preoccupy the mind of a touring cyclist, it is how to get your laundry done. Actually, this is perhaps only the preoccupation of those who cycle in Scotland, where a laundrette is as rare as a sober person in Reform Street in Dundee on a Friday night, i.e. not unknown, but difficult to find, and as a result, a shock to behold. Americans, in their own country, take it for granted that they will be able to wash their clothes at a laundromat and do not fret about it. I had to learn this relaxed behaviour. In Nebraska City, I discovered how not to fuss about a bag of dirty clothes. I also learnt how to be pleased, yet unimpressed, by a bag of clean ones.

In Nebraska City I was also reminded of the wailing I had listened to from a fellow cyclist I had met in the Orkney Islands. There, defeated in her quest to get some laundry done while cycling through Scotland, this American had retreated to her bed with a pile of novels in order to shut out the difficulties of life in this dark and uncomfortable land.

"Why is getting laundry done an all-day experience in this country?" she had cried, covering her head with her duvet. "That is, if you can get it done at all. In my country, it takes an hour. I have never been anywhere where life is so arduous." A fair comment, perhaps, made all the more telling because she had worked in Kosovo and Afghanistan.

On our day off in Nebraska City, Alcy, Wendy and I cycled into town. We left our dirty clothes at the Cider House Laundry on 1st Avenue, had breakfast at Johnny's on Central Avenue and then collected our clothes. They had been washed, dried, folded and bagged up. They were presented to us by the charming gentleman who had done our laundry and who made us feel as if he had been waiting his entire life just to provide this simple service. He was proud to do it. He beamed. He shook our hands. He wished us well. It was still only 8.30am. My laundry bill was $5.

The rest of the day was ours to explore Nebraska City. I chose to go to the Lewis and Clark Interpretive Centre, which is just outside town. I marvelled at the fantastic displays of prairie life and the reproduction of the keelboat in which Lewis and Clark sailed up the Missouri. More importantly, I enjoyed the fact that my head was feeling cooler. I had elected, the afternoon before, to have most of my hair cut off. I hoped this would make riding with a helmet on (which was a tour rule) more comfortable in the excessive temperatures we were experiencing. I might look a fright but who cared?

CHAPTER SEVEN: NEBRASKA CITY, NE TO PIERRE, SD

Days 10 to 16
17th June to 23rd June 2010
479 miles

Rumble Strips

The next day's cycling, 67 miles to Fort Calhoun, Nebraska (pop. 856) should have been an easy one after our rest day, but for me it turned into a nightmare. Our route took us again onto Highway 75 which I hated. I was not used to cycling on such roads. Trucks whizzed by and the debris on the hard shoulder where we were riding made the riding unpleasant at times. By now I was getting used to American 'shoulders' and their associated rumble strips, which formed a barrier between the road and the shoulder. Sometimes these constituted a continuous line of raised, ridged material parallel with the highway, with only an intermittent gap, and never where you needed one. At other times, the rumble strips were at 90° to the road, forming horizontal barriers for the cyclist who had to squeeze in between them and the edge of the shoulder on the right. Occasionally the shoulder disappeared altogether and it was necessary to cycle over these strips, and this set the teeth shaking in the head. Yet the rumble strips did give some protection, however illusory, from the traffic. If you heard a truck on the rumble strip, it was way too close and time for you to get out of the way.

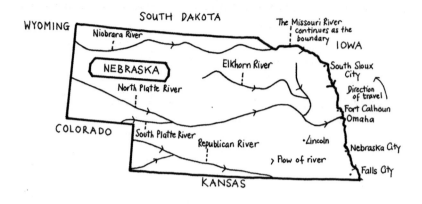

Nebraska

Flats and Boots

Going down a hill on Highway 75 and across a small bridge where the shoulder narrowed almost to nothing, I heard a loud bang and came to a halt. A long, rusty screw had gone through my tyre and had come out the other side. My tyre was well and truly kebab-ed. Fortunately, Karl the bike man was just behind me and he was able to get me going again. This was not a simple matter of getting out the puncture repair kit. Karl said it was the worse 'flat' he had ever seen and that my tyre would need a 'boot'. A boot is a piece of material which lies inside the tyre, at the entrance and exit points of the puncture. It is designed to give some strength to the tyre at the site of the offending tear and, if fitted correctly, stops the inner tube bubbling through with predictable results. The tyre can continue to be used until a new one can be purchased (or until it finally gives up the ghost for good). Karl told me that, in the absence of a proper boot, a dollar bill would do. I thought this was some kind of bike mechanic's mumbo jumbo until I discovered that it is absolutely true; a dollar bill is made of material that can hold pressure without ripping. As far as punctures were concerned, I was lucky. I only had two throughout the entire trip. Mike B.

took the record with nine. On one tour, we were told, one cyclist had nine punctures in one day.

Fixing a Flat

The puncture had unnerved me, as there had been nowhere to get off the road while the trucks pounded by. I had fallen behind because of the delay and so was one of the last to reach Offnut Air Force Base (headquarters of US Strategic Command and where President Bush was taken after 9/11). Here the route instructions told us to get off the road and join the traffic-free Keystone Trail through Omaha City.

Tom had told us to leave the Keystone Trail at Dodge Street, where we would find a shopping centre and some fast food restaurants. It was a long way on the trail and Bev and I, who were cycling together, stopped to read the map, uncertain where we were. As we were figuring out whether we had missed the turn or still had some way to go, we came across the only rude person we met on the entire trip from Missouri to the Pacific – a man jogging on the trail who very vehemently told us to move over, as well as giving us his opinion of what he thought of us. "Assholes!" he shouted.

In fact, we were blocking the trail and should have moved to the right when we stopped, but it was so unusual, indeed, unknown, to encounter bad manners and bad temper that we were shocked. So much for Omaha.

We finally found Dodge Street and emerged from the relative coolness of the cycle trail to a horror of concrete, tarmac and blistering heat. I realise now that I should have skipped lunch, turned around and continued on to Fort Calhoun, but I made the mistake of going into an icy cold, air-conditioned restaurant. The order took ages. Bev and I lingered, enjoying the respite from the heat and discussing whether we should buy a *Wall Street Journal* from the news stand. Neither of us wanted to carry it, so we decided not to buy it, little knowing it was the last *Wall Street Journal* we would see until we reached the Pacific.

When we emerged from the restaurant, I thought I was going to collapse as the full force of the midday sun hit me. I saw a temperature of 96°F displayed on a sign. It was a struggle to get across the parking lot and back down to the cycle track, where the relative drop in temperature revived me. At the next sag stop, at the end of the trail, Tom gave us revised instructions to Fort Calhoun. Bev took our copy and we set off through the northern suburbs of Omaha, until the gradient of North 60th Street brought us both to a full stop. Not for nothing does Omaha, named after the Indian tribe who inhabited the area, mean 'Dwellers on the Bluff'.

Dundee, Nebraska

I had hoped, on this stretch of our trip, to meet the 'Sage of Omaha', a.k.a. Warren Buffett, one of the richest men in the world and Chairman of Berkshire Hathaway. How nice it would have been to find him waiting for us with a pitcher of iced water. It was not to be, although we were still able to admire the wooded affluence of the area in which he lived. Buffett bought his house in Dundee for $31,500 in 1958 and still lives there. He obviously does not go to work on a bicycle though, as the area is murderously hilly.

By now the name of the suburb should not be a surprise. Dundee, Omaha was developed in 1880 by some Kansas builders who had initially been funded by Scottish money to convert the Kansas City Fairgrounds to residential housing, named, of course, Dundee Place. Another Dundee Place was established in St. Louis by Thomas A. Scott, using money from the Dundee Land and Investment Company which allowed the purchase of 22 blocks of land in the city.

I had it in my head that we still had 16 miles to go after we got back onto Highway 75, where I knew there would be no shade. In fact, had we carried on, we would only have had about five more miles to go to Fort Calhoun and it was just about all downhill. But, out of water, we chose to call up the van and get a ride into Fort Calhoun, where we would be staying with Tim and Cheri, friends of Tom, in their ranch house. We found some shade under a tree outside one of the large, detached colonial style houses that ooze privilege and wellbeing for those inside.

When Sue arrived in the sag van to pick us up, her first words were, "I knew you would be under that tree. That is where I stopped and slept for two hours".

Getting a ride was one thing I like to think the Sage would have approved of, because when we got to Tim's, I saw that my legs were very sunburnt. I had to sit with my legs in ice packs, kindly supplied by Tim. I had covered both legs with zinc oxide sun block to ride through Omaha, but even that had not been enough. I realised that, from now, on, I would have to cycle as far as I could before the sun got intolerable, not waste time in air-conditioned buildings at midday, and be prepared to get in the van, rather than soldier on, once the sun moved round in the sky and hit me with full force. I was paying the price for having spent most of my life in North-East Scotland, where sunshine is an event. No one else on the trip had a problem with the sun, although they were all were careful to use sun screen. I had come to the United States well before the trip in order to get acclimatised, but I still was not used to the intensity of the sun. Consequently, I was to suffer a lot from it.

Blackbird Hill

Fort Calhoun is on the Missouri River opposite the site where, on 1st August 1804, Lewis and Clark waited for a meeting with the Oti Indians while they celebrated Clark's 34th birthday. Pudding that day was cherries, plums, raspberries, currants and grapes of a superior quality which they enjoyed after feasting on a saddle of venison and a beaver tail.

Following customary practice formed in Europe and exported elsewhere to those who had to deal with indigenous peoples, Lewis and Clark took with them on the expedition 89 'peace medals'. The most impressive were 'Jefferson' medals. These had a likeness of the President on one side and an engraving of a handshake on the other. They bore the words 'Peace' and 'Friendship' above and below. The purpose of each medal was not just to act as a token of respect and friendliness. By showing the likeness of the ruler, each medal made it clear to the recipient that those who receive should not mess with those who give. The Oti Indians arrived the next day and were graced with such medals from Lewis and Clark.

When we left Fort Calhoun on 18th June 2010, our first objective was the hill, north of the town, where Lewis and Clark had honoured the Chief of the Omaha Indians, Black Bird, by planting a flag on the mound where he was buried. Black Bird had died in a smallpox epidemic four years previously which had killed around 400 members of the tribe. It soon became clear that we were not going to make it directly. By the time we arrived at Blair, ten miles down the road, the skies had darkened ominously. I cycled through the town and caught up with Wendy and Alcy who had stopped at an intersection on the outskirts and who were studying the sky carefully. Just then a huge four-wheeled vehicle passed us by at speed and turned right down a side street. A few seconds later it returned, with tyres screaming, and the driver rolled down the window.

"You all don't know this town, right?" he yelled. "You've got about ten minutes before that thing hits. Turn right around now, get back into town and shelter at the convenience store where you'll also get some food. Get going now!"

He was talking about the storm which we could all see rolling in. Not wishing to dispute his advice, we turned around and pedalled as fast as we could back to the Super Food store. Wendy phoned Tom to tell him where we were and to where anyone coming into town should aim for shelter. It was not a moment too soon – feeling as if I was in some blockbuster Hollywood disaster movie, I watched the sky darken to the extent that it looked like midnight, not early morning. And then the thunder, lightning and rain started. It was a spectacular sight from the porch of the store and lasted a long time. The experience left me with a nagging fear about what would happen if I were caught out in such a storm. Sue said to leave my bike on the road and get down flat, and as low as possible, in a ditch by the side of the road. What about the snakes, I wondered?

Tim, our host in Fort Calhoun

Back in Missouri, I had seen a black rat snake near the Mary Meachum Freedom Crossing where the volunteers were handing out free iced water. It had slithered underneath the benches in the volunteer hut and down the bank into the Mississippi.

I was told by one of the volunteers in the hut that it was not venomous. Later on, I was also told to watch out for copperhead snakes, which are venomous and prolific. Unfortunately, this advice included the helpful hint that I should take care when taking my tent down, as copperheads like to crawl under tents and seek warmth from the inhabitants sleeping above them. Copperheads have two heat sensing pits between the eyes and the nostrils which they use to locate their prey. I was determined not to fall into this category.

No one was more wimpish than me when it came to snakes, unlike my fellow cyclists who were sensible about them and did not regard them with horror. Not even the prospect of rattlesnakes seemed to faze them. I was assured that rattlesnakes were shy creatures, more afraid of us than we were of them. I did not like to think I might have to put this to the test, however. For now, worrying about the weather was enough for me.

Weather Warnings

Whereas in Britain our endless conversation about the weather is a tool to ease social situations, in the United States, I was to find that talk of the weather is a matter of life and death. My hotel room in St. Louis contained a book with detailed instructions about what to do if the tornado sirens sounded. If staying above the 25th floor, you were instructed to go into the bathroom and close the door. If you were below this floor, you had to make your way to the lobby where you would be directed to a place of safety. I was on the 27th floor, but I decided that if the sirens sounded, there was no way I was going to lock myself in the bathroom and sit out the tornado. I was going to hot foot it to the lobby as quickly as possible.

It was with some alarm I had noticed that the supermarkets in St. Charles had baskets of cheap radios for sale, which could be clipped to the belt. They were all pre-tuned to the local weather station and gave minute by minute severe weather warnings. TV and radio programs were also interrupted by such warnings and all towns had prominent signs to storm shelters. This was weather for real.

We were to find that out in Gettysburg, South Dakota ("not that Gettysburg" as the sign going into town states), where the Sheriff came down to the campsite and warned us that a storm was forecast. Seeing a Sheriff at our campsite was not unusual, as it was common for the cops to swing by to say "hallo" and pass the time of day with us. We often provoked a stir in town and I like to think not only because the locals had heard about my new haircut. This Sheriff had weather on his mind and warned us that there was "a big one" coming. Having seen the one in Blair from the safety of the store, I listened to him intently. He added that he would be down to see us in plenty of time before it hit and would evacuate us during the night if need be.

The Sheriff then looked round the campsite and advised some of us to move our tents. That included me. I had pitched my tent under a tree which had looked perfectly alright, indeed, ideal, when I had put the tent pegs in. Now I realised I was camped under a massive dead branch. I had chosen a place which would have been particularly dangerous in a storm. I groaned at the thought of moving my tent. I had been the last into camp. I had missed going to the museum which everyone else had seen. Worst of all, I did not get to the café where everyone except me got to see some real live cowboys, spurs and all, drinking their coffee. I did not mind missing the museum. I could do without a cup of coffee. But I was mad at myself for missing the cowboys.

Many of us spent an anxious night waiting for the storm to hit, which it did at 6am. Fortunately, we had our tents down by then and were under the park shelter, having delayed our departure as we could see the storm rolling in and had no wish to be caught out in it on the road.

It is a law of camping that wherever you pitch your own tent, everyone else chooses a better spot than you. In our group, I noticed that the men who had been in the military always picked a superb camping spot on the highest ground. Why was it that I had failed to spot these sites, seconds before, when I had cast my eye round the campsite? Shade was another issue. I did not have a compass with me, thinking rather stupidly that any fool would know which way west was. That worked when we were cycling along the highways, but at campsites, sometimes arrived at after cycling through towns or winding roads in parks, I was often confused about direction. I would carefully figure out which way the sun was going to move round and then pitch my tent to ensure it would be in shade before too long. The trouble was that I was often 180° out.

Ten days or so into our journey, I was finding it all very exhausting. I wondered whether we would ever have an uneventful day. Would we ever have just one day without sun, storm, flood, accident or punctures in dangerous places? I found it all mentally wearing. I was the most inexperienced cyclist on the trip and the one least accustomed to all the extremes of distance and weather that America had to offer. It had taken me time to master the camp routine. Some of the highways daunted me both in terms of traffic and the unrelenting scale of the road ahead, mile after mile without apparent variation or visual distraction. Without much to look at except tarmac and cornfields, it was easy for the mind to wander into areas where it would have been better not to venture. Often I heard a little voice in my head repeating "How many more miles on this road?" Little did I know then what I would face later in Eastern Montana. There the monotony of the road was such that I had to cover my odometer up. Otherwise I would become fixated on looking at it as the miles rolled slowly by. Or I would tell myself that I would not, under any circumstances, look at it for at least ten miles. I would then be tormented with disbelief to discover, when I looked down, that I had only cycled half a mile. It wasn't as if the directions required careful mileage to be kept. Cycling 50 or 60 miles on the same road does not require precise navigational skills. The odometer was useful, though, approaching or leaving cities, to ensure the correct road was taken at the given mileage point. It was unfortunate for me that I went through four of them on the trip. The first one broke before I left St. Charles. I was lucky to get replacements and, when the third one broke, was able to do so only because Sue asked a friend, driving out to see her at Waitsburg, Washington, to buy an odometer and bring it out to me.

Reservations

When the rain eased off, we left the Super Food convenience store in Blair and set out for Blackbird Hill (one word, unlike the Chief) and then for South Sioux City, Nebraska; not to be confused with Sioux City, Iowa and North Sioux City, South Dakota, which are all in the same metropolitan area on the banks of the Missouri. On the way there we cycled through the Winnebago Indian Reservation, where, according to the tribe's own website, 44% of the Native American population of the reservation lives below the poverty level.[64] The Winnebago Indians are not native to Nebraska. They originated in Wisconsin but were shipped south in the 1860s and purchased land from the Omaha Indians, who wanted a land buffer between themselves and the Lakota (Sioux) Indians to the north.

Today, the Native Americans have a certain amount of "home rule", as the Winnebago Tribe Constitution states in its preamble. Membership of a tribe is by blood, with the exact qualifying amounts laid down in the same documents. The tribes have their own governing bodies or councils, which have wide powers and manage the tribal and communal lands. The Winnebago tribal lands, for example, may not be allotted to individual members of the tribe.

The reservations were a surprise to me, despite having read some Indian history. To read is one thing, but to see it with your own eyes is quite another. Until I cycled through them, I had no concept of the extent of the reservations, the powers of their tribal councils and their economies (the Indians have special taxation privileges and pay no federal or state taxes on the profits of their casino operations, for example). The very idea of the reservation seemed to me the embodiment of a socialist republic, so despised by the rest of America. The manifest deprivation on them was as depressing as their public housing and the general aimlessness of the people standing around the stores. It was all a bit too much like some parts of central Scotland.

Fairy Lights by the Missouri

South Sioux City, Nebraska (pop. 11,925) is on flat land west of a large bend in the Missouri River. I wanted to get there quickly. I had decided not to linger at Blackbird Hill, where Sue had provided an *ad hoc* lunch for us at the van, and had pedalled on, terrified at times by the volume of traffic for the last 14 miles into the city. Even so, I could not quite believe that I was one of the first to arrive at our destination right on the river near the bridge to Iowa. I was looking forward to the camping as I was now the proud owner of a new, two-man Marmot tent, which Tom had bought for me. It could be pitched without the fly, allowing maximum ventilation and a mosquito-free environment in a mesh dome. It could then be turned into a waterproof unit when the fly was put on in anticipation of the inevitable rainstorms.

It might be assumed that sleep would come easy to us after a hard day's riding, but alas, getting through the night at a campsite was sometimes as exhausting as being on the trail. In my tent, I was either frightened of impending storms, anxious about the ride the next day and whether I would cope with the hills and the distance, concerned about my ability to tolerate the sun, or just plain kept awake in a noisy campsite.

The campsite at South Sioux City was such a place. No sooner had we pitched our tents than the campsite filled up with enormous RVs of a size that mercifully we have not yet seen in the UK. Invariably, each monster was towing a tiny little car. On second look, however, that tiny little car turned out to be a huge four-wheel drive vehicle. In case they tired of the jeep, the inhabitants of these vehicles also brought their motor bikes, which they hung from the back of the van. Territory was marked out by stringing fairy lights from tree to tree, or in a circle on the ground around the RV. Not content with that, one family at South Sioux City planted an artificial fir tree outside the door of the RV, complete with fairy lights. The tables and chairs would come out, then the barbeque, the coolers full of beer and the sound system. The children would ride up and down the road on their bicycles through the campsite, shouting. Granted, we were early to bed and we could not expect our fellow campers to sit quietly and read a book when we crawled into our tents. At South Sioux City, though, the carousing started late and continued all night, to the accompaniment of motorcycles racing up and down outside the camp ground. None of us slept well that night in South Sioux City and, when we crossed the bridge into Iowa the next morning, the twenty minutes or so that we were to spend in that state were expressed, peevishly, by some of our party, to be plenty long enough.

Into South Dakota

Along the Iowa shore of the Missouri we passed the monument to Sergeant Charles Floyd, the only man to die on the Lewis and Clark expedition. Floyd, born in Kentucky, had been a mail carrier on the American frontier, and one of the first recruits to the expedition. He fell ill about a thousand miles up the Missouri from St. Louis, appeared to recover slightly and then got very sick with something described as "bilious colic".[65] This was probably appendicitis. Floyd's last words were "I am going to leave you. I want you to write me a letter".[66] He was buried by his fellow expedition members. On the way back from the Pacific, they found his grave had been disturbed by animals and reburied him, something which would have to be repeated on several occasions in the future. Floyd's monument is a 100 foot obelisk made of sandstone from the Kettle River area, near the Iowa bank of the Missouri and the moored steamboat which bears his name.

Stormy Sky in South Dakota

The border with South Dakota is not hard to spot. It's all to do with the fireworks. In Iowa, such things as firecrackers, torpedoes, skyrockets and roman candles cannot be sold to members of the public, who must content themselves with gold sparklers containing no magnesium. In South Dakota, just about anything goes, and so firework shops proliferate at the state line. Here, on the South Dakota side, the only prohibited fireworks are those made from dynamite, nitro-glycerine or giant powder (a blasting explosive). South Dakota is a place where real men are not content with sparklers.

After Charles Floyd's death, the Corps of Discovery had to appoint another sergeant to replace him. At Elk Point (pop. 1,963) where the expedition saw their first buffalo and where we were headed for breakfast after our sleepless night in South Sioux City, the first election in the American West among white men took place. Patrick Gass became sergeant in place of Charles Floyd. At Cody's Café in Elk Point, where we had the chance to study the display of barbed wire while we ate our eggs and hash browns, Cody, the owner, cook and front of house, told us that Patrick Gass had come back to Elk Point after the expedition. In late life he fathered a child, an ability which may or may not have something to do with the fact that he was, as far as anyone knows, the last surviving member of the Lewis and Clark expedition.

Main Street had been impassable in Elk Point, due to road works, and we had cycled through the neat, side streets of this small town with their trim, white clapboard houses. Some of the gardens were adorned with anti-abortion posters. This was an area where feelings about the rights of the unborn run deep. We were to come across numerous anti-abortion billboards, as well as the ubiquitous slogans about salvation through Jesus. The religious billboards got very tedious, especially when there was no salvation from the wind and a hard saddle.

Our destination that day was Chief White Crane State Park, just outside Yankton, South Dakota, where George Shannon had gone missing, nearly dying for want of a bullet. On the way there we cycled through Vermillion (pop. 9,765) where I would have lingered for a few days had I been on my own, in order to enjoy the leafy streets of beautiful colonial-style houses. Lingering was, however, something you could not do on a group trip. Home of the University of South Dakota, Vermillion is named after the Lakota Indian word for 'red stream', and is situated on a bluff overlooking the Missouri, where Lewis and Clark had camped on 24th August 1804. Lewis and Clark had feasted on delicious berries, double the size of a currant, which the Indians called 'rabbit berries'. When they camped that night they found themselves "much annoyed by mosquitoes". We were soon to share that annoyance with these pesky creatures.

Mosquitoes Abound

Our campsite at Chief White Crane State Park was on the far side of Yankton (pop. 13,528). The town is named after the Yankton tribe of the Sioux, and as I passed the cattle yards on the outskirts of the town, I realised our cycling tour was taking us into a different world, that of the old Wild West. Nebraska had seemed pretty civilised compared with this.

Lewis and Clark had met the Yankton Sioux here, near present-day Gavin's Dam, which overlooked our camping area. Clark described them as wearing buffalo robes, leggings and moccasins and decorating themselves with porcupine quills and feathers. My decoration that night was the midge net as our friends the mosquitoes were back in force, only this time they were bigger and more fearsome than those on the Katy Trail. I had brought my net from Scotland and had put it on over my head, covering my face and neck, to exclamations of disbelief from my fellow cyclists. They had never seen such a thing. Shock quickly turned to envy and soon they all wanted one. I reminded myself not to leave it lying around, lest one of my fellow cyclists be tempted to try it on and, having done so, cause an international incident by not giving it back.

A midge net is an essential fashion accessory

Bigger and more fearsome, too, were the inhabitants of the RVs which were parked in this camp ground in South Dakota. Once again, fairy lights delineated their respective territories, but these people were no fairies. Not only did one party keep us awake all night, but we were treated to the views of our fellow campers on Obama, which involved terms such as "Un-American". From here, until the Oregon border, there was, to me at least, a slight air of menace at every place we camped, in the sense that it was obvious that becoming embroiled in an argument would not be prudent unless you were prepared to see guns drawn. (President Bush had lifted the ban on loaded concealed weapons in National Parks and such guns were permitted in State Parks if the laws of the respective state permitted it.) Getting into a heated discussion about Obama with a crowd cooking beans in a Dutch oven over a fire was something I did not fancy, so I kept quiet. I never quite got used to the guns, no matter how commonplace they came to be.

Although we often camped by the Missouri, one of the frustrations about following Lewis and Clark's journey was how seldom we saw the Missouri when we were on the road cycling. There is no bike trail along the river, as there is along the Danube, for example, and even if the road was near the river, it wasn't near enough for us to see it, and far too far away for diversions down one of the dead-end gravel roads to the various landing and recreational areas by the water. When we stopped for the day, it was often far too hot to even consider leaving camp to explore the river. At Chief White Crane, we were only five minutes bike ride from the 74 foot tall embankment of Gavin's Dam, but none of us chose to go and look at Lewis and Clark Lake which the dam encloses, preferring, despite the mosquitoes, to try to ignore the noise from the campsite and rest up for the day ahead.

Wacintaka

The Missouri today is 2,340 miles long and bears little resemblance to the river which Lewis and Clark ascended. Its course has been straightened to remove the biggest of the meanders, slashing its original length in the process. For many miles the river has been channelled. Gavin's Dam is only one of five huge dams upstream from Yankton which were built as part of the Pick-Sloan Plan begun in 1944. The others are the Garrison, Oahe, Big Bend and Fort Randall dams. The Pick-Sloan Plan eventually resulted in 90 dams on the Missouri and its tributaries. It excluded, however, the Yellowstone River, which remains the longest free-flowing river in the continental United States and the largest tributary of the Missouri. We were to see the Oahe Dam a few days later when we left Pierre, South Dakota, as well as the end of the huge lake, 231 miles long, which it created up the Missouri to Bismarck, North Dakota. The dam's associated power plant provides electricity for much of the north-central United States. To build the dam, Indian reservation land was flooded. It was said that the older Indians died of heartache as a result.

It took us two days to get to Pierre from Yankton. The riding was easier, on smaller roads through farmland, with the occasional farmhouse sitting way back off the road, surrounded by a shelter of trees. The first night, after 89 miles cycling, we stopped at Lake Andes (pop. 819) passing by Equal Rights School Road, near Springfield, a name which intrigued me but about which I have been able to find no information. In Lake Andes, historical tornado activity is 84% greater than the US overall average[67] and I was glad we were camping on the gymnasium floor of the Central High School. The corridors of the school were adorned with photographs of the graduating classes going back over time. It was easy to see the story of falling school rolls and population. Like all the schools we camped in on our way to the Pacific, the Lake Andes School was beautifully appointed, with bright classrooms and corridors, good showers and a clean floor for camping.

The next stop was Chamberlain, South Dakota (pop. 2,338) and a ride of nearly 86 miles. We followed a zigzag course east of the Missouri, which we could not see but knew ran at a 45° angle to our left, with huge bends and meanders, which look deceptively nothing on the map. Through Geddes, Platte, Academy and passing by Bijou Hills, there was little traffic, except for convoys of four wheel drive vehicles. Each one was towing a large motor boat and was headed for one of the ramps onto the river at the recreational areas. We were now on much higher ground. The Bijou Hills signify past glaciations in this area[68] and rise to 2,100 feet at the ridgeline. We were riding at about 1,700 feet. We caught our first glimpse of the Missouri as we began the descent into Chamberlain, an exhilarating free wheel into town from the high ground above. The trouble with going down, though, is that it means you have to go up again when you leave. The thought of a massive hill climb out of the other side of town the next morning made me determined to make an early start.

In Chamberlain, we camped in the games room of St. Joseph's Indian School, which was opened in 1927 by a German Catholic Priest, Father Henry Hogebach, a member of the Priests of the Sacred Heart. The first pupils were 53 children from the Cheyenne River Reservation. By 1960, there were 331 pupils boarding at the school in dormitories, but now 200 Indian children live in family units of 12 to 13 children per home. I was shocked to hear that the school takes tiny children away from the reservations, but my judgement was premature. They are not taken from stable families but instead chosen on their need for residential care.[69] The school, which has a waiting list of over 120 children from the Lakota Sioux tribe at any time, certainly had a lovely atmosphere, but it got me thinking about a society where people live in reservations and have their children taken away from them.

The school also runs the Akta Lakota Museum and Cultural Centre, opened in 1991 to honour the Lakota people and promote its culture. Visiting this magnificent museum of life on the plains was inspiring as we began our journey through them and learnt the four values of the Lakota Indians: 'Wacantoqnaka' or generosity', 'Wacintaka' or fortitude, 'Wotitakuye' or kinship and 'Woksape' or wisdom. Wacintaka, especially, was something we would need as we climbed onto the high plains and moved westwards towards the 100th meridian, the great dividing line between land which receives 20 or more inches of rain each year and that which receives less than this. Arable agriculture was traditionally possible on one side but not the other.

I was up and off as the sun rose the next day, and cycled up the long, steep hill on the other side of Chamberlain which took us back onto the plains. I had always imagined the plains to be flat, and they are from a distance. Cycling up to them from the Missouri River and through them, however, you find out about the bluffs, rolling hills, and the up and down gradients to the creeks and gullies which cross the land. All this means hard work for the legs, especially against a prevailing wind. The Great Plains rise from about 1,500 feet in the east to nearly 5,000 feet in the west and, sometimes, it would feel as if we were climbing this far several times each day.

"If the plains were flat, the Indians would not have had to go out to look for buffalo", explained Sue, as it became clear to me how easily thousands of buffalo (more correctly, bison) would have been able to conceal themselves.

Not successfully enough, though, as they were hunted to near extinction in the nineteenth century. Those that were left by the time the transcontinental railroad was finished in 1869 found themselves trapped either north or south of it. The southern herd retreated to the Texas Panhandle. In the north, it was a South Dakotan, born in Dallas in Morayshire, who decided to save the buffalo from extinction there. 'Scotty' Philip bought a herd of 74 buffalo which had been the descendants of 5 calves rescued from a buffalo hunt along the Grand River in 1881. Philip prepared a special pasture for them, north of Pierre, and these buffalo became the basis for restocking the herd throughout the United States. It was said that, on Scotty's death, in 1911, the buffalo came down from the hills as his funeral procession passed.[70]

We were getting into desolate territory, with few services. The only place to eat that day was the casino at Fort Thompson (pop. 1,375) on the Crow Creek Reservation. The Crow Creek Indians are a mixture of Dakota and Lakota Sioux and were originally from Minnesota; casualties of the Indian Wars and enforced relocation. Smallpox finished off many who made the journey in the 1860s. The reservation is near Lake Sharpe on the Missouri, one of the lakes created when it was dammed as part of the Pick-Sloan Plan. Fort Thompson itself had been relocated when the dam was built. It is a sad tale for the people who lived there and I felt the sadness permeated the landscape. Fort Thompson looked poor and its people with it.

Going into a casino at just after 8am in the morning seemed odd to me, but I was intrigued to see the inside of one. The Lode Star was dark, with rows of slot machines. In front of one of them, a large lady with a vacant expression on her face, sat slumped, with her right arm outstretched to push the buttons. A huge mural of a buffalo stampede surrounded the room. Next door, above the gambling tables, another huge mural, "In Honor of all Our Veterans" took up one wall. It showed an American soldier carrying a gun, and a bald eagle draped in an American flag with a tribal head-dress wrapped in its folds. We moved through to the restaurant area and sat down for breakfast. The food was good and very cheap.

Early morning in the casino

We had left our bicycles outside the casino and when we came out most of them had been knocked over. Worse still, Ayako's was missing. We all felt for her. I could imagine how I would have felt. For some reason she had failed to lock it. To be fair it was seldom necessary to lock a bike up, or so we had thought. After that, we did not take a chance. The casino staff felt sure they knew who had taken the bike and promised to retrieve it. Reluctantly, the rest of us cycled on, leaving Ayako with Tom to wait for the return of the bike. We felt bad about that too, as it did not seem right to leave one of our number behind. We learnt later that, after an hour, with no bike in sight, they went to the reservation police who took things in hand and went to the most likely suspect's house, where they found it. It was a great relief for Ayako, as well as a lesson to us all, as we had discovered that it was not easy to buy anything on the trail, much less a bespoke bicycle. Shops were few and far between and, when we did come across one, there wasn't much to buy anyway. It reminded me of the days on the west coast of Scotland when anticipation would give way to despair as entry into a shop would bring sight only of a few carrots and last week's copy of the *Oban Times*.

We hadn't had any rain for a few days, and the sun was bothering me as we neared Pierre (pronounced 'Peer'). To get away from the blistering heat, I decided to ride the last few miles into town in the van, which was intensely annoying as the road was downhill nearly all the way. But I was glad to be off the bike. I needed to get out of the sun and into an air-conditioned room. Most of us chose to stay at the Capital Inn for our rest stop in Pierre, instead of camping in Griffin Park by the Missouri River. Our Griffin did not want to camp at the park either, despite its name. He needed to get out of the sun too. He and Tom shared the room reserved for pets and owners.

House of Commons Green

Our motel, on the outskirts of town, next to a gas station with its own mini-casino, was a favourite with hunters and boat owners. Inside each room, the management supplied rags for use in cleaning guns and knives, so that patrons would not use the towels. All the rooms had external power points and water taps, so that boats could be backed up and hosed down and cleaned. In the cool of the evening – a relative term as it was still insufferably hot – hunters backed their trucks up, put their portable barbeques on the flat beds and cooked their steaks. I liked that about America. No one seemed to mind. People felt free to do what they wanted. It was the more acceptable side of wanting to carry a loaded concealed weapon. There were 12 Harley Davidson motorcycles parked outside my room. I was happy, though. The motel had a laundry (as they all do); I had clean clothes, air-conditioning, TV, a shower and Wi-Fi. I had booked my bike in for a service at the only bike shop in town and had bought a salad in the supermarket. Free coffee was available in the lobby 24 hours a day.

Pierre (pop. 13,646), situated opposite the original American fur trading settlement of Fort Pierre established in 1817, is the capital of South Dakota. Originally, this state was part of the huge Dakota Territory, divided into North and South Dakota in 1889. It is said that President Benjamin Harrison shuffled the papers on his desk before signing the admission documents to ensure he did not influence the order of priority into statehood. In the event, North Dakota beat South Dakota. People had flocked to this area only when railroad links were finished to Yankton and, more importantly, gold was found in the Black Hills in the west of the state. It was a trifle inconvenient that the mineral the gold seekers were after was on territory reserved for the Yankton Sioux when they ceded most of their land to the United States in 1858. Such territory was meant to be inviolate. There are no prizes for guessing who was victorious in the resultant conflict.

The Lakota Sioux dead numbered 153 after the 7th Cavalry opened fire on them at the Battle of Wounded Knee, or, as many now call it, the Massacre of Wounded Knee. The encounter marked the nadir in relationships between the native peoples and the United States Government which had adopted a zero tolerance policy towards Indian land claims.

Not having the firepower of the Federal Government, the Lakota Sioux had chosen to put their faith in powers connected with an item of clothing called the 'Ghost Shirt'. They believed that wearing such a shirt would protect them from the bullets of the white man. If that sounds odd to us, it is perhaps an indication of how desperate the plight of the Indians had become. The Ghost Shirt was of great spiritual significance. Associated with it was the Ghost Dance, part of a new religion which swept through the tribes, offering them assurance that the white man would disappear if they performed the dance.

Sadly, the white men did not go away and the Ghost Shirt was no protection against bullets. After the massacre, it was the Ghost Shirt itself which disappeared. Somewhat improbably, it ended up in Glasgow, Scotland, where it was on display for many years at the Kelvingrove Museum.

How had this come about? The answer is that an Indian called George Crager had visited the site of the massacre while the bodies were still lying on the ground. He had taken some items away, including the Ghost Shirt. A year later he travelled to Europe with Buffalo Bill's Wild West Show and brought the items with him. The show was spending the winter in Glasgow. George wrote to the Director of Glasgow Museums, offering to sell items from his collection of Indian artefacts. The offer was accepted. George also donated 14 other objects, including the Ghost Shirt.

A century later, an American lawyer called John Earl, a Cherokee Indian, was visiting Glasgow when he saw the Ghost Shirt on display at the museum. He knew immediately what it was and was well aware of its spiritual significance. His visit was the catalyst for a formal repatriation request from the Lakota Sioux. They wanted the Ghost Shirt returned to them. It took a long time, but in 1999, at a formal ceremony at the site of the massacre, representatives of the City of Glasgow handed the Ghost Shirt back.[71] It is now at the Museum of the South Dakota Historical Society in Pierre. Seven years after this ceremony a statue of Buffalo Bill was unveiled in Dennistoun, the area of Glasgow where the show had taken place in 1891.

Pierre feels like a cowboy town, or as it calls itself with pride, a 'cow town'. It had its heyday in the era of cross-country cattle drives. Sadly, these cattle drives became obsolete after the introduction of the railroads, but the town memory is full of the times when cattle from as far away as Montana were herded and driven by cowboys to Pierre. Three ferries were used to carry them across the Missouri and into the stockyards which lined the river. In town, there was so much dung that the sidewalks were built two feet up from the ground to prevent the cows from "spattering 'em up", as the Historical Marker in the town narrates. Fourteen salons helped to quench the thirst of the cowboys.

Despite being a cow town, Pierre has beautiful parks on the banks of the Missouri and an elegant State Capitol building made from limestone and marble, which was completed in 1910. Visiting it, I could not help but notice, in one of the arches along the wall on the ground floor, a painting of a wagon train fitted out with cloth from Dundee. I was the only visitor to the State Capitol that lunchtime and the security guard asked me if I wanted to sit in the Governor's chair. Of course I did and it felt pretty good too!

The Missouri near Chamberlain, South Dakota

The guard also asked me if I had noticed that the green carpet, lining the corridors, was "House of Commons Green". I had to admit I had not, ignorant as I was at the time that green is the colour of the carpet in the Commons and red in the House of Lords.[72] He was surprised that I was so poorly informed about my own Parliament, and pointed out that the South Dakota carpet was chosen specially as a tribute to the 'Mother of Parliaments'. Now who felt as if she came from a cow town. I thanked him for his time and went upstairs to the top of the building.

Peering over the balcony into the House of Representatives, the sight of the chairs reserved for the members from the county of Minnehaha took me right back to poetry lessons at school. Walking down the elegant staircase I could see above me, lining the rotunda, the statues of the Greek goddesses that represent South Dakota farming, livestock, mining and family life. In the basement, some aspect of family life was evident in the glass display cases which contain miniature dresses, each one a replica of the dress worn at every single inaugural ball by the wife of the incoming Governor.

South Dakota is hunting country, with an average of a million pheasants killed in the annual shoot. Big game hunting includes antelope, deer, elk, turkey, bighorn sheep, mountain goat and mountain lion and small game American crow, bobtail quail, sage grouse and tree squirrel. There is even a limited number of licenses available to shoot tundra swan.[73] Lynn's Dakotamart on West Sioux Avenue was the place to go to get kitted up for this sport. It sold guns, ammunition, reloading supplies, bows, archery accessories as well as bait for fishing in the form of leeches, crawlers, minnows, chubs and shiners. More importantly, Lynn's Dakotamart sold midge nets. Despite looking at me with amazement when I had put mine on at Chief White Crane State Park, many of our party made sure they bought one. It was the Tour of Discovery's essential fashion accessory.

The day we were in town was 23rd June 2010 and the United States football team was playing Algeria in the World Cup. The game was being shown on the TV, high up in the corner of the crowded coffee shop where I waited while my bike was being serviced. Not a single person was watching. Even when the United States won the match, no one looked up. South Dakota was certainly a different world.

Carrots of Tobacco

Lewis and Clark had a taste of how precarious life could be as they ventured further and further upriver and passed by the site of present day Pierre towards the end of September 1804. Trouble started when three boys from the Teton Sioux tribe swam across the river. They informed the expedition that there were two parties of Sioux in camps further upriver, one in a group of 80 lodges and the other in a group of 60. Lewis and Clark sent the boys away with some tobacco for the chiefs and an invitation to meet the next day.

The Chiefs were Black Buffalo and Black Medicine. Things got off to a poor start when they all met up, even though more gifts in the form of medals, a United States flag, a cocked hat and a laced uniform coat were offered and accepted. Next some feathers were given to the Chiefs. A tour of the keelboat followed and the whiskey bottle came out. The Chiefs enjoyed this refreshment so much that they sucked the bottle dry and overstayed their welcome. Eventually they departed the keelboat, but then refused to leave the pirogue, the smaller boat which had taken them to shore. They hung onto the mast and sat on the rope, preventing the boat from being tied up to shore. The Indians expressed themselves less than satisfied with the quantity of presents and demanded more.

A potentially nasty situation ensued and tempers rose. Clark drew his sword. The Indians took arrows from their quivers and bent their bows. The prow of the boat was turned towards the group of Indians and it was made clear that the expedition members were prepared to fight. All this over whiskey. The Indians wanted more of it and of the tobacco which had been doled out in the usual form of 'the carrot'.

From the *Journals of Lewis and Clark*, I had imagined a 'carrot of tobacco' to be a slang term. I was wrong. It was a standard term for tobacco packaging in the nineteenth century fur trade. The Manitoba Museum has a reproduction of a carrot, donated to the Hudson's Bay Company by the Imperial Tobacco Company. It looks like a long sausage, and weighs about 3 lbs. To make the carrot, tobacco leaves were rolled up tightly, bound up in linen and tied securely with cord.[74]

Giving tobacco away as a gesture of goodwill was commonplace, but for Lewis and Clark, goodwill had its limits. Confronting each other on the banks of the Missouri, with the expedition members making clear their intentions to fight, it was the Teton Sioux who backed down this time. They stepped back to discuss what to do next. Clark went towards them and offered to shake hands, but the chiefs refused his offer. Clark turned to go back to the boat, but, to his surprise, one of the chiefs and two warriors followed him. He hauled them into the boat. Honour satisfied all round, everyone then proceeded upstream. It had been a close encounter and Lewis and Clark were lucky to get away unscathed. Perhaps it was telling the Indians in no uncertain terms that the members of the Corps of Discovery were warriors, not squaws, which had done the trick.

Captains Lewis & Clark holding a Council with the Indians

Lewis and Clark holding a council with the Indians

The next day, cordiality had been restored and, upriver, the expedition was treated to a banquet held in a Teton house; a large shelter covered with skins. About 70 Indians sat round the chief, with two flags laid out on the ground before them – a large Spanish flag and the United States flag which Lewis and Clark had given to the Teton the day before. A peace pipe was displayed on a frame of forked sticks over a bed of swan down. Piles of buffalo meat were indicated to be a gift for the white men. Dog was on the menu, along with pemmican and potato. Platters were prepared and the guests invited to eat from them with horn spoons. The journals record that the men enjoyed the potato and the pemmican but partook "sparingly of the dog".[75] For this meat they had yet to develop a taste. It was to be more easily acquired than that of the Indians for the white men who were to take over their territory.

CHAPTER EIGHT: PIERRE, SD TO WILLISTON, ND

Days 17 to 24
24th June to 1st July 2010
488 miles

Geometry

We took Euclid Avenue out of Pierre early the next morning; another reminder that even in a cow town, the classics must have a place. Our job that day was to cycle the 74 miles to Gettysburg (pop. 1,352). It was here that the Sheriff warned us we might have to evacuate the campsite when the storm hit and where I missed seeing real cowboys.

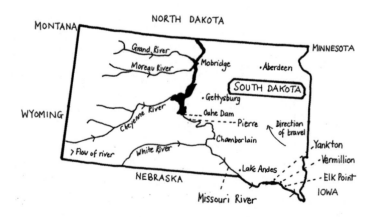

South Dakota

This South Dakota Gettysburg was named after the battle site in Pennsylvania by Civil War veterans who settled in this area of Dakota Territory in 1883. It is a quiet, little town on the prairie, with a few shops and a museum, and peopled by folk who guard their own way of life. When the Oahe Dam was being built, there was a proposal that the town should be the site of a new school run by the Bureau of Indian Affairs. The existing school was to be destroyed by the flood waters of the new dam. The town would also get federal funding to help sort out its water supply. Gettysburg turned down the funding rather than get the school.[76]

We spent the evening in Gettysburg watching children playing baseball in the park and then lining up, team by team, for photographs. Despite the anxiety about the oncoming storm and Sue's pronouncement that it would not be the first time everyone had to spend the night in the toilet block (it being the safest structure around if the storm shelter could not be reached), it was a relaxing time. There was something very attractive about these small, isolated, American towns, where children could ride their bicycles around freely, mums and dads congregated in the park to watch their children play ball and everyone had a friendly word. It was pure Norman Rockwell. Underneath, though, there was an intolerance for difference that was hard to take.

After the storm the next morning we left Gettysburg for Mobridge, South Dakota (pop. 3,465) which lies at the top of Lake Oahe, across the Missouri River from Sitting Bull's grave (although some dispute the remains are actually those of the Lakota warrior). It was a 62-mile day of long, lonely straight roads, big black stormy skies and so hot that it felt as if the air was crackling. We were all glad to stop at the Dakota Maid in Selby after 42 miles and get some food, drink the Dark Canyon coffee on offer and rest up in the cool shade of this little café on Highway 12. There is not much in Selby, but it does ship out, via the nearby railroad, between 5 and 6 million bushels of grain each year.

The air was like a blast from a furnace when we reached Mobridge, freewheeling into town and seeing, at last, the huge

Missouri River on our left. It was probably a routinely hot day for the inhabitants of this town where the record for the same day of the year stands at 108°F. I was glad we did not have to get our tents out and sleep in the park. Instead we were directed to a cool, dark, basement; an answer to a prayer for deliverance from the heat.

Murals in Mobridge

We were camping in the handsome town auditorium, an art deco building designed and built in the 1930s, as a public work, by the Works Progress Administration, the largest of Franklin D. Roosevelt's New Deal agencies. The WPA ensured that millions of Americans, who would otherwise be unemployed, had meaningful work. One of its principles, however, was that no relief through its services should be available to women if they were married and had a husband employed or eligible for WPA work. In rural Missouri, for example, 40% of WPA funds went to women who were married, but with husbands who were disabled, too old to work or had been unemployed for 5 years or more.[77] Other married women had to fend for themselves.

The upstairs gymnasium of the auditorium, which was being refurbished, was decorated with murals by the Sioux artist, Oscar Howe, who became Professor of Art at the University of South Dakota in Vermillion, the little town where I had wanted to linger.

Howe had been born on the Crow Creek Reservation. He was descended from two chiefs, Bone Necklace and White Bear. He exhibited a talent for drawing as a very young child, using charcoal from the fire to draw on the floor when his father, who thought drawing foolish, took his pencils away. Like many others, he was sent away to an Indian Boarding School, this time in Pierre. It was run on military lines which perhaps did not suit him, and he developed a disfiguring skin disease and then trachoma. He had to leave the school but eventually graduated and went to work as a labourer building roads. After a bout of tuberculosis, he ended up at the Santé Fe Indian School. This art school had a worldwide reputation for Indian art, but he caused ripples by departing from what the art world thought Indian painting should be.[78]

The ten murals at Mobridge, each one of which is 16 feet high and 20 feet wide, feature Sioux ceremonies and the history of the Missouri River, including the historic meeting between Lewis and Clark and Sacagawea, the Indian woman who accompanied the tour and the mother of Pomp, the youngest member of the expedition.

Sacagawea, whose name meant 'Bird Woman', was born to the Shoshone Indian tribe in present day Idaho. She was captured, along with several other girls, by a group of Hidatsa Indians when she was about twelve years old. The Hidatsa had originated way up in the north of what is now North Dakota but were forcibly shoved south and west by the Lakota Sioux. They ended up with the Mandan Indians. The Hidatsa raiding party took Sacagawea to what is now Stanton, a village just outside modern Washburn, North Dakota and where we were to camp a few days later. At 13, she was married to Toussaint Charbonneau, the interpreter who accompanied the expedition, becoming his second Shoshone wife. 'Otter Woman', his first wife, did not travel to the Pacific. Who decided this, we do not know. Reading between the lines, though, it was Sacagawea, rather than her husband, who was most needed on the expedition. Charbonneau was not an attractive character. He did not speak English and his Hidatsa was poor, even though he lived among them. Sacagawea's native language skills were good and would be needed when the expedition reached the mountains where her own people lived. Leaving Otter Woman behind, Charbonneau moved into Fort Mandan with Sacagawea but obviously thought he was a cut above everyone else. He did not see why he had to do his share of the chores and he went off in a huff, only to return and plead to be let back on the expedition. Like the pure blooded French-Canadian that he was, though, he could make a good sausage.

Walking Tacos

After a shower in the basement wash rooms of the Mobridge auditorium, I decided to join the other members of our group in the upstairs, air-conditioned foyer and watch Mobridge life through the glass doors. I needed to summon up the courage before facing the sun again. We sat in our picnic chairs, most with a beer, some with a soda (as the Americans call fizzy drinks) and watched South Dakotan life go by.

A man in a cowboy hat drove up and parked opposite the auditorium in his bright yellow Hummer. He got out, did an errand in one store, climbed back into the Hummer and drove 20 yards down the street, where he repeated the whole process. This went on all the way down the street. An elderly couple in a dilapidated, dusky pink 1960's Cadillac drove up and down, up and down. It was Friday and this vehicle heralded the start of the good old American weekend tradition of 'dragging the gut' – driving up and down the main street in town for the hell of it. Perhaps they want to show off their cars or perhaps they do it because there is nothing else to do, but it is so popular in small towns in America that a festival is dedicated to it in McMinnville, Oregon. This has exasperated the city fathers there who have taken steps to outlaw it, making it a traffic violation to pass along or cross the same point in a designated "traffic congested street" four or more times in any direction within a two-hour period. The fine, whether or not a policeman has issued a notice after the third such passing or crossing, is anything up to $150. I felt it would be a long time before the traffic got so bad in Mobridge that dragging the gut was outlawed here.

The world passed by in slow motion in Mobridge. Once again I felt that I was on the stage set of a movie. Shimmering heat, old cars, tatty store fronts, and no one walking. Mobridge looked poor. It was a surprise to me that in the heartland of America I had hardly ever seen a large, smart house; it was a place of trailer camps and run-down wooden houses. I got so used to this that when I saw a huge, modern house on the outskirts of Great Falls in Montana, I was taken aback. I stopped to look at it, resting my arms on my handlebars and musing on its implications. I realised that I had seen little or no house construction since St. Louis. I had also seen few young adults. Nearly everyone we met was ... just like us. Getting on. Depopulation was for real.

Venturing out, Alcy, Wendy and I set off in search of some real food. The modern world had, indeed, come to Mobridge in the form of a coffee shop, but none of us could face a designer brew and a biscotti. It was a long time to dinner and we needed food fit for adventurers and cowboys. We got it in the form of the 'Walking Taco', which a lovely lady, wearing a T-shirt emblazoned "Deadwood, South Dakota", made for us in the ice cream parlour. I can still hear her infectious laugh as she told us about life in Mobridge and how she had had a busy time ferrying her children to Bible school in Aberdeen. At least there are some children around, I thought, reflecting on the fact that apart from the children playing baseball in Gettysburg, we had not seen many young people. I told her I lived near the other Aberdeen in Scotland, but my information was lost on her. She was more concerned, nay flabbergasted, that we had never heard of a Walking Taco. In case anyone else remains in ignorance, here is her recipe:

The Walking Taco
- Buy a bag of Doritos, open it down the side.
- Add cooked ground beef, chilli, salsa, lettuce, tomato, sour cream.
- Stir.
- Eat with a wooden fork whilst walking along the street talking about important stuff such as baseball.

Perhaps if Aberdeen had been named after somewhere with little rainfall, in the Sahara perhaps, and not after the cold, wet, Scottish birthplace of Charles Mitchell, the President of the Chicago, Milwaukee and St. Paul Railroad, it may have had an easier time of it in its early years. The first train into the Aberdeen area, in 1881, heralded a building boom and so, Aberdeen, in common with every other little town on the prairie, soon had a Main Street. Things went well only until it rained heavily, whereupon the worthy citizens of Aberdeen noticed that they had built their town on what came to be known as the "frog pond". Being loath to abandon the site, no doubt because of the proximity of the railroad, they put up with repeated flooding and battled to get rid of the water with only one small pump. An engineering project, which included building an artesian well, was begun in 1884 with the aim of both solving the problem once and for all and providing the town with piped water. Unfortunately for all involved, the pressure of the underground water was so great, it caused a huge explosion of water, flooding the buildings on Main Street good and proper, to a depth of four feet.

The solution was just a simple valve. Once installed, the water system was soon working efficiently and the people of Aberdeen got piped water. It was not the end of the floods, however. As recently as 2007, Aberdeen and the surrounding county were declared a disaster area when nearly ten inches of rain fell in 48 hours. Ironically, when one of Aberdeen's most famous residents, L. Frank Baum, lived there, the area was experiencing a drought. The description of Kansas in his most famous book, *The Wizard of Oz*, was based on his experiences living in Aberdeen, South Dakota.[79]

Entering Desolate Territory

Our stay in Mobridge was a short one. The next morning we had to be up even earlier than usual to cross the Missouri River before it got light. The town is named for the bridge (hence 'Mo' and 'bridge') and Highway 12, which is the route across, was down to a single lane due to road works. At almost a mile long, we knew we did not have enough time to get across the bridge before the traffic lights, controlling the single lane, changed from green to red. The thought of being stuck in the lane with traffic coming towards us was alarming, so the plan was to leave early enough for there to be no traffic on the bridge. That was perhaps optimistic, but the cars we met coming headlong towards us were few in number. We were able to leap off the bikes and get out of the way before they rushed by. It was a relief to get to the other side, despite our arrival bringing on a rainstorm.

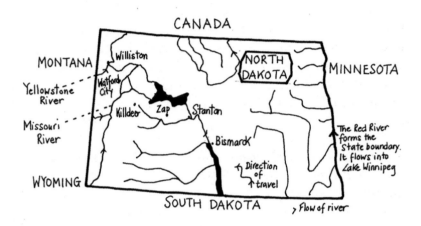

North Dakota

We were entering another world. We passed a large Adventist College on our right, but apart from that and a few ranches, there was little sign of habitation. A large sign at the end of a dirt road leading to a ranch house displayed the names of the owners in large letters. Underneath their names, the sign read "Have a Nice Day. Be safe. No trespassing. Beware of Guard Dog".

I often wondered what would happen if I got stranded and dared to venture up one of these dirt tracks to a ranch house. Bev told me that it wasn't Texas, where I'd be sure to get shot if I attempted anything like that. I thought the bike would give protection, as anyone could see that a cyclist was harmless and probably only wanted water or help with a repair. Even so, I was glad I never had to ask for help. I was more scared of the dogs that might pound down the road towards me than a rancher with a gun.

The bridge across the Missouri had represented more than a physical demarcation in our journey to the Pacific. It signified yet another psychological adjustment to increased scale and isolation. Now we were climbing up to the High Plains of North Dakota, a new landscape of endless grassland and high, rugged buttes. It required nerve not to be spooked by the terrain, and strength to get up the seemingly relentless hills, up and down, up and down, as we gradually gained height. I can remember how my heart sank when each hill appeared before me. Later, in Lewiston in Idaho, I picked up a second-hand copy of a book called *Dakota: A Spiritual Geography* by Kathleen Norris and was relieved to read her description of this journey. She expresses my feelings more eloquently than I can articulate:

> *Passing through Mobridge and crossing the river you take a steep climb through rugged hills onto the high plateau land that extends all the way to the Rockies... You have left the glacial drift plains for a land whose soil is the residue of prehistoric seas that have come and gone, weathered shale and limestone that is far less fertile than the land to the east but good for grazing sheep and cattle. Here, you set your watch to Mountain Time.*

> *Here, also, you may have to combat disorientation and an overwhelming sense of loneliness. Plunged into the pale expanse of shortgrass country, you either get your sea legs or want to bail out.*[80]

That was exactly how I felt, like a small boat in a vast ocean of nothingness. We pedalled 64 miles that day before we found a food stop in the form of the Prairie Knight's Casino on the Standing Rock Sioux Tribe Reservation. This monstrous resort, literally in the middle of nowhere, has over 600 slot machines as well as gaming areas for Blackjack, Craps, Three Card Poker and Ultimate Texas Hold 'Em, where the gambler competes against the dealer, not the other players. It also provides a huge buffet lunch at the knock down price of $7.95 for seniors. There was no competition as to who came out best, the casino or me. I ate heartedly and downed flagons of pink lemonade.

No Time for Tea

Our destination that day, 26th June 2010, was a campsite near Bismarck, North Dakota (pop. 94,791) at Fort Abraham Lincoln, where Colonel Custer and his wife, Libbie had lived from 1873 until his death at the Battle of Little Big Horn in 1876. Also known as Custer's Last Stand, this battle was between the Lakota, Northern Cheyenne and Arapaho Indians on one side and the US 7th Cavalry on the other. The Indians were sure of victory as this had been forecast by Sitting Bull. Sure enough, the Indians overwhelmingly defeated the American troops. US deaths amounted to 268, including Custer, his brother-in-law, two of his brothers and a nephew.

The Fort is now a State Park, gifted to the state of North Dakota in 1907 by President Theodore Roosevelt. I found it to be a civilised place. That is to say, it had what the Americans call a 'primitive' campsite – one without power. The absence of a socket meant it was unattractive to the noisy RV campers, who had plagued many of our nights. For my part, not being able to charge my iPod was a small price to pay for peace and quiet.

There was no time to be lost on reaching Fort Abraham Lincoln and, sadly, no time to visit the reconstructed barracks, which had housed 600 soldiers, or Custer's house, where Libbie must have made life comfortable for him. She was a woman of some fortitude, having spent most of her honeymoon alone and, as she recounts in *Boots and Saddles*, her account of life with Custer, the next twelve years "in fear of some immediate peril, or in dread of some danger that threatened". At times, that was what the Tour of Discovery felt like to me, but the hardships

I endured were nothing to those of Libbie who once spent 36 hours in a blizzard near Yankton, travelled across the Plains in a wagon train with the Army, rising each day before 4am, and then saw her husband killed by Indians.[81]

Elizabeth Custer with her husband, George Armstrong Custer (seated) and his brother

Our haste to make camp was due to the fact that a storm was forecast. As soon as I got my tent up, I hot-footed across the park to find the wash rooms, determined to get clean and dry and under cover before the rain started. Asking directions to the showers from an elderly couple sitting outside a camper van, I was astonished to hear cut-glass English accents in response to my question. Peter and Vi, from Montreal, and who had recently spent a year in St Andrews, spoke the kind of immaculate English only found now among ex-patriots or foreigners. Vi told me that they had been living in Canada for 40 years and were driving home after visiting Theodore Roosevelt National Park, the only one in the nation named after a President. Vi offered me a cup of tea after my shower. As I washed my hair, I imagined her getting out the tea pot and warming it. I felt sure she would pour my tea into a tea cup. I had not seen one since leaving home. Perhaps there would be a Rich Tea biscuit.

I never got to find out. When I emerged from the shower block, a few heavy drops of rain signified that we had only seconds to take shelter. I ran past Peter and Vi's van waving regret as they scuttled around collecting up their picnic chairs and battening down the hatches. They waved back as if to say "No tea now, unfortunately". I felt sad about that and a little homesick. But I did not feel like waking them up at 5.30am when we left camp to ask them if they had any Rich Tea biscuits.

My carefully chosen pitch was soon to turn into a bog

The thunder and lightning which started about 5pm was terrifying. Under the tarpaulin which Sue and Kit had set up by the van, the earth shook beneath us. I noticed with alarm that my impeccably chosen tent site was turning into a bog, then a pond as the water inched nearer and nearer to my tent. I chose to look the other way, reckoning that the storm could not last that long and when it stopped the earth would hiss and steam dry within minutes. I had to wait until midnight for the rain to stop. Thankfully, my tent survived.

Help from the Mandans

Mandan Indian house, Stanton, North Dakota

When Lewis and Clark reached this area in 1804, 1,600 miles from Camp Dubois in Illinois, they found five villages with a population of about 4,400 Indians; mainly Mandans but also Hidatsa and Arahami. Collectively these habitations were known as the Mandan Villages. These Indians lived peacefully together and sometimes joined forces against their mutual enemy, the Sioux. Lewis and Clark were pleased to find the Mandan Village Indians friendly and informative about the route the expedition would take in the spring, and so they decided to overwinter near them. They built a fort six miles south of the Knife River near present day Stanton, North Dakota (pop. 345), our next destination. It was here that Charbonneau and his young wife, Sacagawea, were recruited to the expedition and where Pomp, their son, was born. Lewis recorded that he was a "fine boy", quickly delivered after his mother was given two rings of the rattlesnake to alleviate her tedious labour and violent pain. Here, too, Lewis and Clark prepared the Return Party, which was to leave for St. Louis in the spring with specimens for President Jefferson, including a live prairie dog (actually a large rat), a sharp-tailed grouse and four magpies. The prairie dog and the magpies survived. Not so the Mandan Indians, who were largely wiped out in smallpox and whooping cough epidemics. By 1837 there were only 125 of them left. The last full-blooded Mandan died in 1910.

I sagged the last six miles into Stanton as I wanted to visit the Knife River Indian Villages two miles on the other side of town, where an earth lodge of the Northern Plains Indians has been reconstructed. I was astonished to see how much it resembled the reconstruction of the crannog at Loch Tay in Perthshire, with well laid out areas for storage, sleeping and cooking, and how solid it felt inside. I was tempted to ask permission to stay the night, but instead I freewheeled back to Stanton, with the wind behind me. A huge *Wizard of Oz* Tin Man looked down at me from the roof of one of the small, neat weatherboard houses as I cycled to our campsite by the Knife River. This was the scene of a family party, to which people had journeyed from all over America. When they packed up there was not a single piece of litter left on the grass. It was shaming to think that there is more litter between my house and Arbroath, around twelve miles away, than I saw in all the 2,800 miles I cycled across the United States.

Zip to Zap

After our camp on the Knife River, one of the tributaries of the Missouri, it was to be some days before we saw water again. Instead, we followed Highway 200 which runs east/west, south of the Missouri River and Lake Sacagawea, formed by the Garrison Dam. Our first target was Killdeer (pop. 713). It was a long and tiresome journey there, along an up-and-down road, as straight as a die through grassland, passing by Hazen, Beulah, Zap, Golden Valley, Dodge, Halliday, Werner and Dunn Center. All these little towns were off the highway and we caught only glimpses of them nestled below the road in the hills. Beulah (pop. 3,152) I could easily ignore, put off by the sign on the highway that advertised its 12 churches, but Zap (pop. 231) I would like to have seen. Zap was said to be named after a place in Scotland (although no such place exists) and is famous for 'Zip to Zap' when, as a result of an invitation in a student newspaper, nearly 3,000 people descended on the town on 9th May 1969. It all started when the editor of *The Spectrum*, the student newspaper at the North Dakota State University in Fargo, decided that if college students in the east could go to Florida for their spring break, why couldn't the students in the Dakotas go somewhere equally exotic? He chose Zap to fill this role, a town whose only claim to fame until then was that it featured in the answer to the question "Which towns in North Dakota sound like Kellogg's Rice Krispies?" The answer was Zap, Gackle and Mott.

The people of Zap would probably have preferred to remain in the cereal bowl, but the invitation for students to congregate at Zap for the spring break promised "orgies, brawls, freakouts and arrests" and thus guaranteed trouble for its citizenry. It did not help that the national press got wind of the Zip to Zap invitation. Even students from Florida went to North Dakota for the spring break. Zap had never seen anything like it. Things got out of hand when the beer ran out, despite the two bars in town doubling their prices; a marketing strategy that served only to inflame passions. A fire was started in Main Street (it being somewhat colder in Zap than Florida) and to feed it the students tore down a vacant building. Matters went from bad to worse with unimaginable liquids being spilt and regurgitated onto the street.

Naturally, it all ended in tears. What had started out as a student prank ended with the National Guard being called out to quell the only official riot in the history of North Dakota.[82] No doubt it is to avoid a similar situation developing in McMinnville in response to invitations on Facebook that the city fathers there have taken steps to outlaw conduct which would attract participants to the 'Dragging the Gut Festival'.

There was no sign of a riot when we passed by Zap. In fact, there was no sign of any life at all. The town would have been hard to spot nestled down in the valley had it not been for its name writ large in white letters on the hill behind the town.

Keep on Trucking

North Dakota's oldest rodeo is held each year in Killdeer but trucks, not horses, were to be our companions when we arrived, as we camped adjacent to the gas station on the road into town. Peace was not restored the next morning on the road from Killdeer to Watford City (pop. 1,435), when we were caught up in the ugly side of the North Dakota oil boom. The day had started off calmly enough as we left Killdeer and climbed to over 2,000 feet through the spectacular Badlands of the Killdeer Mountains. The area was the scene of a battle in 1864 between General Sully and the Teton, Yanktonai and Dakota Indians, which resulted in a defeat for the Indians. The US troops burnt over 1,500 Indian lodges and even punctured camp kettles so that the Indians, who had tried to escape into the canyons of the Badlands, would not have any usable materials if they returned.

Pretty soon heavy truck traffic, in both directions, made cycling very unpleasant. Now it was our turn to say, like the citizens of Zap, that we had never seen anything like it. Huge vehicles whooshed by every few seconds, on a road that certainly was not designed for this kind of traffic. They created vortexes of air which almost knocked us off our bikes. The shoulder was narrow and the terrain sloped sharply down to the right off it, making the thought of a quick getaway from the shoulder rather formidable. I did not want to end up in a ditch. The worst vehicles were the flat beds carrying enormous portacabins; when two passed each other on the road, the air currents seemed to suck me off the saddle as I tried to get out of the way. The day before I had thought the nodding donkeys by the road picturesque, but now I began to curse the oil industry. I pressed on at high speed wanting to get to Watford City as soon as possible. Larry and I arrived together and, comparing notes, shook our heads in disbelief at the cycling conditions. To my surprise, we were among the few who made it all the way to Watford City. Most of the group had wisely said "Enough is enough" and had sagged into town when the truck traffic became intolerable.

That evening, safely settled in the basement of the city auditorium where we were camping, with the public library and free internet conveniently above, Tom decided it was too dangerous to cycle to our next destination, Williston. So the next morning we loaded our bikes onto the vans and left Watford City (established in 1913 in anticipation of the Great Northern Railroad extending its line and named after Watford, Ontario, not Watford near London). Our first stop was Alexander, for breakfast. This small community of 217 souls, home to the Ragged Butte Motel, had a sign displaying the Ten Commandments on the road into town, which immediately resulted in a burning intent in my heart to sin. Unfortunately, I could find no outlet to do so and had to make do with hash browns and eggs, rather than strong liquor, and a tour round the Lewis and Clark Trail Museum which left me with no desire to covet my neighbour's goods.

Trucks and cyclists do not mix

Lovingly looked after by a group of enthusiastic volunteers, the museum, housed in an old school, was heartbreakingly run-down. It included old farm machinery, a replica schoolroom complete with slates and various items of North Dakota memorabilia, including certain artefacts to do with Charles Bannon. He allegedly murdered a family of six in 1931 and was the last man to be lynched in North Dakota. In the 'Hall of Fame' on the second floor, glass display cases, each one purchased by a local family or individual, told the story of life on the prairies in the form of photographs, letters, lacework and medals. It was a story of depopulation, moving on, of leaving for a better life. Many of the display cases had not been brought up to date. I wondered if the children of the people who had bought them even knew they were there.

Sightseeing was proving to be more exhausting than cycling. I started to feel a familiar weariness and loathing for it as we moved onto Fort Union, a reconstructed trading post, where, until 1867, Assiniboine, Blackfeet and Crow Indians traded buffalo furs for goods such as pipes, guns and whiskey. My ennui was banished by listening to the sales assistant in the gift shop give us an impromptu lecture on the Indian trade. He pointed out that the traders had abhorred the settlement of the prairies by white farmers as much as the Indians. For both groups it meant the end of a way of life. He gave quite a performance and we learnt that he was a college professor who worked at the fort every summer to supplement his income.

Trade Turns to Oppression

Fort Union had been established three decades after Lewis and Clark passed by the site and, for a time, it was the furthest point on the Missouri River navigable by steamboat. Situated at the very edge of the frontier, it attracted an international tourist trade. In the same way that tourists now might go on safari, camping in enclosures and examining the wildlife from the security of a jeep, important personages of the day made their way to Fort Union by steamer to observe the camping grounds of the Indians on the flat plains outside its high wooden walls. These visitors included John Audubon, the naturalist and painter and Karl Bodmer, the Swiss painter who accompanied Prince Maximilian of Weid on his expedition up the Missouri in 1832 to study the Mandan and Hidatsa tribes. Bodmer's paintings were those I had admired for so long in my copy of *The Journals of Lewis and Clark*.

Tepees at Fort Union

This fort was never a military post but a business establishment run with money from John Jacob Astor, once the richest man in the world, and his American Fur Company. Its manager was Kenneth McKenzie, known as the 'Emperor of the Missouri'. In 1833 he decided to ship a still upriver to the fort. All was well at first: he soon had a working distillery on the go and, with a ready and captive clientele in the form of the Mandan, business looked good. He started to make a lot of money, especially as he was prone to mixing the hard stuff with anything the Indians were prepared to swallow. McKenzie's mistake was to refuse to sell his precious liquor to two passing traders, after he had already annoyed them by charging extortionate prices for supplies. It was illegal to sell liquor to Indians and they promptly reported him to the US authorities when they got back to Fort Leavenworth. Congress passed a law making distilleries illegal in Indian territories. (Today the sale of alcohol on reservations is legal only if state and tribal law permit it.) McKenzie's days as the Emperor were over and he was dismissed.

Fort Union's days became numbered. John Jacob Astor saw that silk, not fur, was becoming the fashionable choice for hats and he sold out. As the prairies became more settled, relations with such Indians that were left alive after the smallpox epidemics, deteriorated. The once mighty Fort Union was demolished and the materials used to build nearby Fort Buford, which was a military fort. Its purpose was not trade, but to tame the area for the white man.

Fort Buford is near the confluence of the Yellowstone and Missouri Rivers. It has been reconstructed for visitors who tramp from the car park in the searing heat to the officers' quarters, doing a North Dakota war dance to try and fend off the mosquitoes. The Fort today is a place of melancholy as befits its history. It is where Sitting Bull surrendered to the US Army Commanding Officer on 19th July 1881, after making his way back to the United States from Saskatchewan where he had been in exile with his people. Sitting Bull's story was not a dignified one after that. Refused permission to go back and forth from Canada to Fort Buford and also to establish his own reservation near the Little Missouri River, he was sent to Standing Rock Agency in South Dakota and then to Fort Randall, where he was held as a political prisoner. Somewhat surprisingly, he was given permission to leave and join Buffalo Bill's Wild West Show which toured the United States and Europe. The show re-enacted, as its final scene, an Indian attack on a cabin on the prairies. The so-called freedom was too hard to bear. Sitting

Bull lasted only four months in the show before he returned to the Standing Rock Agency in South Dakota. There he was shot in the head on 15th December 1890 by the reservation police, during unrest provoked by a warrant for his arrest.

Sitting Bull and his nephew, One Bull

The Confluence of the Missouri with the Yellowstone

After Fort Buford, we drove by the confluence of the Missouri and the Yellowstone Rivers, in more comfort than Lewis and Clark had experienced. The wind had been so violent when they neared this spot in April 1805 (the Indians downriver having told them about it) that the men could not row the boats. A lie-to was ordered. It must have been a welcome respite. Many of the members of the

148

expedition were suffering from sore eyes, caused by the sand from the sandbanks which blew around so extensively that columns of it floated above the river like smoke. The next day, 25th April 1805, was so cold that ice formed on the oars. Lewis was worried because Seaman, his Newfoundland dog, had been missing all night, but thankfully the creature appeared about 8am. Lewis killed a buffalo calf and, leaving Clark and the boats, marched over the hills and found what the French called the 'roche jaune'. He sent a man upriver to explore and report back and they all camped out before rejoining Clark the next day.

Expending less energy than Lewis, we were taken in the vans to Williston (pop. 12,512) where we were to spend two nights camping on the floor of the National Guard Armory, next to the Chamber of Commerce. Blissfully, it was air-conditioned, but, on the first evening, someone in the office turned the air-conditioning off before they went home. That brought the mosquitoes out. I was glad I had followed Hans Ruedi's habit of pitching my tent inside and sleeping under the mosquito net.

Reflections

Williston is situated in a geological feature called the Bakken formation, part of a larger feature called the Williston Basin, where oil was first discovered in the 1920s. New drilling techniques have resulted in a bonanza to exploit the estimated oil resource, estimated by the US Geological Survey to be between 3 and 4.3 billion barrels of oil.[83] It is all on a scale unimaginable to the early pioneers of the oil industry, to whom a plaque on 2nd Avenue in Williston is dedicated. Behind a model of a nodding donkey, the words challenge future energy pioneers to "lay a solid sub-structure upon which tomorrow's energy problems can be addressed and opportunities realised".

These opportunities are currently being realised through a process called hydraulic fracturing or 'fracking', whereby the under surface rocks – typically 8,000 feet or more below ground level – are blasted with sufficient pressure to cause them to fracture. The oil is then encouraged to flow to the surface by means of propping open the fractures. The controversy regarding fracking is whether or not the general water supply can be contaminated by this process, as the liquid which is injected under high pressure to fracture the rock is toxic. Those who support fracking say there is no way the toxic water can leak, as it is recycled for use many thousands of feet below the water table and, in any event, could not, without the high pressure, flow through the rock of the Bakken Formation which is extremely hard.[84] Those against fracking protest over the alleged lack of transparency concerning the composition of the fracking liquid, the dumping of the toxic liquid at surface level as well as general water and air pollution.[85] As soon as I heard about fracking I decided that the Williston water tasted odd. Do not think it cannot also happen here in the UK. Fracking may well be coming to a location near you. Testing has taken place to see if it can be used to extract shale gas near Blackpool. The composition of the additive used with the water has not been disclosed.[86]

Williston was another place that seemed like a stage set, with the railroad line, the huge grain elevators, streets on a grid with low-rise office buildings; the occasional store, enormous car parks and once again, no one walking.

Williston, North Dakota

I decided it isn't just laziness and cheap fuel that keeps Americans in their cars. To me the most precious commodity lacking everywhere I had been was shade. There wasn't any to speak of, apart from the trees in a park or the shade on one side of the street when the sun moved round. It was torture to walk around a town during the day. I wondered whether the severity of the winters in the areas we had cycled through meant that it was impracticable to build shade shelters in car parks or even to provide some relief for the eye with some landscaping. I became convinced that the vast, unshaded, shimmering acres devoted to parking the car must be contributing to global warming. The 'parking lot' came to represent, to me, the modern equivalent of the homestead. Whereas once people had always had the ability to move on, move west, leave what they had and start afresh and farm new land, today there is always land enough for the parking lot to be abandoned in the crumbling down town areas. It can then re-emerge, bigger and uglier, further out in order to serve the huge shopping malls.

Outside Williston Chamber of Commerce

When I saw how much space is devoted to parking in the west, I remembered how shocked I had been in St. Charles to find, in a suburban sub-development, a sign informing all residents that no more than six vehicles were permitted per household in that area. Six! But I could see why a family with teenagers might need six cars. Without a car per person, each individual would be completely marooned. The sub-division was a little island surrounded by what, to me, were monster highways, but which I soon learnt were pretty standard suburban roads.

I had discovered this area by stopping a policewoman and asking her where I could ride my bike. She was on a bike too – a fancy mountain bike of a standard I had hardly seen before. Her job was to patrol the 'business district'. She was looking forward to getting a new one which would have automatic gears. Automatic gears! It is true, as I found out later. You can get automatic gears for a bicycle. Apart from mad touring cyclists such as ourselves, I think she was the last person I saw on a bicycle until we reached Oregon, over 2,000 miles later (not counting the children who rode around the campsites on their bicycles). It was then not a surprise to find that Portland, Oregon has both a bicycle-friendly and a verdant, green, shaded environment, with beautiful avenues of trees. Admittedly it does have the climate for trees, but it does not have the room to spread out or relentlessly pave over the landscape. The next stop is the Pacific. The endless supply of land runs out there. Oregon was the only place in America where you had a faint inkling that people might matter more than cars.

Trailer parks abounded on the outskirts of Williston, from which young men off the oil fields blasted into town in their monster, shiny, new, pick-up trucks. They then raced them up and down the drag where the out-of-town supermarkets were situated. We were told that the last four years had been boom, boom, boom, but it hardly looked like that downtown. After my experience on the road from Killdeer to Watford City, I wanted reflective clothing. There was nothing downtown so I cycled the few miles out of town to Wal-Mart, which I felt sure would sell workmen's gear for the rigs. I bought a highly fluorescent, orange, net safety vest which would be cool to wear over a cycling shirt. There would be no mistaking me on the road now.

In the café there, I met a young man, dressed in new clothes from the store, who was changing into new boots. His old clothes and boots he put in a bag. He told me he had been in Williston for six months working on the rigs nearby and was clearing out of town before he drank himself to death.

CHAPTER NINE: WILLISTON, ND TO GREAT FALLS, MT

Days 25 to 31
25th June to 8th July 2010
414 miles

Along the Hi-Line

A large sign at the state line with Montana on Highway 2 informed us that transport of invasive species across the state of Montana was prohibited. I wondered what they had in mind. Soon we were on the Fort Peck Indian Reservation, which at over three million square miles is the ninth largest reservation in the United States. In the 2000 census, it had a population of only 10,321. Our destination that day was the Community School at Poplar (pop. 911) where we were to camp on the gymnasium floor. Poplar, we were told, is the murder capital of Montana, a claim that is widely repeated on the internet. From what I have been able to find out, this is not true, but it was the location for the killing, in June 1979, of Kimberly Ann Nees, who was attacked in her pick-up truck. Her body was dumped in the Poplar River. A local man, Barry Beach, was convicted on his confession alone and was sentenced to 100 years imprisonment. Many in Poplar are convinced of his innocence, believing that the confession was the result of coercion and pointing out that there was no evidence to link him to the crime. The case has become a cause célèbre. Finally, in November 2011, a judge granted Barry Beach the right to a new trial. He was released from prison, where he had been incarcerated since 1984, pending this new trial.

Sign at Montana border

A burial was going on in the small cemetery on our left as we cycled into town, with rifle shots into the sky echoing over the road. It looked like a military burial and I wondered whether it was a soldier from Iraq or Afghanistan. A few days after we left town, we discovered that Poplar had lived up to its reputation, with three stabbings in ten days, including the murder, on Independence Day, of a 21-year-old soldier, Ryan Buckles, on home leave before being posted to Afghanistan. The alleged perpetrator, Curtis Eder, was also 21 and had grown up with Buckles. He was charged with murder and aggravated assault in the tribal court. The last entry he posted on Facebook before his arrest was "On my way home to raise some hell".

Living in Scotland as I do, where alcohol plays a significant part in crime, it was not a shock to learn that drink was a factor in two of these three stabbings in Montana. I had seen its effects already. All down the highway, at various intervals, were little white crosses by the side of the road. Each cross represented a road fatality. I hated these little white crosses. They were meant to act as speed deterrents, but I could not see how. There were so many of them and, juxtaposed alongside the billboards urging the inhabitants of the reservation to abstain from drink and drugs, they began to look ridiculous. Six crosses on a post represented six deaths. It almost seemed like a target. And how could a cross by the side of a highway be permitted in a country that enshrined the separation of church and state? I was to discover I was not alone in my irritation. Legal moves are afoot to prohibit these crosses. In Utah, crosses erected to commemorate State Troopers who have died have been declared unconstitutional by the federal appeals court. I hope this eventually means the end of them in Montana, too.

It had been a good ride to Poplar, with a tailwind and fine clear skies. I covered the 77 miles there by just after midday and enjoyed the rolling ride on the straight road. Poplar, however, was not a place to wander around in and I spent most of the afternoon chilling out in the school, thinking of the ride ahead through Eastern Montana. I had thought North Dakota desolate, but this landscape was to test me further. Kathleen Norris had written:

> ... there is so much nothing to take in, so much open land that evokes in many people a panicked desire to get through it as quickly as possible. A writer, whose name I had forgotten, once remarked "Driving through Eastern Montana is like Waiting for Godot".[87]

We were in the Hi-Line, that area of northern Montana near the Canadian border where the track of the Burlington, Northern and Santé Fe Railroad (BNSF) runs parallel to Highway 2. This railroad is the result of the merger of many railroad companies over the last 150 years, particularly that, in 1995, of the Burlington Northern and the Santé Fe Pacific. It is now under the new ownership of Berkshire Hathaway, whose Chairman, Warren Buffett from Omaha, claims "When traffic travels by rail, society benefits".[88]

156

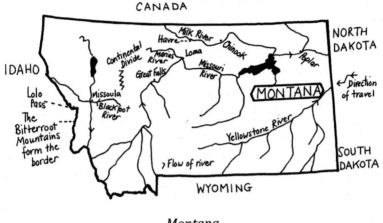

Montana

There were times along the Hi-Line when I thought how good it would be to get on a train. Montana has the third lowest population density of any state in the United States, with 6.699 persons per square mile. Even North Dakota, which was as empty as the ocean, has 9.378 per square mile. The Hi-Line stretches for 650 miles and the BNSF defines many of them. I would wave if I heard a BNSF engine coming up behind me or saw one approaching me on the track, about 200 yards from the road. If the driver sounded the siren by way of acknowledgement, I was ecstatic. If I was ignored – misery. What a rotter to pass me by on this long and lonely road and not even wave!

The road west was harder going after Poplar as we experienced the first of the debilitating headwinds which would plague us all the way through Montana and down the Columbia Gorge. Fierce dogs, rain (again) and the relentless monotony of the Plains all made for some tough times on the saddle. We were now firmly in Mountain Time, two time zones from where we had started in Missouri, which is in Central Time. In North Dakota, some places keep Central Standard Time and some Mountain Time, with the division roughly following the course of the Missouri River. To save changing our watches we had kept camp time to Central Standard Time while we were in North

Dakota. Our last time zone would be Pacific Time in Oregon, but we had a long way to go before we would need to change our watches to that.

The Scotties

Glasgow, Montana (pop. 3,253) where the football team are called the Scotties and the cheerleaders wear kilts, was 72 miles from Poplar. A miserable campsite awaited us, with goose thorn cacti underfoot, strong enough to shred bicycle tyres if ridden on. My fellow campers shouted at me to get off my bike as I rode into the campsite, oblivious to the damage these little plants could cause. To make matters worse, the mosquitoes were out and were fulfilling the promise that the further west we rode, the bigger the mosquitoes. It was time to put on the midge nets again.

I had had a chance to look around Glasgow, named after its Scottish namesake. It is a place which once flourished; when President Roosevelt ordered the construction of Fort Peck Dam on the Missouri and again during the Vietnam War when it was home to the Glasgow Air Force Base. It is pretty run down now, but one of the buildings took my eye. It was faced with green tiles, of a sort and design that you can find in many tenement closes in Glasgow, Scotland. I wondered who had put them there, imagining them to have been brought over from the west coast of Scotland and then overland by train to Montana.

My exploration of Glasgow did not go unnoticed. First, I heard a car horn beeping at me repeatedly from the other side of the street. The two people inside the car were beaming at me and waving. I was used to this by now. The sight of a cyclist seemed to make people happy, or perhaps it was because I looked so odd, with my zinc oxide war paint on. I waved back and turned left towards the campsite. The car door opened and they started yelling, "We saw you! We saw you! Come back! Come back!"

I got off the bike and walked back to the car. It was Patricia White Cloud and her husband who explained that they lived in

Poplar and had seen us there. They had wanted to talk to us and, well, here I was. Could I tell them where we were going? Where had we come from? How long had we been on the road? And would I send her a card when we got to the Pacific?

I felt bad about our impression of Poplar in the face of all this enthusiasm. We had been told that some groups of cyclists won't stop there at all as they consider it too dangerous. Now I felt the people had been labelled and put in a box. No one would ever be able to say they were from Poplar without seeing an expression on the listener's face, "O God! Not Poplar".

It is true that the Hi-Line country we were cycling through does not correspond with the conventional idea of Montana. There are no snow-topped mountain peaks and lush green valleys. The countryside here probably appears flat to those who are not on a bike. It is featureless and windswept, but it has the certain charm of many supposedly unprepossessing areas at the end of the world. I liked it, but just about everyone we met had a chip on the shoulder about Eastern Montana and acted as if they had to apologise for it. Everyone needed to explain why they were there and not in Western Montana, which does look like the place of the movies.

Later, at the museum in Seaside, Oregon, the guide told me she was originally from Montana. She was most reluctant to tell me her home town, first of all saying, "I'm not from the pretty part" and, when I pressed her further, she took it for granted that it was, as she said, "Nowhere you would ever have heard of". She finally admitted she was from Glasgow. I like to think I made her day by not pulling a face but telling her with pride that we had cycled along Highway 2 and had stopped there.

An Encounter with Elvis

After a night in Glasgow amongst the goose thorn, I was determined to get away before the wind got up the next day. Until precisely 8.15am, I congratulated myself on my good sense. Within seconds the wind was up and then doubled in intensity within minutes. Near Hinsdale, we crossed the Milk River – so named by Lewis because it was the colour of a cup of tea with a spoonful of milk – and soldiered on to Saco (pop. 224), where Sue and Kit had made lunch for us at the van, parked by the railroad tracks. A huge grain elevator towered over us. The town was absolutely dead and looked like a stage set for a western. This unlikely place was established only because a place for a water tank was needed by the railroad. It probably felt that it needed to make its mark on the world and did so by making the world's largest hamburger, which took the meat from 17 cattle. I dread to think what it looked like, but it got the town into the *Guinness Book of Records*. It was probably made from Angus beef, as all the cattle I had seen were Aberdeen Angus.

That night, the campsite at Malta, Montana (pop. 2,120) was right next to, indeed, almost under, the railroad tracks which went over a bridge at the end of the site. Like Saco, its neighbour along the track, Malta's name had been chosen by a railroad official spinning a globe and choosing the name of the place where his finger came to rest, in Maine for Saco and in the Mediterranean for Malta.[89] It was a good job his finger had not landed in Hungary or Finland. That was not the only claim to fame Malta had. One of the largest dinosaur fossils ever discovered, that of a brachylophosaurus, was excavated near the town. It is 77 million years old, lives at the Judith River Dinosaur Institute and is called Elvis. Feeling about that old, I was more interested to discover that there was a motel at the campsite. I took the opportunity to get out of the heat and sleep in a proper bed. My Marmot tent had not let me down, but my stamina for camping was waning. I was not alone.

Tour Routines

By now we had been on the road for nearly a month. Malta was where some of us celebrated Independence Day on 4th July by sleeping in air-conditioning and not venturing into town for the fireworks. The trip so far had been a test of endurance for me.

It wasn't that I did not enjoy it as, despite the long days on the saddle and the demands of the loneliness of the landscape, I was having the time of my life. It was just that, compared to the other riders on the Tour of Discovery, I felt pretty pathetic. I had quickly discovered that cycling on your own through Europe, when you can stop as you please and there are services every few miles (including several bicycle shops in every German town), was very different from cycling in the United States where you can cycle 60, 70 or 80 miles without coming across a shop or a café, or indeed any sign of human life whatsoever. The Plains were not, as in the days of Lewis and Clark, teeming with Indians, buffalo, elk and antelope. We could not, as Lewis and Clark had done, stop where we liked to camp, as private property renders this impossible except in designated areas. Ironically, the vast open spaces posed their own restrictions. On a bicycle it was not possible to follow the signs to places of interest off the road, as a car or motor bike was needed to make such detours. I began to appreciate the allure of the Harley Davidson, offering the freedom of the open road, with the convenience of being able to explore off it.

Our support vans stopped, leapfrog style, every 15 or 20 miles up the highway, so we always knew we could get water and a snack and have a chat with someone at the next sag stop. I had no idea how the lone cyclists managed this trip. How did they carry enough water for what could be 80 or 100 miles? How did they keep sane in this expanse of nothingness? I did not know and did not wish to contemplate it. So many little motels, cafés and stores were now closed, I wondered if, in the future, cycling without support would even be possible.

The sag van always waited until the last rider had gone through before moving on, to ensure that we were all 'counted in'. This was a great comfort as you knew you were not going to be abandoned on the highway. It also meant, however, that it was good manners not to get too far behind or else the riders up front would get too far ahead and the sag system would not be able to run efficiently. When the sag van passed you on the road, you did not have to acknowledge it, but if you needed assistance, you had to pat the top of your helmet with your hand. The van would stop as soon as practicable and give assistance. I usually waved when the sag van passed, as I liked to hear the toot of the horn and see the driver wave.

I was often first or second out of camp in the morning and would make pretty good progress while it was cool. Soon, however, Wendy and Alcy would overtake me, then Mike B., then Jay and Hans Ruedi and Ayako, then Larry. Mike B. would usually lead the riders strung out far along the road. He was a marvellously efficient rider who made it all look effortless. After a while, Judy and Mike M. would overtake me, and I would then stay behind them, with Bev and Ken behind me. My favourite riding position was to be a few hundred yards behind Judy and Mike and happiness was to arrive at camp at the same time as them. I managed this twice, once at Killdeer and once at Poplar.

What I really did not like was to be the last rider on the road. This happened when those behind me would be asked to sag a stage (i.e. get in the van) so that the whole tour would not fall too far behind. Sometimes I wouldn't know this had happened until I got to the next sag stop, where I would find that I was last through. I would then get terribly anxious that I would hold everyone up. This was an entirely self-imposed anxiety as no one ever made me feel bad about being slow on the road, but it would sap my strength. Rather than torture myself with this anxiety, I would sometimes choose, then, to sag a stage and keep up. I was relieved that I was never required to sag a stage.

The important things on the trip were not to get dehydrated, not to get too tired and to keep clean and cheerful. It was much more sensible to sag for a few miles, than arrive at camp tearful or cranky and too late in the day to have time to rest up. When you are in a group for 44 days, it is essential not to be a pain, or as Tom would have said, a "disharmonious influence".

Bev was a tremendously experienced bike rider, who had crossed the United States twice. At 77, she was an example of fortitude and perseverance. She had the ability, which I did not, of staying at the back on her own and keeping a steady pace until she reached camp. If she got tired in the headwinds, she would stop and recite a Shakespearean sonnet. She claimed the time it took to do this was the requisite rest time she needed. In Glasgow, Montana, we challenged her to exhibit her knowledge of these sonnets and, of course, she passed with flying colours.

Shakespeare on the Trail

Ken, the other slow rider, was usually way behind; in part because he liked to stop and look at every information board and historical marker on the trail, but he was a generally slow rider anyway. A few times he was asked to sag or accept he would be on his own if he refused to do so. Sometimes, he would come into camp hours behind everyone else. I don't know how he did this. I would have been scared to be out on the highway without support and I had quickly learnt that if I stopped too many times to look at stuff, I would lose resolve it was then hard to regain.

Wendy and Alcy were a good team. In the mornings, before they shot ahead, I cycled near them and was comforted by their yellow jackets in front of me. They were great riders. When things got tough, they just put their heads down and kept going. Alcy never moved on her saddle, whereas I noticed that Wendy shuffled around like me. Jay and Hans Ruedi never seemed to get tired and Larry was a superb consistent rider. I tried to emulate his style, which was steady, steady, steady. Ayako was a marvel. Over 70, she was like a machine on wheels. She and I often cycled together when we had to negotiate our way out of a large town after a day off. She claimed she had no sense of direction. I was happy to go ahead of her, pleased for once to be better at something than someone else. Once we were on the main road I would wave her on and she didn't need any persuasion. Like a flash she would pass me and soon be out of sight.

I doubt whether I would have managed to finish the journey without the tremendous enthusiasm and support of my fellow riders and the staff. Talk about encouragement! That was what kept me going. Karl told me that, at first, he wasn't sure if I was going to be able to hack the whole journey, but then said "You're doing great. You listen and you learn". You bet I did. I was too frightened not to! Tom's view was that you had to do a long distance trip in America to learn how to do one. Nothing could properly prepare you for it. That I agreed with too!

"Everyone sags at some time," Sue explained. "Sometimes it takes more courage to say 'I have had enough' than to press on."

She was right. I could not believe my eyes one day when, on the road and battling against the wind in Montana, the van stopped and, to my utter amazement, inside I saw Hans Ruedi. The great man himself was taking a ride. And even Bev would sometimes take a day out and travel in the van.

I had also found getting used to the camp routine more exacting than I had anticipated. Americans are very efficient and there was no hanging around. We got up before 5am, got our tents down and had a first breakfast of bagels, fruit, oatmeal and coffee, prepared by Sue and Kit who were never late with the food. Unlike the British, who would have hung around chatting over a second cup of coffee, Americans move out within minutes. I needed no persuasion to do that as fear of the sun coming up propelled me out of camp ahead of the pack. Our daily route instructions would tell us where we could get food, and we would all agree to stop at the same place. This wasn't difficult as there was usually no choice about where to stop. Here we would have a second breakfast of eggs, bacon and hash browns, or pancakes, or biscuits and gravy. In America, a biscuit is a cross between a muffin and a scone. Good to eat, hot, on its own, but I could not face the white gloopy mess that was poured on top and called 'gravy'. Again, there would be no hanging around and the Americans would eat, pay and clear out. Often I was reminded of stories of how astonished American troops were, during World War II, to find that the British downed weapons and made a cup of tea at every opportunity. I often felt like some hapless Brit in the face of all this American efficiency. I would have been the one crouching behind a hedge in Normandy making a brew while the Americans marched on.

The West Is Another Place.

"You know you are in the American West when you automatically get hash browns with your breakfast," Bev explained.

How true this is. The hash brown line marks the division between east and west. If you ask for bacon and eggs in Johnny's or Shorty's, or Cody's or Dotty's or Debbie's, or any one of the small, 'family restaurants' in the west, you always get bacon and eggs, hash browns, toast and as much coffee as you can drink. "You can drink it all day," was Hans Ruedi's comment on the coffee, which was incredibly weak and tasteless, but for which I acquired a certain affection as mug after mug was poured for me, usually by an elderly waitress in a pinnie who called me "Hun". Sadly, these family restaurants are in decline as the little towns on the trail crumble into decay. Many times we would anticipate stopping at one of them during the day to find that it was now closed. My heart would sink if I saw the van coming back towards me along the road. Kit would stick her head out of the window and yell, "No food at [whatever the place was]. Go on for 8 miles [or 10 miles or 12 miles] and we'll give you lunch at the van". Sue and Kit made a good lunch, but it was not the same as eating at one of these little restaurants with their friendly staff. At Alexander, where we had stopped when it was too dangerous to ride from Watford City to Williston, the look on the face of the only member of staff in the restaurant, who was cook, waitress and front of house, was a picture when 16 of us walked in! To help her out, I went into the kitchen and served all the coffees.

Invariably, we would get talking to the locals also eating breakfast. Jay was the kind of person who could instantly put anyone at ease, with his natural charm, good manners and genuine interest in other people. At Touchet, in Washington State, an old man called Harry was glad to talk to Jay, while the local ladies meeting up for coffee all toasted our journey and wished us well on the road. "Good grief!" was usually the reaction when we told people how far we were cycling.

After second breakfast we would pedal onto our destination and, if possible, get ice cream when we neared our campsite. If there was a Dairy Queen in town, its location would be detailed on our daily route sheets (at first, I had had to ask what 'DQ' meant). After putting up our tents and before dinner we would, of course, shower and wash our clothes out. Despite the terrible rainstorms, we did not have days of relentless rain. This was not the west coast of Scotland. Within minutes of the rain stopping, the ground would be frizzling with heat. The sun was so hot, it was possible to wash padded cycling shorts out in the shower, hang them on a bush and take them down dry by bedtime (no later than 8pm if the temperature in the tent permitted). There was only one day on the trip, at Fort Abraham Lincoln, where my clothes did not dry the same afternoon.

At camp, dinner would be at 6pm, cooked by Sue and Kit in a camp kitchen. There was always a salad with rice and beans or pasta and vegetables or fried chicken or pizza or tacos. Our favourite was a hobo supper, and here is the recipe:

Hobo Supper

- Find a camping ground with a fire pit or barbeque.
- Light the coals and leave them to get white hot.
- Erect a trestle table.
- On the trestle table put a stack of large sheets of aluminium foil, about 18 inches by 24 inches.
- Next to the foil put a bottle of olive oil.
- Along one edge of the table, put, in individual plastic boxes all or any of the following: ground beef, tomatoes, celery, potatoes, carrots, onions, garlic plus anything else you want to use up.
- Take a sheet of foil and cover one half of it lightly with olive oil.
- On top of the olive oil, put any or all of the above ingredients to your own choosing.
- Season with salt and pepper, tomato ketchup or barbeque sauce.
- Wrap up your supper tightly in the foil, making sure nothing can escape from your sealed parcel.
- Write your initials on the outside with a magic marker.
- Hand to the person in charge of the fire pit who will put your parcel in the coals.
- After 25 minutes, retrieve from the fire pit, open and eat.
- If possible eat with a green salad on which you have poured Dorothy Lynch's Salad Dressing, a Nebraska delicacy.

This routine left little time during the day and I often felt I was short of time, both on the road and in camp. I would have liked to hang around in many of the places we camped at, but that would have turned a 44-day trip into an 88-day trip. So there was nothing for it but to keep going, pondering often that I would have to come back and explore at my leisure some of the places we cycled through.

The Spirit of America

By now it was 5th July and we had been on the trail since 8th June. In two days' time, we would have a day off at Great Falls, but first we had to get to Chinook and Loma. The wind was up for real as we pressed on towards Chinook on Highway 2, riding parallel to the railroad and passing Wagner, where Kid Curry and the Butch Cassidy gang had held up a Union Pacific train and pocketed over $60,000 in cash. I was glad to stop for a self-service coffee at Dodson at the rundown convenience store. Not for the first time on the trip, I found that the old boy serving in the store could not understand a word I said. I was accustomed to having to repeat everything at least twice while the recipient of the information tuned into my strange accent. Usually, people thought I was Australian, because, so I was told, if cyclists passing through were not American, they were from Down Under. Here in Dodson, on learning that I was from Britain, the old boy told me that he had difficulty understanding me because my English was "a little outta date".

My fellow cyclists were keen to ensure that I spoke properly, making me learn an Oregon drawl before we crossed the state line. The attempt was not that successful, especially when my vocabulary let me down. Kit looked at me in horror when I asked her for the kitchen roll (paper towels) and thought I had gone mad on our day off when I said I was off to the hole in the wall.

After Dodson, it was off to Harlem, Montana (pop. 848) where, in the local café, a list was posted on the wall by the cash desk, naming and shaming those who had passed 'bad checks'. Anyone who had done so, however, had a whole Indian Reservation in which to make their escape. Harlem is just on the edge of Fort Belknap Indian Reservation, homeland to the Gros Ventre and Assiniboine Indians. It is the seventh largest reservation in the United States, at 28 miles wide and 35 miles long.

Chinook (pop. 1,386) on the Montana plains had not been, to my surprise, the home of the Chinook Indians who, as master

The list of 'bad checks'

boat builders and fisherman, had occupied the banks of the Columbia River and the Pacific Coast. Now there are only about 2,000 Chinook Indians left, on reservations in Oregon and Washington.

But definitely associated with this Chinook, up towards the Canadian border, is the wind of the same name. This warm wind or foehn, characteristic of the weather east of the Rocky Mountains, is common in winter. It occurs when the prevailing westerly wind dumps rain on the westward slopes of the mountains and the resultant, drier air moves over the leeward slopes. The Chinook leads to dramatic rises in temperature east of the mountains. Loma, where we were heading the next day, once held the record for the greatest temperature change in one day (minus 54°F to 49°F, a change of 103°).

Our campsite at Chinook had an idyllic setting; a flat, clean grassy area on the banks of the Milk River and by the water plant for the town, where we could get a shower. One thing marred it though; the most terrible stench which permeated our clothes and clogged our airways. At first we thought we had been misinformed about the plant and exclaimed that it must be for sewage, not water, but we were assured this was not the case. The stench came from slurry which had been spread on the nearby fields to discourage the breeding of mosquitoes. I found this hard to believe, but apparently the nitrogen content in slurry discourages mosquito breeding, provided that the slurry is not too diluted with water. Whatever the reason, it made our stay by the Milk River a memorable one. It was also ferociously windy. Tom had put tarpaulins up around the campsite shelter, to give us some respite from the wind, but these started to flap with a deafening rattle and we had to take them down before they blew away. The wind did not bode well for the morning and even a sing-song under the shelter, led by Sue with her beautiful soprano voice, did not affect the gods determined to make life difficult for those on two wheels. Nothing fazed Sue; I admired her so. I could imagine her on a wagon train, or on a homestead, working in the fields, chopping wood, cooking the food which she had grown and, in the evenings, making clothes for the children. In between all this she would have killed a coyote, fought off some Indians, written her diary, sang hymns and translated a book from the German. In comparison with these capable, self-reliant Americans, I felt like a soft, flabby, pathetic creature born of a far-off welfare state.

It was drizzling when I left our camp by the Milk River before the sun started to rise, ignoring Sue's plea to stay put, have some breakfast and wait until light. I wanted to get on the road as soon as possible. But I was desperate for a coffee. Seeing lights on, I knocked on the door of the local bakery. It was opened by a young man who told me they did not open for another hour, but that I should bring my bike inside, out of the rain. He would make me a coffee and give me the local paper to read. This was Jean's Bakery, where the walls displayed a photograph of every man and woman in the town, dead and alive, who had served or was serving in the US military.

I liked the fact that bicycles were usually welcomed in America. It went without saying that you could take your bike into your motel room. In fact, if you enquired whether you could do this, the reception staff looked at you as if you were mad for asking. So, here in Chinook, it was fitting that my bike was propped up under a large sign, 'The Spirit of America', displayed on the wall above the photographs. These had been my words of thanks to Jean's son when he unlocked the door at 5.30am and told me to come on in out of the rain.

Chinook Bakery

Coffee at Jean's Bakery was the best part of the day. Highway 2 that day was noisy and dangerous as truck after truck raced by on the road. It was also wet and windy. By Havre, Montana (pop. 9,621) where we stopped for something to eat, after 22 miles, I was already tired. Havre, so named after a vote of the original French homesteaders, was incorporated in 1893 as Bullhook Bottoms. Its inhabitants determined to change its name to something less graphic, but the change to Havre was achieved painfully and only after the first meeting to discuss the name change ended in a brawl. The casino in town is still called Bulhook Bottoms and, forgetting its Gallic roots, the town is pronounced 'Havv-er' (and Chinook is pronounced 'Chinn-uck').

Through the Rocky Boys

Worsening conditions were ours when we left Havre and turned left onto Highway 87, where the road through the Rocky Boy's Reservation was covered with broken glass and debris. The road stretched relentlessly ahead, bordered on each side by telegraph poles and the railroad off to the right. This road was an ugly scar in beautiful countryside, with the Bear's Paw Mountains as a backdrop. The smallest Indian reservation in Montana, Rocky Boy is the home of the Chippewa-Cree. Originally two tribes, they came together when the reservation was established in 1916. Both tribes had felt badly treated by the US Government. The Cree had been deported to Canada when they initially refused to settle on a reservation. They returned, however, in time to hunt the last of the buffalo but were homeless until they agreed to join the Chippewa.

About two weeks before we passed through, rain had caused major flooding on the reservation, leaving 300 homes without running water and necessitating the evacuation of 30 families. It was still raining. I was slow on the road, due to the headwind, a puncture and repeatedly stopping to put my waterproofs on and take them off. This was a kind of displacement activity designed to keep my mind off the traffic and the headwind, but it achieved nothing as it meant I got further and further behind. I needed no persuasion when the van stopped and Sue asked me if I wanted a ride. I was taken to the convenience store on the reservation, which leapfrogged me ahead of many of my fellow cyclists. The store was a miserable place. It reminded me of a shop on a housing estate in a poor part of Central Scotland. Booze was much in evidence. I bought a Magnum ice-cream. Not for the first time I felt a deep sense of shame at the fate of the Indians and other deprived peoples.

When I set off again from the store, I was near the front of the pack and I could see Hans Ruedi a few hundred yards ahead of me. Within 20 minutes or so, the sky to the right began to darken. I felt my level of anxiety go up a notch. Within a few minutes, a full blown electric storm, with torrential rain, thunder, and streaks of lightning was rolling towards me. I pedalled faster, trying to get ahead of the storm. In this part of the world, the wind can be strong enough to de-rail a freight train. Perhaps not quite that strong that day, it was still hard to pedal, but, against the wind and with torrential rain in my face, I got up to a magnificent 12 miles an hour as I tried to catch up with Hans Ruedi. I did not want to be out alone in the storm.

Hand Ruedi, however, was oblivious to the exertions behind him, or perhaps he was trying to get away from me as well as the storm. I couldn't catch him. I saw the van approaching. My spirits soared as the word 'Rescue' came into my head. Immediately afterwards, I despaired as the van passed Hans Ruedi.

"Oh, no," I thought, "They are not going to pick us up".

But I was wrong. The van stopped on the other side of the road. Tom leapt out, yelling above the noise of the storm,

"You can't be out in this. Get in the van while we put your bike on the roof".

"What about Hans Ruedi?" I asked.

"He'll be fine. He's tough. He can look after himself," was Tom's answer.

Get in the Van!

And so, leaving Hans Ruedi to his fate (which was immediately to be picked up by a motorist and taken to a warm, dry café at Loma, our destination for the day), I got in the van and we retraced our route back along Highway 87, picking up cyclists as we went and stashing the bikes in and on the van.

Ardus Mo

The campsite at Loma (pop. 92) was behind what looked to be a derelict motel. It was what Judy would have called an ARDUS MO, in honour of a terrible motel she and Mike had stayed in, where nothing worked, including the neon signs outside. Here there was no neon. I was cold as a result of sitting in the van in wet clothes. The campsite was waterlogged and the mosquitoes came out as the rain finally came to a stop. It was time, again, for the midge nets.

To our astonishment, the motel still seemed to be functioning. Wendy, Alcy and I looked through every window of every cabin and there were beds in some of them. Others were piled high with junk. One cabin was open for us to use the shower. Right there and then, we three determined to get one of the usable cabins and dry out, but we had to wait outside until the owner returned to the motel after her shift in the local grocery store. The longer we waited, the more sinister Loma looked to me and the more I thought about Bates Motel. I wondered if there were shower curtains in the cabins. I was relieved when Wendy asked for one with a bath.

"I'm real lazy," the owner said, when we finally got into the motel office, brandishing dollar bills in the hope that she would quickly get organised and give us a key to a cabin.

We could have replied, "Yes, we can see that", but even a cabin where the rubbish had not been emptied was a respite from the rigours of the day, despite the $62 which we had to fork out for the privilege of sleeping in it. Actually, I had the best night's sleep of the trip which I put down to sharing with two capable people. I slept like a baby, knowing if a grizzly appeared, as it had done when Lewis and Clark had camped upriver, Wendy and Alcy, who had earlier fixed my puncture, would deal with it.

I was pretty tired at Loma and decided that I never wanted – ever – to see the Great Plains again. They had beaten me. Now, of course, if I were given the chance to do the journey again, I would jump at it, as I find myself longing for the things I found so difficult to cope with at the time; the vastness and the solitude, the skies and just the sheer challenge of it all. However cold and tired I was though, this was nothing compared to the excitement that I was actually at Loma. Loma was, of course, where Lewis had made the correct choice of which fork of the river to follow. This was the confluence of the Missouri and the Marias. I felt the hand of history on me.

Shep the Wonder Dog

As if in recompense, the weather the next day was glorious. I remember 7th July 2010 as one of the best days of the tour; the kind of day when all the hardships of previous days are forgotten and elation sets in. Our first stop was to be Fort Benton, and the road climbed through bluffs to the right and left and then into the open ground, before we took a left turn and freewheeled down the hill to this lovely small town by the Missouri.

Fort Benton (pop. 1,594) was a shock. After being in small, run-down towns for weeks, there was an air of prosperity here to which we were unaccustomed. The café where we had breakfast was not the usual family restaurant, but a smart, trendy eating house that served strong coffee to smart, trendy people. There was a strawberry on the plate with my vegetable wrap. I felt like a tramp and immediately wanted to get some new clothes, get my hair done and do nothing but drink coffee whilst reading the paper. Even the *Billings Gazette* would do. That was not to be, as we had miles to go.

Fort Benton was once the furthest fur trading post on the Missouri River, and had been founded by members of the

Chouteau family of St. Louis in 1847. In 1860, the American Army had built a road, called the Mullan Road, from Fort Benton to Fort Walla Walla, on the other side of the Rocky Mountains. It comprised part of the plan to prevent the Europeans, in the form of Britain, France and Russia, making a claim on the territories west of the mountains. This was, of course, years after the Lewis and Clark expedition, which just goes to show how the issues of 1803 were still pertinent over 50 years later. The US Government hoped that the road would encourage civilian emigration, which it did until the railroads superseded the wagon trains. The first year the road was completed, 20,000 people travelled along it.

Nine days later, we too would be at Walla Walla, which was 642 miles on the Mullan Road. Our route would not take us along it, as today little is left to be seen. We had to cross the Missouri and take a right onto Highway 228, but first we had to see the statue of Shep, near the Grand Union Hotel.

Shep the Wonder Dog

Shep is the Montana equivalent of Greyfriars Bobby. He belonged to a cowboy whose body, when he died, was put on a train east. That day of the shipment of the deceased, and every day thereafter, Shep appeared at the station in Fort Benton. Shep met every incoming train, looking for his master. Tragically, six years later, Shep was killed by a train he was waiting for, as he had his paws on the rails but was looking the other way. He was hit by the train. Everyone in town went to his funeral and a bronze of Shep now overlooks the Missouri.

Highway 228 climbed to over 3,500 feet out of Fort Benton before we dropped down to Highwood, Montana (pop. 189) and then up again to 3,800 feet where we met the main road into Great Falls. Even the huge gradients did not matter that day. With the Highwood Mountains to the left, the sun shining and, for once, not too much wind, it was a ride of which dreams are made. At last, this countryside looked like my idea of Montana. I felt euphoric, at least until I reached the intersection with Highway 3 and followed the hot, baking, white tarmac six miles into town through the eyesores of the fast-food restaurants, motor shops and out of town outlets.

Wrapped up well on the way to Great Falls

Great Falls was where we were to stay for two nights and have a day off. Our accommodation was student housing, just off 10th Avenue, a continuation of Highway 3 and where the huge supermarkets and drug stores were situated. I shared a pretty run-down and ill-equipped apartment with Ayako, but we were near the supermarket. It was good to stop and prepare ourselves for the next leg of the journey which was to take us across the Continental Divide. That was something I was too scared to think about, as for weeks Ken had been saying to me, "Jeez, Sheila, this is nothing; we have to get over the Continental Divide. You're pretty strong, but Jeez, Sheila, those guys ...".

I felt unnerved by Ken's predictions that he and I were just too feeble to hack the Divide, compared with the other riders. I was strong in parts, but I was not a consistent, steady rider and I did not have the stamina of the others, especially in intense sun and temperatures over 90°F.

Great Falls (pop. 56,690) is a big town. That is, although it has a population of about one third of my nearest big town at home, Dundee, it must spread out twenty times as far. It was a long way on the bike from our apartments to what passes in Great Falls for downtown. It is all far too vast to even contemplate walking. When I first saw Great Falls, I hated it. The scale was just too much for me. Within 24 hours I liked it so much I could happily have stayed there, bought a house and settled there, at least for the summer. The record of 117.5 inches of snow in 1988/89 rather put me off a winter sojourn.[90] Instead of the daunting space, I began to see the lovely tree-lined avenues, the impressive public buildings, and the fantastic museums, of which the one dedicated to C. M. Russell takes the prize.

C. M. Russell (the 'M' stands for Marion, but there is no evidence that this Marion tried to change his name to Wayne) was a rich boy from St. Louis who was fascinated by the Wild West. When he was 16 he went to work on a ranch in Montana. One day, during the harsh winter of 1886-87, the ranch foreman received a letter from the owner, asking him how the cattle were coping with the conditions. Badly, was the answer. The Chinook had blown through, melting the top cover of snow which had then frozen solid when the temperature had plummeted. There was nothing for the cattle to eat as they could not break through the ice. Many had been eaten by wolves. Those that survived were emaciated. The ranch hands were waiting anxiously for another warm wind to melt the ice. When the foreman sat down to reply to the letter, Charlie Russell offered to draw a sketch of the conditions to enclose with it. When he saw the sketch, the foreman said "Hell, he don't need a letter, this will be enough". The sketch was called 'Waiting for the Chinook'.[91] The rest is history. Charlie Russell became one of the foremost painters in America.

In his works, C.M. Russell created an idealised version of the Wild West. It was one that greatly appealed to me as it did not contain trucks and monster RVs. He painted Indians, buffalo, cowboys, horses and even Lewis and Clark meeting the Flathead Indians. The museum, air-conditioned of course, was a wonderful place to spend the day. Ayako and I went there together and were pleased to be greeted like visiting dignitaries as the staff had heard the Lewis and Clark cyclists were in town.

The Empire Builder

Originally there were five great waterfalls on the Missouri near the present day town of Great Falls. Lewis and Clark named four of them when the Corps of Discovery reached this area on 13th June 1805: Crooked Falls, Great Falls, Beautiful Cascade and Upper Pitch. The last two falls later changed their names to Rainbow Falls and Black Eagle Falls. The Missouri dropped over 600 feet from the first falls to the last and this necessitated a portage of 18 miles, whereby the boats were hauled on trucks and wheels made by the men. By 29th June, when the portage was still going on, a terrific storm with huge hailstones knocked the men to the ground.

After Lewis and Clark, it was not until 1880 that the white men returned to this area of the Missouri. This visit was prompted by a man called Paris Gibson who realised that the power of the falls could be harnessed for hydroelectricity. He persuaded a friend, James J. Hill, to make the necessary investment and extend his railroad, the Great Northern Railway, through the town. By 1887, 1200 people lived in the town and no doubt they all turned out in their Sunday best to see the arrival of the railroad that year. The first dam was completed in 1888 at Black Eagle. Today, all the falls except one have been dammed. It is no longer possible to see them as Lewis and Clark did. However, if you travel today by train from Portland, Oregon to Chicago, Illinois, a distance of 2,255 miles which takes 46 hours and 55 minutes, you will do the journey on the 'Empire Builder'. This is what James J. Hill, the man who started it all off, was known as in his time.

CHAPTER TEN: GREAT FALLS, MT TO LEWISTON, ID

Days 32 to 37
9th July to 14th July 2010
388 miles

Lunch Stop

There were three distinct parts to the 92-mile day which was to get us across the Continental Divide. First we were to take the frontage road (a road parallel to a major highway) out of Great Falls to Vaughn. Then there was a long slog through the foothills to the mountains. And finally, a push up to the Continental Divide at Roger's Pass and down the other side to Lincoln, Montana, where we were to camp that night.

The first part of the journey was easy enough as the road to and through Vaughn (pop. 701) was flat. Slowly, the gradient increased. Worse was to follow. The foothills lived up to their name; they are a range of very frustrating hills. No sooner had we got to the top of one hill than we went down the other side, losing much of the height we had just gained. The road was like an extended, narrow piece of corrugated iron. I kept remembering what Sue had said about the ride to Lincoln. On their own, the foothills would be fine. On its own, Roger's Pass would be fine. But put the two together and it is the hardest day of the trip.

There was nowhere to stop for lunch and, instead, it was to be provided at the sag van, which I was very pleased to reach after the latest in a series of what seemed to me brutal climbs.

By then, I thought I was third from the back of the pack, with Bev and Ken behind me. I was surprised to see there wasn't much food on the table under the tarp, which had been put up to give some shade. I took a little food, not wanting to guzzle what was left, as that would have meant meagre pickings for Bev and Ken. I was puzzled, then, to find Sue and Tom packing the lunch things away, dismantling the table and taking down the tarp.

"What about Bev and Ken?" I enquired.

"Oh, they sagged here from Vaughn. They have had lunch and they set off a while ago" was the answer.

I was horrified. My worst scenario had occurred. If I set off now, I was bound to be last on the trail, as the others who were still here would soon catch me up and overtake me. It was already past noon and the sun was high in the sky. There was still a long way to go. How would I get over the pass if I cycled all the way there in this heat and was last in the pack? Ken had predicted I was too weak to do the whole ride that day.

This was a classic example of how the mind can sap energy from the body. Tom put out the call for anyone who wanted to sag the next stage to come now. His plan was to drive those who wanted to sag fifteen miles or so and drop them off at the bottom of the pass. I had to make a quick decision and decided to go with Tom, as did Ayako and Mike B. who said he was not feeling too well. His decision surprised me as he was an amazing rider. But, as Sue had often reminded us, everyone sags sometime. I think he was missing his wife, who had driven up from Colorado and had spent the time off in Great Falls with him. Later, I regretted sagging that day as I missed a spectacular descent before the final climb to Roger's Pass and did not have the satisfaction of saying that I had done Great Falls to Lincoln by pedal power. Perhaps it was the right decision, as the sun would have fried me before I got to the pass, but it was also a lesson on not listening to pessimism. What Ken had said rang in my ears and had lessened my resolve. Next time, I shall do better.

When we were dropped off at the foot of the pass, Ayako was away like a machine. I was next and Mike B. was some way behind. The road was a killer and, to make matters worse, it looked as if we were cycling downhill, even though we were going uphill. No one had told me about this optical illusion and I thought I was going mad. I stopped twice to see if my brakes had jammed on, as my eyes told me I should not be pedalling. At the top, Sue, who was waiting with Kit in the van, told me that when she cycled that stretch of Roger's Pass, she stopped and poured water from her water bottle on the road to test the slope, as she too had thought she was going crazy.

The Divide

After a while, Mike B. passed me, saying the same thing he said every day when he overtook me, "Hey, you are doing great, Sheila. You're going so fast I couldn't catch you". He was such a nice man. His encouragement always gave me a boost. With those words, of course, he pedalled past, making it all look effortless.

Roger's Pass holds the record for the place with the lowest ever recorded temperature in the United States, excepting Alaska.[92] When it broke the record, it was January 1954 and the mercury dropped to minus 70°F. Now it was July 2010 and in the mid-90s. Despite being above the tree line, there was no shade on the road. All the trees were some way back from the tarmac, with no overhanging limbs to make life more comfortable for those who wanted to stop to take a break. I had completely covered my legs and face with zinc oxide and looked like a creature from another planet. In fact, my fellow cyclists called me the Maori, which I took as a compliment, as these people are brave and warrior-like. I was hot and the last few miles to the top were torture.

We crossed the Divide about six miles from where Lewis and Clark crossed it at Lemhi Pass. That pass is not suitable for ordinary vehicular traffic, let alone a bike. Modern travellers have to check with the local ranger about the road conditions before they attempt the climb to Lemhi Pass on the single lane gravel road and are warned that engines may overheat.

No doubt those who do attempt the Lemhi Pass route are rewarded with a view as near as possible to that which Lewis saw on 12th August 1805, but for Lewis the effort to get to the top did not bring him the sight he had hoped – that of a clear descent to the Pacific. Instead he saw range after range of mountains. Lewis recorded in his journal that, at the fountain of the Missouri two miles before the Divide, he halted for a few moments and thought of the toilsome days and restless nights they had suffered on the way. These were my thoughts exactly when I got to the top of Roger's Pass at 5,610 feet. But any hardship I had felt was extinguished by the exhilaration of having made it so far and knowing that, in 12 days' time, we would be at the Pacific. I cycled the remaining miles, through the forest, down to Lincoln, in good spirits.

I had been surprised, though, to find that the Continental Divide was marked only by a sign giving the elevation. Americans, unlike the British, do not need to validate their historic and cultural experiences with the presence of a tea room. Neither the Lewis and Clark Interpretive Center in Nebraska City, nor the C.M. Russell Museum in Great Falls had a tea room, which would have been unthinkable in institutions of similar size and quality in the UK. A soda machine was about as good as it got. It seemed to me to be part of the cultural inability of the Americans to linger.

A Lot of History Goes with this Location

The campsite at Lincoln (pop. 1,100) was about a thousand feet below the pass and situated by a stream at the RV park at the end of town. It could not have been more idyllic. After the High Plains, where little offers relief to the eye, the intensity of the green landscape, with mountains as a backdrop, was almost painful to behold. I pitched my tent right by a stream, dangled my feet in the freezing water, and thought how lucky I was to be in Montana. It wasn't quite yet the country of Marlboro Man, but it was close.

However, all was not as it seemed. Marlboro had originally been a brand of filter cigarettes considered fit for women only and sold with the strap line "Mild as May". The red strip on the cigarette paper was designed to conceal the discerning, cigarette-smoking woman's lipstick stains. To increase sales, the image of the tough, independent cowboy was grafted onto the brand, which had Americanised the name of the Duke of Marlborough for the transatlantic market. Marlboro Man was born. When the original Marlboro Man retired, the cigarette company, Philip Morris, spent millions of dollars looking for someone to replace him. All in all, there were three, consecutive, Marlboro Men. Reputedly, they all died from lung cancer.[93]

So, too, Lincoln turned out to be something more than a quiet, little town. Late at night, when we were all in our tents, the noise of motorbikes woke us up. This was Harley Davidson country proper, where real men smoke cigarettes on their Fat Boy Lo machines ("Fat, dark and strong, this down and dirty version of the custom icon is the new big dog on the road"). It is a far cry from Netherton Cottage near Aberlemno, near my home in Angus, from where Arthur Davidson's grandfather, Sandy, had emigrated to the United States in the 1850s. A current project is underway to create a legacy visitor centre and museum at the now ruined cottage at Aberlemno. No doubt it will have a tea room.[94]

The motorbikers who stopped us sleeping were using Highway 200 next to the campsite as a race track and they went up and down all night. It was what Meriwether Lewis would have called a restless night, and a short one at that, as we had to be up at 5am.

"Where the hell was the Sheriff?" we muttered at breakfast.

Having been visited many times by law enforcement representatives on our trip, there was no one available when we really needed them.

When I was trying, fruitlessly, to get some sleep in Lincoln, I did not then know that a man called Theodore Kaczynski had been arrested there in April 1996. There are no "Welcome to Lincoln, where Ted Kaczynski lived" signs on the way into town, nor does the town website mention his name. This is not surprising, as Ted was the 'Unabomber' who sent mail bombs which killed three people and injured 23. The name 'Unabomber' derived from 'UNABOM', used by the FBI to refer to the unknown person sending bombs to universities and airlines and going undetected for nearly 20 years.

Ted was a bright child. He got into Harvard at 16 and attained his doctorate in mathematics from the University of Michigan, before becoming an assistant professor at the University of California, Berkeley, where he was the youngest person ever to be hired to that office. He gave all that up to live in a remote cabin near Lincoln and become a survivalist. Well, accounts of Ted's life story call the cabin remote, with no running water or electricity, but the marker on Google Earth shows the location of it just off Highway 200 and perilously close to the campsite where we spent the night. In the autumn of 2010, the land where Ted's cabin stood was put on the market for $69,500 dollars, reduced from $154,500. The particulars from John Pistelak Realty stated "A lot of history goes with this location".[95]

Ted became dangerously radicalised when he discovered that a road was being built in one of his favourite areas in the wilderness. He determined on revenge and the mail bombings were the result. He was caught after he sent a 35,000 word essay to the media and demanded it be published. The FBI agreed to its publication in the hope that someone might be able to identify the writer. This is precisely what happened. His brother, who already had his suspicions that Ted was the bomber, had these deepened when he read the 'Unabomber Manifesto'. He first hired a private investigator to make enquiries about Ted, from whom he had been estranged for ten years, and eventually talked to the FBI. Ted is currently serving life imprisonment without parole in a prison in Colorado.

The Stray Bullet Café

We had left the stifling humidity behind a long time ago, but, so far, we had had little release from the heat. That changed at

Lincoln. It was cold, very cold, when we left early in the morning. We had to put on as many clothes as possible commensurate with still being able to ride a bike, including long tights, hats, gloves and several layers of jumpers. We were headed for Missoula, Montana (pop. 64,081) a full 1,300 feet lower than Lincoln. Theoretically, it should have been a free wheel all the way. That was not to be, because of the wind, and several hills to get up and down to the other side, but the cycling was not difficult. It was so much easier, psychologically, to cycle alongside the Blackfoot River, following its enormous sweeps and bends through the mountains, than on the straight-as-a-die roads of the Great Plains.

The Stray Bullet Café

By Ovando (pop. 71) we were through the first range and, within minutes of arrival, had to strip off layers of clothes and apply sun screen (or, in my case, zinc oxide). Breakfast was at the Stray Bullet Café, so named because one is lodged in a wall of the building, a memento of the days when it was a saloon and cowboys brawled the nights away, taking pot shots at each other. This was my kind of place. There were cowboy pictures

187

on the wall, men in checked shirts at the tables and an espresso coffee machine at the counter. I loved the Wild West as conjured up by the Stray Bullet Café. It was so much easier than the real thing.

Ovando was originally going to be called Sadiesville. Once you know that, it sort of destroys the whole Wild West spirit of the place. One of the first settlers of the area in the 1880s, Ovando Hoyt, was chosen by his peers to write to the Federal Government in Washington, DC, requesting a post office and a mail service to the new town. The men at the big post office back east took one look at the name 'Sadiesville' and thought "Perhaps not". They named the town Ovando (which comes from the town, Obando, in the Extremadura part of Spain), looking only as far as the name on the form for inspiration.[96]

Customers at Ovando

Independent Minds in Montana

We were headed for Missoula, and it was a fair ride apart from the one, long hill which we had to get up and over about halfway there. 'Tubing' in the Blackfoot River is a popular sport in these parts and I could not believe my eyes when cars started to come towards me with huge, tractor-sized inner tubes, fully inflated, tied to the backs of the vehicles. The drivers and their passengers were hell-bent on launching these things into the waters of the Blackfoot. Every 'tuber', as these daredevils are called, had two tyres: one to lie in and, attached to it, one for emergencies to which the beer was attached. From the road, it did look appealing to be quietly flowing down the river with a beer, but only where the river was benign. The rapids and eddies would not have been for me.

This was Montana, where people want to do as they please and not be told by others what to do. Nowhere is this more apparent than on the roads, as the tale of Rudy Stanko illustrates. One day, in March 1996, a policeman called Kenneth Breidenbach was driving along Highway 200 and saw, in his car mirror, a vehicle approaching from behind. It was a 1996 Camero sports car, with a suspension system designed for high speed. The sports car overtook him. He tailed it for about eight miles and then signalled to the driver to pull over. He then gave the driver, Rudy Stanko, a speeding ticket, claiming he had clocked the car doing 85 miles an hour. Rudy Stanko appealed against the speeding conviction for which he was found guilty. His appeal failed and he appealed to the Supreme Court of Montana.

Now, originally, Montana had no set speed limit on its roads. Between 1973 and 1995, however, the Federal Government introduced a maximum speed limit of 55 mph throughout the United States. Some argued that it had no power to do this (remember the Constitution) but the Federal Government had anticipated this response. It told the various states in the Union that if they refused to implement the speed limit, they would not get any funding for their roads. No doubt kicking and screaming, individualistic Montana introduced the speed limit of 55 mph. It also made the fine for being caught speeding a token $5.

It was shortly after the federally imposed speed limit came to an end that Rudy Stanko was stopped in his Camero. There was, once again, no set speed limit and instead, a person operating a vehicle had to drive it in a "careful and prudent manner" and at a rate of speed no greater than was "reasonable and proper" given all the conditions. The conditions included the state of the road and the type of vehicle.

Rudy Stanko claimed that he had been driving carefully and prudently in his Camero. He was a good driver, he had never had an accident and the car was almost new and in perfect condition. But just in case that argument did not wash, he also claimed that Montana's "careful and prudent" principle was so vague as to be unconstitutional. Poor Officer Breidenbach could only say that he regarded Rudy Stanko to be speeding at 85mph, but was unable to say what speed he would have regarded careful and prudent in all the circumstances.

One of the appeal judges thought Rudy Stanko's argument ridiculous. After all, no other Montana driver had any problem understanding what "careful and prudent" meant and the statute had been on the books for 43 years. But the court as a whole backed Rudy Stanko and said that the provision was unconstitutional. No Montanan should be punished for speed alone, without first being notified of the speed at which their conduct violates the law.[97]

The consequence of all this fuss was that a statute had to be passed bringing into force specific speed limits and now Montana has a maximum state speed limit of 75 mph. It is said that the fatal accident rate on the roads doubled when, as a result of Rudy Stanko's case, this limit was introduced.

Old Griz

I sagged the last seven miles into Missoula, as within seconds of getting to the sag stop at Milltown, a torrential rainstorm started, with thunder and lightning.

"Get in the van," shouted Tom.

I did not argue. Our accommodation that night was Knowles Hall at the University of Montana in Missoula. Ayako and I shared a room. What a pleasure it was to put the clean, white, crisp sheets which had been handed to us by the helpful reception staff onto the bed and have the best shower of the trip. We got free use of the laundry and internet. On each of our doors, a welcome sign was displayed, showing Old Griz, the grizzly bear mascot of the university, on a bicycle on the Lewis and Clark Trail.

I liked Missoula (pop. 66,788). At Knowles Hall, there were no screens on the windows which meant either the students were immune to mosquito bites, left for home each year before the mosquito season started or, improbably, that the mosquito had not discovered Missoula. Perhaps it was too cold for them in the winter and they had decided not to return. In the winter of 1996 Missoula had over 200 inches of snow.

At the back of the beautiful university campus, bounded by elegant, faculty housing, was an enormous hill. A path zigzagging up its steep slope ended at a large white 'M', painted onto the ground. It was a mark of honour to climb up to the 'M', but for us, far too hot to do so and honour went by the by. Sue told us that the scratches we could see on the hill were evidence of Glacial Lake Missoula, a prehistoric lake formed at the end of the last ice age behind a huge ice dam at the southern end of the Cordilleran Ice Sheet. The Columbia River Gorge had been formed as a result of this dam rupturing and the floodwaters forging relentlessly westward. When later I saw the Willamette Valley in Oregon, before returning to Scotland, I was reminded that its fertility was due, in no small part, to the mass of sediment carried down in those floods and dumped there.

Missoula left us in good spirits for our journey the next day. Our objective was to climb the road up to Lolo Pass (elevation 5,233 feet) in the Bitterroot Mountains and cross the Idaho border to Lochsa Lodge, in the Idaho National Forest.

It is 44 miles from Missoula to the summit at Lolo Pass, but only the last four miles are difficult. It was a glorious ride through majestic, forested countryside with mountains looming above the tree line. I was so overcome with the joy of it all that I did not even see the sag van parked in a recreational area in the trees off the road. Ayako and I sailed by regardless and did not get counted in until we stopped for food at Lolo Hot Springs.

A brown bear had met those up ahead of us, but true to form I had missed it.

Lolo is where, on 13th September 1805, Clark had discovered the water from the rock was, indeed, so hot that he could not bear to touch it. Lewis had other things on his mind, as he had lost his horse. He stayed behind on the trail with four men to look for it, and then two men had to be sent back by Clark to continue the search. Missing the sag van seemed pretty tame in comparison.

The next days were to test the Lewis and Clark expedition to its limits. The route over the Bitterroot Mountains was punishing, with fallen trees and rocky gorges. On 15th September several horses slipped and rolled down a steep hill. One of them was carrying Clark's desk, which was broken when the horse lost its footing.[98] The desk tumbled down the mountain side, stopping only when a tree broke its descent. A few days later, during which finding, feeding, caring for and worrying about the horses seemed to have preoccupied much of their thoughts, another of their mounts fell a hundred yards down a near perpendicular slope into a creek, dodging rocks all the way down. To the astonishment of all, the horse stood up, shook himself down and, after a twenty-minute rest, was able to carry on.

Portable Soup

Such was the severity of this part of the journey that Lewis and Clark decided to split the party into two groups, no doubt to lessen the risk of them all getting lost, or all falling down the side of a mountain. Clark went ahead with six men. By the time Lewis and the rest of the expedition caught up with them at the Nez Perce Indian villages on 18th September 1805, they were done in. They had been eating their portable soup, the forerunner of Knorr stock pots. The men hated it.

Portable soup was made by repeatedly reducing stock until it formed a gelatinous mass. This was then dried out so it could be put in a box and easily transported. Lewis had purchased 193 pounds of the stuff before the expedition started and was not alone in being an advocate for it. It was also a favourite of Captain Cook and of the Royal Navy which administered it to its sailors on a daily basis on board ship until canning was invented. A small amount of the portable soup was added to hot water and stirred. We do not know if the members of the Corps of Discovery had to hold their noses when drinking it, but they all must have accepted that it was an occupational hazard of life away from home.

Mrs Beeton's Portable Soup

- 2 knuckles of veal
- 3 shins of beef
- 1 large faggot of herbs
- 2 bay leaves
- 2 heads of celery
- 3 onions and 3 carrots
- 2 blades of mace and 6 cloves
- A teaspoonful of salt
- Sufficient water to cover all the ingredients

Take the marrow from the bones; put all the ingredients in a stock pot, and simmer slowly for 12 hours, or more, if the meat be not done to rags; strain it off, and put it in a very cool place; take off all the fat, reduce the liquor in a shallow pan, by setting it over a sharp fire, but be particular that it does not burn; boil it fast and uncovered for 8 hours, and keep it stirred. Put it into a deep dish, and set it by for a day. Have ready a stew pan of boiling water, place the dish in it, and keep it boiling; stir occasionally, and when the soup is thick and ropy, it is done. Form it into little cakes by pouring a small quantity on to the bottom of cups or basins; when cold, turn them out on a flannel to dry. Keep them from the air in tin canisters. Note: soup can be made in 5 minutes with this, by dissolving a small piece, about the size of a walnut, in a pint of warm water, and simmering for

2 minutes. Vermicelli, macaroni, or other Italian pastes [pasta], may be added.[99]

Through the Idaho National Forest

Our journey through the Bitterroots was less exacting than that experienced by Lewis and Clark. There was even a visitor centre at Lolo Pass and free coffee on tap. I decided I liked Idaho. From the pass it was a 99-mile ride downhill along a winding road. At least that is what the sign at the top said. Pedaling against the wind, though, it did not always feel as if we were going downhill.

Winding road west from the Idaho border

Lochsa Lodge was a resort complex set in the forest near Powell Junction, where there was a ranger station. The lodge had a restaurant, a bar, the obligatory gift shop, a backpackers' store (outside) and showers (again outside). There was an adjacent campground near the river which was to be our home for the night. It was 11th July 2010 and the final of the World Cup was on in the bar in the resort when I arrived and headed inside for a cold drink. Four people were watching it. Two of them asked if anyone knew the rules.

The resort was packed, with more motorbikes than I could count, all ridden by huge men. They all sported long hair, red bandanas, tattoos, little or no protective clothing, and all had revolvers at their hips. Each biker had an equally large girlfriend on the back in jeans and a bikini top.

Scared of the bikers in Idaho

In the small backpackers' store, the sales assistant handed me a bulging wallet, saying a cyclist had left it and assuming the owner to be of one of our party. He and I looked inside the wallet. Someone's life was in there, but the wallet did not belong to anyone on the Tour of Discovery. I left the wallet in the store and went round the resort calling out the name of the owner – to no avail. I felt sick for the person who had left it behind and hoped that they were cycling towards Montana. The pedal west back to the lodge to retrieve it would be a lot easier than the pedal east, even if they had to then climb the hill again to the pass. The thought of getting to the bottom of the road, 99 miles from the pass, and *then* finding out you had lost your wallet, would be trying indeed.

As if I had not cycled far enough that day, I missed the turning to the campsite and carried on until I neared the Ranger Station at Powell. I was preoccupied, thinking about someone I did not know and who probably did not yet even know they had lost their wallet.

Retracing my steps, I found our campsite to be more sedate than the presence of the bikers had made me fear. There was no power, so we escaped the fairy light campers, and, for once, we did not have to seek shade for the tents. We were in the forest, under a canopy of trees. Nearby was the fast flowing Lochsa River whose headwaters were just upriver from our camp at Powell Junction. The river takes its name from the Nez Perce Indian words for 'rough water' and is one of the best rivers in the world for white-water sports.

Idaho

Next day, it was back on Highway 12, the road we were following through the Bitterroot Mountains. These are named after the bitterroot, the small pink state flower of Montana (*Lewisia rediviva*). Who discovered and named the flower is probably obvious. A low-growing, extremely beautiful pink flower, the bitterroot is also known as the 'resurrection flower' as it is hardy, perennial, and can live for a year without water. It has then all the characteristics of the typical Montanan. The root was prized as good eating, in the days before a traveller could get a hamburger at Lochsa Lodge, and the Indian tribes planned their migrations across the mountains to ensure the plant root was at the right stage to be dug up, pulverised and cooked. If you wanted a sack of the stuff, you had to be prepared to give a horse in exchange.[100]

Highway 12 parallels the Lochsa downstream, following the enormous bends in the river and the 60 rapids between Powell Junction and Lowell. We were pedalling through the Clearwater National Forest, dense with coniferous trees, impenetrable from the road, except for where a few trail heads led up the steep slopes through the trees.

I heard a voice behind me as I cycled down this road. It was Mike M., catching up with me (an unusual occurrence as it was usually I who was trying to catch up with Judy and Mike). He wanted to explain to me the difference between a National Park and a National Forest: the former are for recreational use only and have as their prime objective the preservation of the natural landscape and any historic features in the area bounded by the park. John Muir, the Scots-American who was one of the world's first environmentalists, was inspirational in their creation and the first park established was Yellowstone National Park in 1872. President Ulysses S. Grant signed the bill bringing it into effect after Theodore Roosevelt badgered his fellow politicians to agree to it. The National Park system covers 84 million acres and is managed by the National Park Service under the Department of the Interior.[101]

National Forests, however, permit multiple use, with recreation going on alongside lumber operations, cattle grazing and the exploitation of mineral reserves. They were created in 1891 when some Californian businessmen became concerned about over-exploitation of natural resources. Now, these multiple use areas cover 193 million acres.[102] National Forests are managed, not without controversy between the differing interests, by the Department of Agriculture and the US Forest Service.

The Clearwater National Forest covers 1.8 million acres from the top of the Bitterroot Mountains to the Palouse, which we were to come to later. Those areas which are designated for recreational use only are, like most of the National Forests west of the Rocky Mountains, original forests, and this mass blanket of dark green continued many miles down the river to Lowell.

A Tale of a Pump

Lowell is at the confluence of the Lochsa and the Selway, 2,000 feet lower than the headwaters of the Lochsa at Powell Junction. The rivers meet here to become the Clearwater River, which gives its name to the National Forest. We then followed the Clearwater down to Kooskia, bringing our total cycling that day to 89 miles. Our camp was at the Clearwater Elementary School at Kooskia (pop. 675 and pronounced 'Cous-key') on the Nez Perce Indian Reservation. I parked my bike, along with some others, in a corridor of the school and put my sleeping bag down by the bikes. I was happy because I had found a rubber bracelet in the general store in Kooskia which was impregnated with mosquito repellent. I put it round my ankle and wore it like a talisman, confident in its powers.

Dinner was always at 6pm and that evening at Kooskia, two of our party had not arrived by that time. Bev's son, Tad, who had joined us in Great Falls, to spend the last two weeks of the tour with us, was missing along with his mother. Surely they were still not out on the road? The wind was fierce and the heat sapping. A rescue party had to be sent to find them. Now there are two roads into Kooskia and no sooner had the van left to find them than they turned up on the other road. They had been at Lowell, where they had met two cyclists going west/east up the pass (i.e. up the 99-mile hill). Each of these cyclists had been riding a bike with a different tyre valve fitting and one of their pumps had broken. They had not wanted to risk going over Lolo Pass without a working pump for each bike and had been at Lowell for six days waiting for a replacement pump to arrive. Tad's pump was just what they needed and, with no faith that the replacement pump would indeed arrive, they offered to buy it. All the hanging around had been due to waiting for the stranded cyclists to get cash to pay Tad when the campsite office opened. Bev and Tad had been in the campsite when the sag vans passed and, as they had forgotten to leave their bicycles on the road, the sag vans had passed by without counting them in.

Kooskia, Idaho

It was a tour rule to leave your bikes on the road if you departed off it for any reason. It was strange how quickly we learnt to recognise the bicycles from a long, long distance away. The country is so empty that a bike by the side of the road stands out like a lit beacon marking out who was where. So too, a speck on the horizon could easily be identified as everyone has a unique stance on a bike which is like a name badge.

We all thought selling his pump was very worthy of Tad, but his good deed for the day, albeit transacted on a commercial basis, left him pump-less. His plan was to cycle ahead of his mother. If he had a puncture he would use her pump when she caught up with him. That, of course, is exactly what happened the next day, except Ken was the first to catch him up, not his mother. I wonder if he cursed himself for giving up his pump as he sat by the roadside and waited.

The Lands of the Nez Perce

Lowell had been a pleasant place for them to spend the afternoon with attractions such as white-water rafting, fishing, and trail walking. Tad even had a plunge into the Selway. I remember it as the only place on the trip which had a European-style loo, with two buttons on top for the flush. This had intrigued Kit, who had never seen one, and wondered what the buttons were for. The loo was obviously a stand against the topsy-turvy world of America, where light switches were up for on and down for off and shower taps were designed to tax one's sanity. Each one seemed to be different. Taps that looked as if they should be turned, only worked if you pulled them out and then pushed them up. Taps that looked as if they should operate with a pull, worked only if you managed to move them in the right direction by accident. In Gettysburg, South Dakota I had a cold shower because for the life of me I could not find out how to get it to run hot. Bev said soothingly that it was "counter-intuitive". In Glasgow, Montana, at the mosquito-infested campsite, I had to get dressed, walk to the camp office, disturb the manager and his wife and ask for instructions on how to get water from the shower. I could not understand what the manager mimed I should do, so he, plus daughter Isabel, walked me back to the shower room and gave me a demonstration. Their opinion of me needs no recording.

Without the help of the Nez Perce Indians (Nez Perce means 'pierced nose' something these Indians did not do) Lewis and Clark and the rest of the expedition would surely have starved to death on the Bitterroot Mountains. The Indians gave them quawmash roots and fish to eat, which led to some of them getting sick. Lewis felt so unwell, he could hardly sit on his horse. Rush's pills, which had survived the journey so far, were administered to those who had to lie down on the trail, too weak to continue.[103] Quawmash was the edible bulb of the Common Camus, which has a blue flower and is not to be confused with that of the poisonous Death Camus, with a white flower, and which the Indians pulped and used on their arrow heads. Luckily for the members of the expedition, their stomach aches were caused by greed and not poison.

The Nez Perce Indians also built canoes for the expedition and agreed to look after their horses, which they had obtained from the Shoshone Indians, Sacagawea's tribe, on the eastern flanks of the Rockies. It had been an emotional reunion for Sacagawea with her own people, from whom she had been captured by the Hidatsa. Lewis had been introduced to the chief, Cameahwait, by the first Shoshone he came across – a group of women who had never seen a white man before. Lewis got across to the women that he came in peace. This was just as well as he only had three men with him and the group of Shoshone warriors, including Cameahwait, who then arrived on the scene, outnumbered Lewis and his men by 20 to 1. It was Cameahwait who broke the news to Lewis that he would not find a water route to the Pacific and would need horses to attempt the journey over the mountains. Agreeing to negotiate the same with Clark, the Shoshone chief and Lewis went to find the rest of the Corps of Discovery. There, where Clark had camped, Sacagawea recognised the chief as her brother. Sacagawea was overcome and, not surprisingly, the negotiations for horses were halted frequently as Sacagawea wept and was unable to translate from Shoshone into English for her tears.

After that, it was no contest. The Shoshone agreed to sell horses to the expedition. They wanted guns in return. They had been hounded off the plains by hostile tribes and did not, as Cameahwait explained, like living in the mountains eating berries like bears. They were men of the plains who should be on horseback hunting buffalo. The chief's name meant, indeed, 'he who never walks'. Lewis told him that he could expect more white men to come with everything the Shoshone could desire. It was not to be. The Shoshone suffered horribly as their life in the mountains became intolerable and they were removed to a reservation which was too small to be sustainable. In 1905 they were moved again by force to Fort Hall in Idaho where the remnants of the tribe now live with those of the Bannock Indians.

The Nez Perce once inhabited a huge area round the Snake, Salmon and Clearwater Rivers but are now confined to the reservation through which we were cycling. It is a still a large area, at over 1,000 square miles, but a fraction of the original tribal lands. In the nineteenth century, part of the Nez Perce tribe resisted being moved onto a reservation, before surrendering to the US 7th Cavalry in 1877 near Chinook in Montana, where we had camped by the Milk River. Before this surrender they fought 13 battles with the US Army as they tried to move north to Canada for refuge. They almost made it. Chinook is only 63 miles from the border. On surrender, their Chief Joseph, said

Hear me, my chiefs. My heart is sick and sad. From where the sun now stands, I will fight no more forever.[104]

Joseph was captured as a prisoner-of-war, and, in the dead of winter, taken, with 400 members of the defeated tribe, in an unheated railway wagon to Fort Leavenworth.

Oversized Trucks

Orofino (pop. 3,247), the biggest town on the Nez Perce Reservation was our first target after an early start from Kooskia.

Not that the early start did me much good, as I had to cycle back to the school to find my iPod which I had left charging in the corridor. Bev had already retrieved it and had it in safe keeping. I should have had more faith and cycled on in the knowledge that someone would find it, making the journey to Lewiston via Orofino a little shorter for me than I managed to contrive.

I was sorry to leave Kooskia. I liked it a lot. Tom had parked the vans in the street outside the school and Sue and Kit had set up trestle tables in the street for dinner. We had sat in the shade under the trees lining the street. No one had bothered us. I had contemplated the land of the free. I did not miss the nanny state.

From Kooskia, we continued on Highway 12 which, between 1943 and 1945, was constructed by many of the 265 males of Japanese ancestry held at the Kooskia Internment Camp, six

Wishing I had the road to myself

miles east of Lowell. These men had been interned elsewhere in the United States after Pearl Harbour and had volunteered to go to Kooskia; a "paradise in mountains", according to one of the internees, who had been a landscape gardener in Santa Cruz. Some worked in the camp, but most were paid to work on the road.[105]

Highway 12 has its own controversy today, as there are proposals to permit its use by oversize trucks. These trucks will carry equipment which is destined for the tar sands in Alberta, where oil exploration is going on. The plan is to ship the equipment from Korea to Vancouver, Washington State and then up the Columbia River by barge to Lewiston, where it will be loaded onto the oversized trucks to continue on up Highway 12 and over Lolo Pass and thence to Canada.

On the way down the highway, we had seen numerous placards protesting against this proposal. One householder had even measured out the size of the trucks by stringing lines down the highway to show their length and height. From what we could read in the *Billings Gazette*, the Nez Perce were opposed to the proposal. I, too, was appalled at the thought of enormous trucks going up to Lolo. How would they even fit on the road? How would they deal with the gradient to the summit? What would happen if one broke down? It was inevitable that trucks of this size pounding up and down the road would change the wilderness. It would certainly be the end of cycling the Lewis and Clark Trail (at least for me). I noted that there would be three stops for the trucks on the way up Highway 12, at Orofino, Kooskia and Lochsa, all places where we had stopped on our way downriver.

When we cycled down Highway 12, no permit had been granted to allow these trucks. The matter was the subject of litigation in the Idaho courts. It has now been resolved. On 15th December 2011, the Idaho Department of Transportation announced that a giant megaload would travel on Highway 12, east to west, the following night. The load was a pipe, 95 feet long, 22 feet wide and 17.5 feet high. It weighed 185,000 pounds. It was to travel accompanied by three traffic control flaggers, three pilot vehicles, an ambulance and a service vehicle.[106] I am glad I was not on the road at the time.

Orofino (literally 'fine gold') is on the Clearwater and was named after a gold-mining camp established in 1861 on the

Orofino Creek. We had a good run there, cycling by the fast flowing Clearwater. However, the dense, impenetrable forest had given way to more open forest and areas of commercial development, as well as residential buildings displaying "Obama sucks" signs. Worst of all, it was all too clear that we were out of the protected areas of the National Forest and into logging country. We started to be passed by huge logging trucks, which, after Orofino, increased in number horribly. I found the cycling terrifying. Highway 12 is only two lanes and we were on a narrow shoulder (which sometimes disappeared altogether) between the right-hand lane and the metal barrier, which was our only protection against falling down the steep slope to the river. I had soldiered on cycling between Killdeer and Watford City in terrible truck traffic, but it was not something I wished to repeat. I had found myself lying in my tent at night, seeing the trucks whizzing by in my mind's eye. I needed no more of that. I did not want to be 'Cracknelled', although at the time I could not express my fears in those terms as James Cracknell, the Olympic athlete, did not have his encounter with a truck in Arizona until a few months later. So, at the first sag stop after Orofino, I decided to sag the rest of the way to Lewiston. Later, in the bike shop in Lewiston, I was told that no local person would cycle the stretch from Lewiston to Orofino. It is considered far too dangerous.

I don't know why I expected green forest all the way to the Pacific. But my ignorance of the country through which we were to cycle, as we followed the Clearwater further and further down, resulted in a profound shock on discovering that we had left trees behind and were back into bare, open country with no shade.

Lewiston (pop. 31,293) where we had our last day off before making the final push for the Pacific, is at the confluence of the Clearwater and Snake Rivers and on the edge of the Palouse. It is on an area of hilly, silt dunes and now a major wheat-producing area in the United States. Sue had once driven a combine in this area, but when the crop was peas. "No one eats peas anymore," she claimed, explaining the change to wheat.

The first white men to visit this area were not Lewis and Clark, but those on an expedition led by David Thompson in 1803. His objective was to set up fur trading posts for the North West Company, another huge fur trading empire, which would eventually merge with the Hudson's Bay Company in 1821. Thompson, who had left London at the age of 14 bound for Canada, had explored vast areas of North America, but from the British territory in the north, rather than the Atlantic coast. He reached as far south and east as the Mandan villages, where Lewis and Clark had overwintered on their way to the Pacific. He was given short shrift by the Nez Perce after he tried to persuade them to take up trapping. The men of the tribe considered this to be work fit only for women and made this known to him. The women, in turn, made it clear that they had quite enough to do, thank you, without adding trapping to their duties. So much for Thompson. Soon after, Lewis and Clark came through the area. Perhaps someone warned them not to suggest trapping.

A Bad Hair Day

Camping had been arranged for us at Hells Canyon State Park near Lewiston, but this was a way out of town and we all elected to stay downtown at the Guesthouse Inn and Suites Motel, where the prospect of air conditioning was much more attractive than going to Hell.

Hells Canyon is the deepest gorge in North America, 8,000 feet at its deepest (dwarfing the depth of the Grand Canyon). It was carved out by the waters of the Snake River and is largely inaccessible by road. In 1806, on the way back to Missouri, Lewis and Clark had taken one look at Hells Canyon from the Salmon River and had turned back. So I did not feel too bad about spurning the park for a motel room that overlooked the Lewiston railroad yards and the Clearwater River.

Downtown Lewiston is low-lying and flat, even though its elevation above sea level, at the Clearwater River, is nearly 750 feet. The downtown areas were enough for me. I did not even seek to explore those areas of the town which rise sharply up to 1,500 feet from the riverbanks. It was just too hot. I never did figure out why it was so much easier to cycle in high temperatures than walk and, having put my bike in for a service, there was no way I was going to walk up hills.

Having had most of my hair cut off in Nebraska City, I now considered myself to look like a decaying hedgehog. I was determined to get my hair tidied up and coloured. Lewiston, perhaps, had not quite caught up with the most fashionable hairdressing techniques of the modern world, but once over the threshold of a Lewiston hairdressing salon, I did not have the nerve to back out. Before my hair was done I had to complete a detailed questionnaire and discuss my hair issues with a fierce-looking woman who wanted to know my percentage of grey hair. The first question on the sheet, to which I was required to give written answers, was, "What do you find challenging about your hair?"

I emerged looking like a bleached, decaying hedgehog. It was, perhaps, a good thing that we were required to wear cycle helmets.

What do you find challenging about your hair?

Recreation Trail at Lewiston, Idaho

At 465 miles from the Pacific Ocean, Lewiston is still a seaport. Timber and other products are shipped down the Snake (the Clearwater giving up its name at the confluence) to the Columbia and thence to the Pacific. By the same token, equipment and goods are sent upstream and unloaded at Lewiston, as we knew from the over-sized truck controversy. Levees built along the rivers make for a good walking and cycling path which takes you to the old historical area. Here you can find a little museum about life in Lewiston, including information about those who came to Lewiston during the gold rush.

The Gold Rush

In October 1886, 34 Chinese men left Lewiston and took their mining tools 65 miles up the Snake River by dragging flat-bottomed boats upriver. There they set up camp on the Oregon side of the river, against the walls of the cliffs, at a place called Deep Creek. By August 1887, they were all dead, murdered by a gang who threw their bodies into the Snake and took their gold.

At that time, there was a lot of ill-feeling against the Chinese. It was said that they worked for less than white men and refused to assimilate. The Chinese were not generally, however, immigrants after the American Dream. They were workers looking to make money and go home. The killings on the Snake River were not the first. Twenty-eight Chinese coal miners had been killed at Rock Springs in Wyoming Territory in 1885 and there had been unrest against the Chinese in many places, including Portland, Oregon, where an attempt to expel them from the city was unsuccessful. Feelings were such that, despite the entreaties of Rev. Henry Ward Beecher (he who had paraded John Brown's chains from the pulpit and who now added Chinese immigration to his many causes), the Chinese Exclusion Act was passed in 1882. This barred entry to further Chinese immigrants for ten years, although those still in the United States could stay.

The gang who killed the Chinese near Lewiston was led by Bruce "Blue" Evans, a horse thief prone to stealing the beasts in Oregon and swimming them across the Snake River to Idaho Territory. The youngest member of his gang, Robert McMillan, was only 15 years old. Evans was arrested soon after the killings came to light but for rustling, not murder, as nothing was known of his involvement in the fate of the Chinese. There being no jail, he was confined to an upstairs room in a Lewiston hotel. Tiring of hotel life, he made his escape.

There was no justice for the Chinese until one of the members of the gang, Frank Vaughan, was persuaded to confess. It did him good to get it off his chest, as he was not brought to trial. Only three of the gang, the youngster, McMillan, Hiram Maynard and Hezekiah "Carl" Hughes ended up in court. By then Vaughan had done the dirty on the rest of the gang too and they had all absconded. They were never to be found. Those who stood trial were found not guilty and the gold the killers stole has never been found.[107]

CHAPTER ELEVEN: LEWISTON, ID TO SEASIDE, OR

Days 37 to 44
15th July to 21st July 2010
478 miles

Jawbone Flats

Highway 12 continued as we left Lewiston, Idaho on 15th July 2010, crossing the Snake River to Clarkson, (pop. 7,337) which was incorporated in 1902 in an area known as Jawbone Flats. The folk of Jawbone Flats obviously had an eye on marketing when they named the town Clarkson, trading on the more established Lewiston next door, or perhaps they just wanted to annoy their neighbours across the water. Neither William Clark, nor any member of the Corps of Discovery, ever crossed the river to what is now Clarkson. We were now in Washington State, our ninth state of the trip, and we followed the Snake upstream until we turned off left, away from the water, to begin the huge climb to Alpowa Summit (2,785 feet) and into the Palouse.

Distinct from the Nez Perce, although they spoke the same language, the Palouse Indians were also horse breeders. The name of the Indians is most closely associated now with the Appaloosa breed of horse with its distinctive spotted coat. It was on these horses that the Nez Perce and Chief Joseph tried to flee to Canada before being defeated at the Battle of Bear Paw near Chinook. A consequence of the defeat was that the horses were taken by the 7th Cavalry; some were sold, many were shot. The breed went into decline until the 1930s when the Appaloosa Horse Club was formed and steps were taken to revitalise it.

Washington State

The Palouse

Tom had told us that the sag van would be at the summit, at the 20-mile point of our ride. It was a slog up to it, far worse than the road to Lolo Pass and, having climbed it, I was not expecting more brutal hills that day. I was wrong. After stopping for food at Pomeroy (pop. 1,517) after a well-deserved downhill run, we made another left turn to climb up and down, up and down, towards Dayton (pop. 2,655). I thought the hills would never end, but the pain was rewarded by the vistas of the wheat fields, brown and yellow, in the sun, like huge abstract paintings. They might be more properly described as wheat hills, as how the agricultural machinery managed on the gradients was a mystery. Before Dayton, we passed a sign to Starbuck. It was near here that Clark had recorded in his journal on 13th October 1805 that Sacagawea was a token of peace. The fact that they were travelling with a woman gave a signal to the Indian tribes that they meant no ill.

This Starbuck has nothing to do with coffee, as the Starbuck with an 's' was named after the first mate in *Moby Dick*. Instead, this Starbuck (pop. 130) was named after a railroad official, W.H. Starbuck. The town originally stood on the line of the Oregon Railroad and Navigation Company. No longer. The only bank in town went bust in 1929, the High School closed in 1956 and the railroad station shut in 1961.

By the time I got to Dayton (pop. 2,655), near to where Lewis and Clark had camped on their way back from the Pacific to St. Louis, I was ready for further refreshment. I found it a delightful town, not least of all because in Home Baked Goodness I was given my coffee by Carolyn in a dainty cup and saucer, the only ones I saw in America. This fortified me enough to press onto the Fairground at Waitsburg (pop. 1,212) where we would camp for the night. It had been a hot, windy, hilly, 79-mile day and, when I arrived, my fellow cyclists gave me a round of applause.

An American Fairground, I discovered, is what we would call a Showground. I was so hot when I got off my bike, only to discover there was no fair, that I took one end of a hose I saw connected to a standpipe and held it above my head, luxuriating in the freezing cold water. I decided I liked the Palouse. Before darkness fell, I stood for a moment with the setting sun at my back and thought how I would miss all this and, having suffered so much from the sun, I knew I would be longing for it when I got back to Scotland.

My affection for the Palouse grew as we cycled up and down hill into the winery country of Washington State, passing Walla Walla, the end of the Mullan Road from Fort Benton, and onto Touchet.

Dr Marcus Whitman, whose restored mission house lies two miles or so from the main road from Walla Walla to Touchet, was a Presbyterian missionary who, with his wife, Narcissi, had established a mission which became a stopping off point on the Oregon Trail. Narcissi was made of strong stuff. She was one of the first white women to cross the continent and she was the first white woman to give birth in Oregon Territory. Unfortunately, the child drowned when she was two after walking down to a river with her cup to get a drink.

The Whitmans lived among the Nez Perce and Cayuse Indians and inevitably this contact led to the transmission of disease, especially measles, to which the Indians had no immunity. In 1847, many of the Indians died from measles and the tribe blamed the missionaries. The result was a massacre, in which the Whitmans were killed along with eleven others at the mission. Over 50 women and children were taken hostage and spent a month or so in captivity before their release was negotiated. It led to an ongoing war with the Indians who were driven inexorably into the mountains. Three years later five men were hanged for the massacre.

All of us except Ken declined to go to the mission. The wind was against us and picking up force. We wanted to make as much headway as we could. For my part, I had seen so many churches cycling through America and so many billboards advertising Christianity, I couldn't face going anywhere with a remotely missionary message. I was on the side of the Indians and was anxious to get to Touchet (pop. 396) before I took a break.

The Gorge

From Touchet it was a short ride to our first glimpse of the Columbia River. Nothing prepares you for the immensity of this river where the Snake flows into it and the drama increases as you proceed west down the gorge which extends for over 80 miles with gorge walls up to 3,000 feet high. The average width of the river down the gorge is a mile. With the ferocious headwinds for which it is renowned, cycling along the gorge is hard going. It must have been worse for Lewis and Clark though. They were in canoes.

Six days to the Pacific. It was 16th July 2010 and today we would enter Oregon, our tenth state and the final one of the tour. Our campsite that night was at Umatilla (pop. 70,548). We pitched our tents on the banks of the Columbia, by the McNary Highway Bridge and near the Umatilla Chemical Depot, run by the US Army, where stocks of chemical weapons are stored for safe disposal.[108] The map of the facility on the internet shows that we had pitched our tents in the "Immediate Response Zone" so it was some comfort to learn later that the depot has won the Army's Exceptional Safety Award for 2010 and has not lost time due to an accident since July 2006.

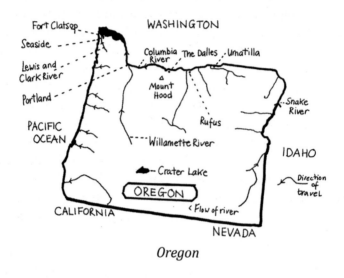

Oregon

Safety was my concern for the next part of the journey, which took us onto Interstate 84, still on the Oregon side of the Columbia. Highway 14 on the Washington side of the river looked, from a distance, a far more benign road for cyclists; however, Tom said there was no shoulder to cycle on, a complete lack of services and lots of truck traffic. Information available on the internet about cycling the Columbia Gorge also states that Highway 14 is dangerous, which goes to show that the grass is always greener on the other side of the fence, or, in this case, the road on the other side of the river always looks easier than the one you are on.

Not all states in America permit bicycles on the interstates, where jurisdiction falls to the federal government, not the respective states. Oregon does permit cyclists on interstates, however, and theoretically the shoulder should have been wide enough and sufficiently free of debris to make cycling on it relatively straightforward. It was, in places, but we also came across a lot glass, rubber and general road detritus and, in some places, the shoulder narrowed to an alarming level. This road was to be our route, off and on for the next three days, and it was pretty scary at times.

I had got over my general fear of American highways and had learnt how to cycle safely across huge intersections and how to negotiate the road when a slip road joined from the right. On this interstate, the slip road issue was magnified because the traffic seemed to be that much more profuse and that much faster. After a while I felt murderous towards the drivers of the gigantic RVs, the predominant vehicles on the highway. Trucks were bad, but those driving them were generally polite, expert drivers. The octogenarians driving the RVs were the ones which worried me. Some of these things were as big as Greyhound buses and no special licence was needed to pound down the highways in them, towing, of course, the obligatory 4x4.

The intensity of the headwind was the last ingredient in the mix which made today's ride an experience best forgotten. At least, I thought this was the worst thing until we had to cycle round a dead elk, which had obviously been killed by a truck (or perhaps an RV driven by an octogenarian). It was lying at the apex of the shoulder where a slip road came in from the right. Its head had been partially decapitated. It was smelly. There was nothing for it except to close one's mouth, stop breathing, avert one's eyes and get past it as best as possible. The sight of that dead elk haunted some of us. It was like the horse in the bed scene from the *Godfather*, writ large on the highway.

At one of the interstate service areas where the sag van had stopped, I declined the snacks at our van and wandered over to a kiosk that advertised coffee and cookies. This was one of the interstate refreshment stands run by local charities that are given a pitch at a rest area in return for promising to man them over weekends. Commercial enterprises are generally banned at such areas in order not to poach trade from local businesses off the interstate. Charities join a long waiting list to get the opportunity to man a kiosk, as thousands of dollars can be made over a long weekend. This one was obviously popular as there was nothing left to buy except for the same type of cookies which were available at our sag van for nothing.

At Rufus (pop. 268) our camp was in the former public school building. It was not air-conditioned and very stuffy inside so I chose to camp outside on the grass by the road, opposite an apricot tree. My greatest pleasure that evening was watching a huge RV come down the road in search of the local RV park. The driver stopped and asked me for directions. I told him, truthfully, that he had missed the turning and would have to go back as the road he was on was a dead end. That operation took many manoeuvres. He had to unhitch the massive Toyota 4x4 he was towing and drive it out of the way, reverse the RV, drive it forward and out, and hitch up the Toyota again. It took ages as the road was narrow with few places to reverse into. His wife was stony faced. I looked on. Revenge is sweet.

At times, the affluence of the RV culture in the United States really got me down, especially when I learnt that it is subsidised by the ordinary non-RV owning sector of the population. It is, under US tax law, an inalienable right for the mortgage interest, on not one, but two "dwelling units" to be treated as a deductible allowance for the purposes of personal taxation. But what is a "dwelling unit?" The answer is that it is a house, apartment, condominium, mobile home, boat, or similar property.

In 1980, a man called Ronald L. Haberkorn went to law and successfully argued that his 22 foot long, mini-motor home qualified as a dwelling unit and, accordingly, that the interest on the loan secured against it was tax deductible.[109] His mini-motor home had a double sink, a medicine cabinet and a commode. It enjoyed a living area equipped with a three-way dinette, where he could sit and watch his wife cook on the four-burner cooker. When he had finished eating he could lie down on a sofa and then go to bed in an overcab sleeper. No doubt he slept well, as he made tax law history and millions of Americans must now say a prayer of thanks to him when they go to sleep in their vehicles at night. The tax break even extends to pop-up campers.

The conditions are only that the vehicle or boat must be used as security for the loan, the interest must exceed what we would call the personal allowance, and the vehicle or boat must be used personally for more than 14 days each year (or, if rented out, used personally for a period equal to 10% of the number of days it is rented out). The final condition is that the vehicle or boat must have basic sleeping, cooking and toilet facilities. No wonder so many Americans buy campers and RVs. As one advertisement for them stated, "all you need is a simple stove and a porta-potty". Coming from a country where the citizen no longer enjoys mortgage interest allowance on a principal residence, I found all this hard to swallow and realised it would take more than the price of gasoline to stop Americans buying bigger and more luxurious RVs.

Bike at Rufus

Before dark that evening I cycled back through Rufus and under the interstate to the shore of the Columbia River and stood by Preacher's Eddy, a 'Treaty Fishing Access Site', where access, as I saw from a sign on a fence, is restricted to members of the Nez Perce Tribe, members of the Confederated Tribes of the

Umatilla Reservation, members of the Confederated Tribes of the Warm Springs Reservation in Oregon and the Confederated Tribes and Bands of the Yakama Nation.

Near here, on 21st October 1805, Lewis and Clark had been "received with great kindness" by the local Indians from whom they purchased some wood and breakfast. According to Clark, the male Indians wore short robes of deer or goat skin. The women dressed in skin which hung from the neck and extended as low as the waist, as well as other skins round their waist and drawn tight between their legs. The Indians were drying fish which they had caught, their access to the river not restricted as it is now to that part of it behind a chain fence.

The Vice-Admiral's Mountain

To the west, I caught my first glimpse of Mount Hood. As with the gorge, nothing prepares you for it, as the snow-topped peak seems to hover in the sky, appearing out of nowhere to hang, far in the distance, over the river. It is the highest mountain in Oregon, although the exact height is open to debate as seismic activity causes it to expand or shrink. Of all the volcanic mountains in Oregon, this is the one most likely to erupt. Mount Hood was named after British Vice-Admiral Samuel Hood, by a British sea captain, William Broughton. In 1792 he sailed up the Columbia River, six months after the American, Robert Gray had named the river after his ship and had produced charts of what he found.

I like to think that when Broughton reached what he named Barings River (now Sandy River), where it flowed into the Columbia, further upstream than Gray had explored, he turned round and, like me, gasped when he saw the mountain. Broughton's commanding officer was George Vancouver, the same man who had disagreed with Robert Gray's suggestion that a major river might lie beyond the sandbars at latitude 47° 17' north on the Pacific Coast. Vancouver had seen the mouth of the river, but the sandbanks had confused him and led him to believe no great river lay beyond them. Had he gone to explore for himself, the river might have been called the Discovery after Vancouver's ship and the British, not the Americans, would have made the first claim to the gateway to the continent from the west.

So Lewis and Clark were the first Americans to see Mount Hood, not the first white men. On 18th October 1805, a cool morning with a fair wind from the south-east (lucky them, that meant a tailwind), they killed a prairie cock. Indians, paddling their canoes, came to visit and, after a council, Lewis and Clark bought 40 dogs (to eat) in exchange for bells, thimbles, knitting pins, brass wire and beads. They proceeded downstream, passing more Indians drying fish on scaffolds by the river. Clark recorded that they observed a mountain to the south-west, the "form of which is conical, and its top covered with snow"[110]. My edition of the journals has square bracketed this entry with the information that this was Mount St. Helens, but I am sure this is not correct. Later on, we would suffer a similar confusion at Crown Point, mistaking the view of Mount Adams for Mount St. Helens.

From the banks of the Columbia at Rufus, looking east, a dead-end road led to the John Day Dam, one of the 14 dams on the Columbia River system and the last one to be completed, in 1971. When it was finished, it was the second largest hydroelectric generator in the world and now, at full capacity, it can power two cities the size of Seattle. A 650-foot navigation lock, 86 feet wide, allows barges and other craft through the dam, lifting them up to 113 feet, the highest lift of any lock in the United States. Fish go through by means of the fish ladders, built, like the dam itself, by the US Army Corps of Engineers. An average of one million salmon make their way upstream each year.

Each one of these dams holds back a lake, created on the course of the Columbia by rising waters after completion of each dam. In the case of the John Day dam, this is Lake Umatilla, 74 miles long. West of the dam, Lake Celilo, 24 miles long, was formed when The Dalles Dam was finished in 1957 and, as its waters rose, it obliterated the falls and rapids at Celilo. This was one of the best fishing areas along the Columbia and in 1957, fish scaffolds were still being used by the local Indians, all probably little changed since the days of Lewis and Clark.

The Dalles was the first town we arrived at the next day after a miserable ride, in the fierce headwind, to Biggs Junction. There had been no solace for us as we rode past the Front Door Chapel, a trailer church just outside Rufus. Where the road met Interstate 84, the van was waiting and Wendy, Alcy and I decided to sag rather than risk the traffic. A wise choice, as it turned out. Roadworks on the way meant that the highway was down to one lane and the shoulder disappeared.

The Dalles

The first thing I had to learn about The Dalles was that the definite article was part of the name and it was pronounced 'the Dahls'. The name comes from the French 'dalle' which means flagstone and refers to the basalt rocks along the course of the river.

We had adjusted our watches to Pacific Time in Idaho, but it was not until we crossed the state line into Oregon that I felt we were entering a different time zone. For a start, just over the Oregon border, there were stalls by the side of the road selling cherries. These were the first produce stalls we had seen on the trip. And, now, at The Dalles, it was clear we were entering the modern world again. We stopped for breakfast at Petit Provencal, which we ate with relish after we finished gawping at the breads and cheeses, the patisserie selection and the cakes. I felt disorientated, as if I were entering a strange world from another planet. This feeling was to become acute in Hood River, further down the road, where the smart and trendy from Portland move *en masse* to enjoy a Sunday excess of consumerism around the boutiques, craft shops, bars and restaurants. I wandered around staring at these strange creatures, like some hick who had come down from the mountains, which is exactly what I was.

On 25th October 1805, Lewis and Clark reached the area where The Dalles was later to be established. By that time, the canoes, which they had obtained from the Nez Perce, had begun to leak, as they had been dragged over so many rocks on the way downriver. Six men were sent out the next day to collect resin to pitch the canoes. They noticed that the water level on the river rose eight inches, which they put down to wind. Below them there were falls, so tide could not account for this rise. On the 28th, when they left the area, after much contact with the local Indians (including giving red handkerchiefs to the chiefs), they were forced to make camp because of the strength of the west wind. They had just come across an Indian family, in whose house they saw a British musket, a cutlass and several brass tea kettles. This must have given them confidence that they were nearing the Pacific Ocean. They noticed as well, that although the wind had forced them to stop, the Indians were still able to canoe on the Columbia and navigate it successfully without mishap.

The Dalles had been a fur trading town, with the name first recorded by the French fur trader, Gabriel Franchere, in 1814. Its main attraction was the amount of relatively flat ground beside the river which gave room for construction of river barges and other cargo vessels. It was also a stopping off point on a massive journey, undertaken twice a year, by employees of the Hudson's Bay Company.

In the spring, between 40 and 75 men would leave Fort Vancouver, downstream from The Dalles, and make their way to York Factory, the HBC headquarters, 2,500 miles away in Manitoba. They would carry supplies, brought in by sea to Fort Vancouver, for the various trading forts along the route and exchange them for furs. This group was known as the York Factory Express.

In the autumn, a similar group, or brigade, called the Columbia Express, would leave York Factory and make its way to the

Pacific, picking up furs along the way in exchange for trading goods, which had also been shipped by sea, but this time, into York Factory. The two groups would meet in the middle of the route. Furs which ended up in Fort Vancouver would largely go to China, where they were traded for Chinese items wanted by the British. Furs which ended up at York Factory went to London.

By the early 1840s, the HBC monopoly over the vast area it controlled in Canada and the Pacific North West was under threat. Wagon trains were bringing the first settlers in on the Oregon Trail (including the ill-fated Dr Whitman and his family) and over-exploitation of the beavers was resulting in their demise.

Settlers and the fur trade did not mix. Dr John McLoughlin, who had established Fort Vancouver for the HBC, violated official company policy not to extend assistance to the settlers, when a group of them demanded help in 1841. He probably saved his own skin and his fort as a result, as the settlers were not inclined to take no for an answer. He might even have prevented war between Britain and the United States, as feelings were running very high about the control of Oregon.

Britain and the HBC began to realise that possession was nine-tenths of the law. The influx of settlers would inevitably mean control by the United States. McLoughlin was told to move the Columbia headquarters of the company north to Vancouver Island in Canada, but instead, he ordered one of the employees to relocate it to what is now Victoria, British Columbia. He refused to move there himself.

Wrangling over Oregon continued until 1846, when, as we know, Britain and the United States came to an agreement for the United States to take control south of the 49th Parallel. That was the end of the York Factory Express and the HBC's hegemony in the area. McLouglin resigned from the Company, moved to Oregon City on the Willamette River and opened a store which became a lifeline for settlers at the end of the Oregon Trail. He became a US citizen in 1849 and is known as the 'Father of Oregon'.[111]

The Columbia River Highway

The horrors of cycling on Interstate 84 along the Columbia are mitigated, in part, by the stretches of the Historic Columbia River Highway which have been restored and which allow the cyclist to come off the main road. This historic highway, which extends from The Dalles to Troutdale, just outside Portland, is mercifully too narrow for the massive RVs and trucks which pound along the interstate. There are even stretches from Moosier to Hood River and from Cascade Locks to Moffat Creek Falls which are only for pedestrians and bicycles. It owes its existence to two visionary gentlemen.

In 1908, these two Oregon gentlemen, Samuel C. Lancaster, an engineer, and Samuel Hill, an investor with an interest in roads, went to Europe and saw there how the Swiss went about road building. They decided to build a road along the Columbia Gorge. It was a fantastic feat of engineering. Sam Lancaster had learnt well from the Swiss. He blasted rock along the gorge for tunnels and, by means of wide, elegant loops down the impossibly steep gradient to the river, built a road which was perfect for the vehicle of the moment, the Model T Ford. The highway was obsolete almost as soon as it was finished in 1922, as people wanted to move faster along the Columbia, and in bigger vehicles.[112]

The construction of dams on this stretch of the Columbia River, shortly after completion of the highway, heralded the end of the beautiful road built by the two Sams. An enormous amount of construction work was undertaken to move the railroad away from the higher water levels which resulted from the damming of the river, and a newer, much bigger road – now Interstate 84 – was built near the new line of the railroad. Sections of the new road encroached upon the old Columbia Highway and parts of Sam Lancaster's engineering marvel were closed. Then rock falls closed some of the tunnels. The old road was closed and so it remained until a restoration project was begun with a view to making much of it pedestrian and bicycle friendly.

This Historic Columbia River Highway transformed the experience of cycling the Columbia Gorge for me and was about as near to an idyllic ride as I experienced on the journey to the Pacific. There were two huge climbs, to Rowena Crest, west of The Dalles and to Crown Point, west of Cascade Locks, but the road is so beautifully designed that you sweep higher and higher up the loops which line the gorge wall, feeling energised by the scenery and by the efforts of those who made the road. The views from the top of these crests are unsurpassed. It was with a thrill that I saw Beacon Rock, the rocky outcrop on the river where, on 2nd November 1805, Lewis and Clark realised they were near the Pacific. It was here that the expedition observed a rise and fall which could only have been tidal.

A Windy Place and the Bridge of the Gods

The views were magnificent, but when we saw that we were to camp at Viento State Park on the Columbia River, hearts sank. 'Viento' means windy in Spanish. Viento lived up to its windy expectations, but was in fact named after three railroad men, Villard, Endicott and Tollman.[113] This was the same Villard who had clashed with the Dundee solicitor, Reid, over the building of the railroad south of Portland and who had persuaded the Dundee investors to back him and not Reid. Once upon a time there had been a railroad station here at Viento. It was now closed, but the trains still ran through on the tracks, about 30 feet from our tents. I crossed the line and walked down, through the trees, to the rocky beach on the shore of the Columbia River. There I was almost knocked over by the wind and, looking west, for the first time I saw in the distance the characteristic clouds of the Pacific coast.

Access to and from the Viento was only by means of Interstate 84 and, as we left the camp-ground early in the morning of 19th July, I saw a lady's bicycle lying just off the shoulder. It looked as if it had been thrown from a moving vehicle. I said a fervent prayer of thanks that none of us had been cycling past at the time. We stayed on the interstate for nine miles or so until we reached Cascade Locks.

Legend has it that two sons of an Indian Chief travelled down the Columbia River peacefully by canoe but argued when they got to the area which is now Cascade Locks. Their father shot two arrows into the sky. One son followed the arrow north (to present day Washington) and the other to the south (to present day Oregon). Their father then built a bridge across the river, so their respective families could meet. This was called Bridge of the Gods. Unfortunately, both sons fell in love with the same girl and she could not make up her mind which son she preferred. They fought over her and the earth responded with force, causing the bridge over the river to crumble. Where there had been a bridge, now there were only rapids.[114]

In fact, what happened was that a natural bridge across the Columbia was formed by a huge landslide called the Bonneville Slide. No one knows exactly when this happened, but it could have been as recently as the eighteenth century. It was definitely before Lewis and Clark went down the river. As a result of this landslide, the Columbia was blocked by a natural dam, over three miles long and about 200 feet high. The river broke through the blockage and formed the rapids, which were a major feature of this river until the Bonneville Dam, four miles downstream, was completed in 1938.

At Cascade Locks (pop. 115) we joined the traffic-free bicycle trail which starts near the modern Bridge of the Gods, a cantilever toll bridge which provides the only vehicular route across the river between Portland and Hood River. Just past Eagle Creek, we had to climb a very steep flight of steps to get onto the high-level bike trail. A groove was provided at the side of the steps to facilitate pushing the bike up, but the gradient was so steep, I doubted whether I could hold the bike at the angle of the slope. Instead I carried my bike up, grateful that my luggage was in the van and not in pannier bags on the back of the bike.

It was obvious that we were cycling into the more populated areas west of the Cascades. Highway 30 took us along a route by Oregon's spectacular waterfalls, including Horsetail Falls and

Multnomah Falls, 620 feet high, which millions of people visit each year. The car park opposite the falls was full of camper vans and cars and the lodge, where we went to eat, was buzzing with people buying souvenirs. Kit, Sue and I went into the restaurant, where most of our party were already ordering their meals. We had left Ayako downstairs sorting out her gear and we expected her to join us within the minute. The waitress politely, but coldly, refused to give us a table for four, insisting we could only have a table for three, even though we explained the last person would be with us directly. I could not believe my ears. After all the kindness and decency of the family restaurants we had stopped at on the way, here was some jobsworth at an ersatz hunting lodge making life difficult. I felt like making a scene and telling her she was un-American, which was the most insulting thing I could think of, and the favoured description used of Obama by the campers we had met at Yankton. I kept my mouth shut. Ayako appeared and we got a table for four.

A long way up

That night we camped on the outskirts of Portland, which of course did not exist when Lewis and Clark made their way to the Pacific. Now there is a city of over half a million people near the confluence of the Columbia River with the Willamette. Portland has free public transport for all in the city centre, a cricket league and Powell's, the continent's largest independent bookshop.

We had once again met up with the Columbia River, having cycled through Troutdale from the top of the gorge wall at Crown Point and then down onto Marine Drive, where we followed the river past the airport. Our destination was the Portland International Raceway, built on the site of an area of public housing called Vanport, which had been obliterated when the Columbia flooded in 1948 after the flood defences failed. A few hours before the river dyke burst, the inhabitants had been told not to get excited as they would have plenty of time to leave. Many left anyway and only 15 people were killed.

The Raceway was the unlikely location for our night's camping. I was one of the last to arrive, so I missed the motorbike racing in the afternoon but was treated to the cycle racing practice sessions in the evening. Fortunately, our tents were not pitched on the racetrack. The directions to the Raceway had been a trifle difficult to follow, or maybe Tad and I, who had met up on the way, were too stupid to follow them. We had backtracked to find the right road, but our confusion had not been helped by some helpful Portland citizen turning a street sign around, which had taken us off course for a while.

The Clatskanie General Store

Ken was the last to arrive at the speedway track and announced that he was giving up. He wanted to fly home for a baseball match, or some such sporting event, and did not want to continue to the Pacific. I was astonished. We only had two more days to go. What was the point of not finishing? I think he was done in. The day before, he had arrived at Viento looking exhausted. He had spent a long time at the Columbia Gorge Interpretive Center Museum, which we had passed on Historic Highway 30. I had decided against visiting it as I knew I could not spend much time there, and the thought of coming out, back onto the bike and into the wind, was enough for me to give it a miss. Ken was cross he did not see all that he wanted to in the museum and no doubt suffered the loss of resolve that I had wanted to avoid. Perhaps cycling past the airport, to which he would return, in three days' time, was just too much. Tom took him to a motel so he could fly home the next day. I was sorry to see him go. I thought he might regret it later and it was a shame that we did not finish as a complete group.

An early start took us through the suburbs of Portland and over the Willamette River at St. John's Bridge, a suspension bridge which was built just after the crash of 1929. As well as replacing the last ferry across the Willamette, construction of this bridge had given many local people work in a time of great unemployment.

It was my first glimpse of the river which had made the early settlers from Scotland homesick for the Vale of Strathmore. The traffic on the bridge made it impossible to stop and gaze over the side to look at the waters, which William Broughton of the George Vancouver expedition had seen in 1792. Having missed the Columbia, it might have been some small consolation to Vancouver to know that when Lewis and Clark canoed down the Columbia, they missed the mouth of the Willamette.

It was then a matter of following the highway to Scappoose (pop. 4,976) for breakfast. There we met a cyclist who had been participating in the annual Seattle to Portland Bicycle Classic which had just taken place. It is a distance of 200 miles between the cities and most riders choose to do it in two days. This one, however, like a minority of participants, had done it in one day. She was in a state of post-ride euphoria, which her parents, who had driven down to collect her, were proudly sharing. I was really thrilled when, outside Ichabod's restaurant, she took one look at my bike and said, "Wow! You have a Surly". For a second I basked in her glory, feeling like a real cyclist and not a plodder. The Seattle to Portland Bicycle Classic is a ride, not a race, unlike the Race Across America in which participants compete to ride across the United States in one go, with no rest days. Solo competitors expect to finish the 3,000 mile race in 9 to 12 days and have to decide when and where to sleep in order to make their target time. Bev told me that hallucinations on the saddle are common as riders are so exhausted.

After Scappoose, it was more of Highway 30 to St. Helens (pop. 10,019) of volcanic eruption fame. Actually this town was called Plymouth and only changed its name to cash in on the supposed view of the volcano from the town. George Vancouver caught sight of the mountain as he sailed past the mouth of the river which he thought too puny to be the gateway to the continent, thus leaving Gray to take the glory of sailing up it and naming the river Columbia. Vancouver named the volcano Mount St. Helens after his friend Alleyne FitzHerbert, shortly after the same was made the first baron St. Helens. Perhaps if Vancouver had paid more attention to the water and not the sky, he would have thought more of what was beyond the sandbanks at 47° 17' north.

It was cold and foggy at St. Helens and we could not see the volcano, 39 miles away in Washington State. Instead, the first of two monster climbs awaited us. My heart sank as I saw the gradient and size of hill before us and a nasty little slip road on the right, bringing traffic over from the other side of the water. This slip road meant I could not get a good run at the hill, but had to hang around until there was a break in the traffic. I found it hard to start pedalling when I finally got to the right side of the road. Mercifully, there was a view point halfway up the hill and I waited there for a while, talking to two women who had done the Seattle to Portland Bicycle Classic in two days and were now cycling home to Seattle via Astoria. Their bikes were fully laden touring bikes. I meant to ask them how they managed to do the Classic carrying all that stuff.

I had not quite appreciated that, before we got to the Pacific, we still had to get over the Oregon Coast Range. This range of mountains, which extends 200 miles south from the Columbia River near Portland varies from 30 to 60 miles wide, with an average height above sea level of 1,500 feet. Highway 30 climbs and dips and climbs and dips through it, but the maximum height we reached on the road was only 655 feet, at Bradley Hill, the next day. It seemed a lot more, but I suppose we were continually going down to near sea level, only to have to climb up again. The road is a brute in places. In winter, motorists are required to carry chains or traction tyres regardless of the conditions, before they attempt the hills we were cycling up, as they are in many other places in Oregon, Idaho and Montana. Even in the height of summer, it was bitterly cold. Despite wearing thick gloves, I could hardly feel my hands on the downhill runs. The typical damp fog that permeates the deciduous forests of the coastal range had not yet burnt off and I had to cycle in Scottish levels of winter clothing.

Our last campsite was at Clatskanie (pop. 1,528), birthplace, in 1938, of the novelist Raymond Carver and home to the Cultivator General Store which proved indeed that we were in Oregon. Here it wasn't eggs and hash browns, or biscuits and gravy, or pancakes and maple syrup, but organic vegetable soup, homemade bread and good strong coffee.

A typical lunch menu at the Cultivator General Store

- Tomato Florentine Soup w/salad and pesto bread;
- Polenta stacks of veggies and cheese with a roasted tomato sauce w/salad and pesto bread;
- Cultivator Roll Ups: collard green leaves with lemon hummus and all sorts of veggies served with a sesame shitake dripping sauce;
- Spinach salad tossed with marinated gigante beans, feta, cucumber, mushrooms, and balsamic w/salad and our pesto bread.

Cultivator General Store, Clatskanie

We pitched our tents in the City Park and stripped off our layers of clothing as the fog burnt away and the blistering sun came out again. It was a bittersweet afternoon. Tomorrow we would be at the Pacific and then disperse. There were mixed feelings. It was good to be within striking distance of our objective, but, after 44 days on the road together, life had become the camp routine, the relentless pursuit of each day's objective on the bicycle and the camaraderie of the group. Tonight, we would recognise this with a special meal of sockeye salmon, made by Sue and Kit in a fire pit. There would be no time for such thoughts tomorrow as the outside world would intrude at Seaside, in the form of meetings with children, unpacking the sag vans, claiming stuff better left behind, and making arrangements to get back to the airport at Portland. As the sun set, we retreated to our tents for the last time. Soon our happy evenings at the campsites, doing our chores and enjoying each other's company, would be no more than memories.

On 5th November 1805, the Corps of Discovery stopped at an island on the Columbia, which they named Deer Island. As well as dining on venison, they enjoyed a swan, several ducks and a brant (a small goose). They were probably feeling tired and somewhat miserable. The night before they had been serenaded non-stop "with a confusion of noises". This was the geese, swan-ducks and other wild fowl squawking incessantly. Then it had started to rain. They had broken camp and set off early, no doubt muttering evil thoughts about the birds in the same way that we had complained about the motorbikers at Lincoln. The next day they overtook some Indians in two canoes. One of the Indians spoke some English and told Lewis and Clark that they traded with a Mr Haley. That meant fur traders were around. They were near the coast.

On 7th November 1805, Clark recorded his thoughts at seeing the objective which they had worked so hard to achieve, the Pacific Ocean. "O! The Joy!," he wrote.[115] The celebrations were premature. It was not the "ocian", as Clark was said to have spelt it, but still the Columbia estuary and they had another 20 miles to go. They had to wait until 15th November to see the ocean proper, and endure, in the meantime, rain that soaked them through in their miserable camps on the banks of the Columbia. Then reaching open water, they established camp at Haley's Bay, named after the fur trader the Indians had told them about. After eleven days of solid rain, they were able to dry out their gear and equipment on 16th November, which was a fine and clear day.

It was not until 15th December 1805 that the Corps of Discovery decided upon the site of a permanent winter base. For this decision, even Sacagawea and York got a vote and the result was that the expedition established itself on what is now the Oregon side of the Columbia estuary. The men thought there was more game on the south side of the estuary. The spot they chose was relatively sheltered and it gave them easy access to the coast where they could make enough salt to last them over the winter. It was to this salt-making place on the coast, present day Seaside, Oregon, that we were headed, on the last day of our Tour of Discovery, as it marks the official end of the Lewis and Clark Trail.

Lewis and Clark at the mouth of the Columbia River

We set off early to cycle our final 62 miles, braving a horrible hill out of Clatskanie as our first test of endurance. We cycled as quickly as possible, in order to keep warm and made our way to Astoria, Oregon, near the mouth of the Columbia, where we rendezvoused at the Pig n' Pancake for food. This town (pop. 9,813) was founded as Fort Astoria in 1811 and named after Jacob Astor who owned the Pacific Fur Company. It was the first permanent United States settlement on the Pacific Coast, even though it did not remain in American hands for very long. In 1812, a nasty little war erupted between Britain and the United States. Those in Fort Astoria knew that the British had the upper hand on the Oregon coast by virtue of their superior sea power and feared that it would not be too long before the British seized the fort. While the going was good, they decided to sell out to the British, in the form of the North West Company. The negotiations took some time, with the Americans no doubt keeping an eye out to sea for British warships. Before the deal was done, they received a visit from David Thompson, the man who had tried to persuade the Nez Perce to take up trapping. He seems to have had a talent for misunderstanding. He was convinced that the North West Company already had a stake in the American operation. Indeed, like Chamberlain, he had a piece of paper in his pocket telling him so. But the Americans knew that there had, as yet, been no such deal. They played along with him, weighing up whether he was friend or foe. In the end, in 1813, the Americans sold the fort and its contents to the British for what they could get, which was less than the value of the furs inside. The British later took the fort and renamed it Fort George.

There was more to the War of 1812 than mere squabbles amongst fur traders on the Pacific Coast. Little is a comparative term, too, as the hostilities were fought at sea in the Atlantic Ocean and all over the American continent. War was, in fact, declared by the United States, a brave thing to do as it was a puny nation at the time. However, it was extremely irritated with the power from which it had broken free.

Britain, thinking of itself as 'best of breed', had told the United States that it could not trade with France. That must have been annoying to the Americans. It also thought Americans should work on British ships to make up for labour shortages. When Americans exhibited some reluctance to sign up for service, the British just went ahead and forcibly took them from captured American ships anyway. That made the Americans even more unhappy. Most of all, the British thought that the Americans were getting a bit too uppity with all this talk of creating a nation from sea to sea. They made sure that if there was any friction between the United States and the Indians, they were going to be right in there fermenting it. That really distressed the Americans. They felt they had a right to a country which extended from the Atlantic to the Pacific. No one was going to get in their way. And who started it all off? Jefferson. How different things would have been had he stuck to his vegetables and his manure.

William Clark also got involved in the war. His job was to move up the Mississippi into what is present day Wisconsin and establish Fort Shelby as a bulwark against British attack from the north. He failed. The British captured the post and promptly renamed it Fort McKay.

As usual, the conflict ended in a tiresome treaty, this time signed in Ghent. It was all very boring for the British who, despite having burnt down the White House in 1814, had so many other things on their minds that the war with the United States barely registered on their radar. The Americans, however, regarded it as a home victory, even though they were left with exactly the same territory they had when the war began. It did perhaps show that the Americans could flex their muscles when necessary. It probably made them feel more like equals when they sat down with the British to agree joint occupation of Oregon territory in 1818 and 1846.

Fort Clatsop and Salt

Fort Clatsop, the winter quarters of the Lewis and Clark expedition on the Pacific and our diversion on the last day to Seaside, is tucked away south of the Columbia River estuary. It sits on a tributary of the Columbia which in 1805 was called the Netul and is now the Lewis and Clark River.

It took the Corps of Discovery over three weeks to build the original fort; the construction of which was carried out in the almost continuous rain, for which the Pacific Coast is renowned in the winter. They moved into it on Christmas Day 1805. Clark records that firearms were discharged and a song sung by the men to celebrate the occasion. They divided their remaining tobacco, which amounted to "twelve carrots" (probably about 36 lbs) into two parts. Those who smoked got a share and those who did not received a present of a handkerchief. It was so wet that they stayed inside and picked on what was left of an elk. It was not in the best condition and they ate it only because they had to, no turkey or Christmas pudding being available.

Mosquitoes had plagued them for much of their journey and now, on the Pacific Coast, fleas tormented them. They had picked them up near Great Falls, when they had had to portage their equipment upstream, and the creatures had enjoyed a free ride to the ocean. There, they met their cousins, the Pacific fleas, who probably outdid them in nuisance value. Clark recorded that once these fleas took up residence in an Indian hut, they became the masters in it and it was impossible to expel them. In an attempt to get rid of the fleas, the Indians built second homes and moved out of the long huts to stay in them in order to get some relief. At Fort Clatsop, the members of the expedition had to search through their blankets for these pesky creatures every night before they attempted sleep.

What struck me about Fort Clatsop, which has been reconstructed by the National Parks Service, was how small it was. Two rows of huts faced onto a parade ground, only 20 feet by 48 feet. There was one room fitted out with a double bed, occupied that winter by Charbonneau, Sacagawea and Pomp. Lewis and Clark probably had rooms next to them. On the other side of the parade ground, the men bunked up in the rest of the huts. How cooped up they must have felt in their cramped quarters in the trees near the Netul River, especially as it rained for 94 out of the 106 days they occupied the Fort.[116]

It must have been some comfort that the local Clatsop Indians were friendly. Their name meant 'dried salmon', but the expedition had little appetite for salmon, having suffered from eating rotten salmon in what is present day Idaho. They preferred dog. In any event, they were there at the wrong time of year for fresh salmon and no doubt they could not face the dried variety. They existed by killing elk and deer and eating wapato, a tuber known as Indian potato. They also had some berries and tried whale blubber, which, as Clark recorded, was "esteemed by the Indians as an excellent food".[117] It looked like pork and tasted like beaver. By now Clark had overcome his initial aversion to dog, which was just as well as the men clamoured for it. The Indians were happy to oblige in providing dogs and Clark noted that when the members of the expedition subsisted on it, they were "fatter and stronger"[118] and healthier than at any time since leaving the home of the buffalo east of the Rocky Mountains.

Jefferson had thought, optimistically, that Lewis and Clark would find a huge mountain of salt on the journey up the Missouri. He was to be disappointed and, after news of the safe return of the expedition reached the east coast, he was derided for his foolishness in a Massachusetts newspaper which dug up this early prediction. He was not wrong to be preoccupied with salt though.

Salt was essential for the preservation of meat, although some craved it more than others; Clark being one who could take it or leave it. As Fort Clatsop was not on the ocean, it was necessary for men to be sent to the open sea to find a place where they could make salt. Five men were dispatched. They were away for so long, the rest of the expedition wondered where they had got to, but then two returned. They explained that they had gone to the mouth of the Columbia and then some distance southwards, before they found somewhere suitable for salt production.

This was present day Seaside. The Indians were friendly there and good salt was capable of being produced. The two men who returned brought back a gallon of white, fine, salt. It was also these men who introduced the Corps of Discovery to whale blubber, as the Indians at the coast had given them some as a gift. Clark determined to set off for the salt camp at the ocean to see what it was like there for himself. He ordered canoes to be made ready and men prepared for the trip. At this point Sacagawea spoke up. I can almost see her pout, stamp her foot and cry out, "It's not fair. What about me?"

She had not, she said, come all this way only to be denied, now, the opportunity of seeing the great ocean. And furthermore, with all this talk of a whale, why shouldn't she see it too?

Sacagawea and Pomp

Lewis recorded that the request was a reasonable one and it was hard that she should not "see the ocean or the whale".[119] So she, her husband, Charbonneau and, no doubt Pomp, too, set off with Clark and twelve men for the coast. By the time they got there, most of the whale had gone, but the salt party stayed, living in tents and producing a gallon of salt a day, by boiling forty gallons of seawater in five kettles on top of a stone oven. It was backbreaking work, made more difficult by exposure to the full force of the ocean. It nearly broke some of the men, who laboured there until 20th February 1806, by which time they had roughly 28 gallons of salt. They then went back to Fort Clatsop, from where the whole expedition left on 23rd March to make its way back to St. Louis. Before he left, Lewis made the list of all those on the expedition and left it there for posterity.

Fort Clatsop is a tourist attraction. I felt as I always did on the Tour of Discovery when we interacted with the real world of families and their vehicles, sanitised history in the form of displays and films and, of course, the ubiquitous gift shop. Naturally, there was no tea room at Fort Clatsop where I could contemplate the fact that we only had fifteen or so miles to go. Soon it would all be over. On the way out of the fort, I looked at the statue of Sacagawea carrying Pomp on her back and thought, "Good on you, girl. I don't know how you did it". I was glad that, along with York, she had posthumously been made an honorary sergeant in the Corps of Discovery by President Clinton shortly before he left office.

In comparison with this young Shoshone Indian girl, I was truly a weakling. Her life of hardship and endurance was to continue. In 1806, she and her family returned to the Mandan Villages with the Corps of Discovery. Clark had obviously taken a shine to Pomp and asked his parents whether he could take him to St. Louis and bring him up as his own. He was too young to leave his mother, Charbonneau told Clark. But three years later, the whole family moved to St. Louis. When his parents decided they were tired of city life and longed for open spaces again, Pomp was left with Clark. Clark arranged for Charbonneau and Sacagawea to settle at Fort Manuel, near present day Mobridge, South Dakota, and procured employment for Charbonneau as an interpreter. There Sacagawea gave birth to a daughter, Lisette.[120]

Sacagawea died in 1814 and Clark legally adopted Pomp and his sister after it was feared Charbonneau had been killed when away from the fort on a trading expedition. In fact, the old rogue was alive and kicking and lived for 30 more years, and had had five wives in all to his name when he died. But by the time they found out he was alive, Pomp was well established in St. Louis with Clark and was enjoying himself in the way only Jefferson knew how, by learning Latin and Greek. He now answered to Baptiste, having been formally named Jean Baptiste when his mother gave birth to him in the Mandan Village. His days as Pomp were over.

For someone who was born in an Indian tent, Baptiste Charbonneau was to go on to keep exalted company. The boy who had journeyed to the Pacific on his mother's back now came across the Duke of Württemberg who was touring Kansas along with other members of European titled households. Baptiste returned to Europe with the Duke and lived there for six years, travelling with him throughout Europe and North Africa. He could already speak French and English and he added German and Spanish to his repertoire.

Perhaps there was something about his early life on the Lewis and Clark expedition that called him back to the wilderness. Baptiste returned to St. Louis, signed up with the American Fur Company and spent the next few years trapping his way across the continent working for it and the Rocky Mountain Fur Company. But it was not just in European languages that Baptiste was fluent; the Indian languages came naturally to the son of a Shoshone and a French interpreter. He became a scout for the American army, protecting supplies and settlers on their way west by wagon train, and then, like a Viceroy, ran, on behalf of the United States, a tract of land in present day California, after the end of the Mexican-American War.

This was another tiresome conflict which had its roots in too many Americans wanting to live in Mexico, in a curious reversal of what is happening now on the border between the two countries. In those days, Mexico extended somewhat further north than it does now and included what is now Texas. In 1836, there were so many Americans in Texas, wanting to do their own thing, that they declared UDI and ran the place as an independent republic until Texas was admitted to the United States as the 28th State in 1845. Not surprisingly, admission to the Union heralded a crisis after a long period of ill-feeling and unhappiness. Bad feelings with Mexico had festered and had sometimes resulted in armed skirmishes. Now things were to come to a head. In 1846, the United States invaded more territory belonging to Mexico in what is now New Mexico and parts of California. As these things usually do, this conflict ended in one side paying off the other. The United States paid $18 million for the land, Mexico swallowed its pride and the Rio Grande became the border.

For Baptiste, it was now nearly 1848, a date synonymous with gold, and he joined the California gold rush. He made sufficient money to be able to boast that he was fed up of panning for gold and getting cold hands in running water. He changed tack and worked as a hotel manager in the gold fields until 1861 when, again, he answered the call of the wild and set off back east into the mountains. Who knows what he did then. Perhaps he followed the gold, or just responded to his wanderlust. Not much is known about him until five years later when, in what some think a re-run of what happened to Meriwether Lewis's father, he died from a bad case of the chills, or pneumonia. There is speculation that he, too, like Lewis' father, might have fallen from a horse into a river before taking ill. Little Pomp, Jean-Baptiste Charbonneau, died on 16th May 1866.[121]

O! The Joy!

Seaside (pop. 5,900) is where Portlanders go when it is too hot east of the Oregon Coastal Range. It has lost the lustre of its early days, when the women and children of Portland were sent there for the summer and they all turned out at the railroad station on a Friday evening to meet the 'Daddy train' from the city.[122] The trains are long gone and today, if you are not driving or cycling, you have to take a bus from Portland to visit this rundown resort, with its tacky gift shops, ice cream parlours and take-away food outlets.

Dundee's Donuts, Seaside

A block away from the centre of town though, is the old Seaside, along the Necanicum River, the first river we had seen for many miles that was not a tributary of the Columbia. This is the Seaside of fine old wooden houses, gardens running down to the riverbank and lazy afternoons in the sun on the front porch.

So down towards the ocean we rode, past Dooger's Seafood Bar and Grill, Dundee's Donuts, Norma's Ocean Diner and Sam's Seaside Café, to get to the official end of the Lewis and Clark trail, where Broadway meets the beach boardwalk and the Pacific Ocean. The route was such that the ocean was not visible until we reached the statue of Lewis and Clark with, of course, Seaman, the Newfoundland dog who went all the way to the Pacific and back. What happened to Seaman after the expedition no one knows.

Arrival at the Pacific

Suddenly there it was. As Clark had said, "O! The Joy!". But this was indeed the Pacific Ocean, not the Columbia estuary. The Pacific Ocean! Not a turbulent sea with waves crashing at our feet, but a thin blue-grey line, barely visible in the mist, far away over the long, flat, expanse of yellow sand which is the beach at Seaside.

Then, as if on cue, the sea mist swirled and lifted. As the sun came out and all the riders on the Tour of Discovery 2010 arrived one by one, the realisation that we had done it began to appear on our faces. It had been a wonderful ride in the footsteps of two great people in history, Meriwether Lewis and William Clark.

AFTERWORD

I had admired the *Journals of Meriwether Lewis and William Clark* before I signed up to cycle the Lewis and Clark Trail. By the time I got to the Pacific, I marvelled that Lewis and Clark had managed to write such substantial accounts on the go, and leave to us such a wealth of beautifully constructed and informative prose. I found it difficult, on the way to the Pacific, to write more than a few words in my notebook each evening and I had nothing to do and no responsibility. These two had to keep an expedition together for 7,689 miles, ensure food and provisions and keep everyone healthy; navigate a course, find new means of transport along the way, deal with indigenous peoples whose languages they did not speak, keep the peace with them, procure specimens to take home, record detailed observations and draw maps. How they had the tenacity to do this and to wait up night after night to take longitudinal measurements by the stars beats me.

William Clark, who died in 1838 at the age of 69, is buried in what is now Bellefontaine Cemetery in St. Louis, Missouri.

Meriwether Lewis, who met his end at Grinder's Stand, was buried nearby. A memorial erected by the State of Tennessee bears a Latin inscription which translates as:

I died before my time, but thou O great and good Republic, live out my years while you live out your own.

NOTE ON SKETCH MAPS, PHOTOGRAPHS AND ILLUSTRATIONS

Sketch Maps

The sketch maps in this book are the author's own work. They are not to scale.

Photographs

The photograph 'A director of the Alliance Trust sits amongst the cowhands' and 'William Reid' are reproduced by kind permission of Alliance Trust PLC, 8 West Marketgait, Dundee DD1 1QN.

The photograph entitled 'Mother receiving wisdom from Mrs. Hubbell' is the property of Alison Russell.

Other photographs and illustrations

The line drawings are © 2012 June Coveney

All photographs, unless otherwise stated, ©2012 Sheila Ruckley

Due to book size limitations, it was not possible to include all the images taken on the Tour of Discovery. To view the complete set of photos, please visit www.historyonabike.co.uk

The prints/photographs of Thomas Jefferson, Meriwether Lewis, William Clark, Dred Scott, John Brown holding hostages inside the Armory at Harper's Ferry, Henry Ward Beecher, Lewis and Clark holding a council with the Indians, Elizabeth Custer with her husband and brother, Sitting Bull with his nephew, One Bull and Lewis and Clark at the mouth of the Columbia River have all been downloaded from the US Library of Congress website www.loc.gov and are in the public domain as the copyright has expired. (PDUS). Full attribution is given below.

Thomas Jefferson

Thomas Jefferson, 3rd President of the United States / on stone by A. Newsam; P.S. Duval Lith., Philadelphia
Library of Congress Prints and Photographs Division Washington, D.C. 20540 USA http://hdl.loc.gov/loc.pnp/pp.print
http://www.loc.gov/pictures/item/2009631979/

Meriwether Lewis

Meriwether Lewis. Portrait, bust, facing left. Reproduction of painting by C.W. Peale in Independence Hall, Philadelphia, Pa.
Library of Congress Prints and Photographs Division Washington, D.C. 20540 USA
http://www.loc.gov/pictures/item/2004672073/

William Clark

William Clark. Portrait, bust, facing right.
Library of Congress Prints and Photographs Division Washington, D.C. 20540 USA.
http://www.loc.gov/pictures/item/2004671922/

Dred Scott

Dred Scott. Portrait, bust, facing left. Wood engraving in 'Century Magazine', 1887.
Library of Congress Prints and Photographs Division Washington, D.C. 20540 USA
http://www.loc.gov/pictures/item/2004672784/

John Brown holds hostages inside the Armory at Harper's Ferry

Harper's Ferry insurrection – Interior of the Engine-House, just before the gate is broken down by the storming party – Col. Washington and his associates as captives, held by Brown as hostages.
1859 print: wood engraving. Illus. in: Frank Leslie's illustrated newspaper, v. 8, no. 205 (1859 Nov. 5), p. 359.
Library of Congress Prints and Photographs Division Washington, D.C. 20540 USA
http://www.loc.gov/pictures/item/2002735881/

Henry Ward Beecher

Henry Ward Beecher. Three-quarter length portrait, standing next to table, facing front, holding paper in right hand] / painted by T. Hicks, N.A.; engraved by J.C. McRae, N.Y.

New York: Published by J.C. McRae, c1853 Nov. 1st (Printed by H. Peters)
Library of Congress Prints and Photographs Division Washington, D.C. 20540 USA
http://www.loc.gov/pictures/item/2004670117/

Lewis and Clark holding a council with the Indians

Lewis and Clark holding a council with the Indians. Philadelphia: printed for Matthew Carey, 1810. Illus. in: a journal of the voyages and travels of a corps of discovery: under the command of Capt. Lewis and Capt. Clarke of the Army of the United States [...] during the years 1804, 1805 and 1806 [...] by Patrick Gass. Philadelphia: printed for Matthew Carey, 1810, p. 26.
Library of Congress Washington, D.C. 20540 USA. Illus. in F592.5 .G2 [General Collections]
http://www.loc.gov/pictures/item/2001699652/

Elizabeth Custer with her husband, George Armstrong Custer (seated) and his brother

George Armstrong Custer, in uniform, seated with his wife, Elizabeth "Libbie" Bacon Custer, and his brother, Thomas W. Custer, standing.
Photographed between ca. 1864 and 1870, printed later.
US National Archives no. B-1923. Print made in 1960s(?) from the glass negative at the US National Archives.
http://www.loc.gov/pictures/item/95512236/

Sitting Bull and his nephew, One Bull

Sitting Bull and nephew, One Bull. 1 photographic print on card mount: albumen. Palmquist & Jurgens, photographer. St. Paul, Minn.: Palmquist & Jurgens, c1884.
Library of Congress Prints and Photographs Division Washington, D.C. 20540 USA
http://www.loc.gov/pictures/item/99402370/

Lewis and Clark at the mouth of the Columbia River

Lewis and Clark at the mouth of the Columbia River. 1805. Created/published 1906. Halftone repro. of drawing by Frederic Remington in Collier's Magazine, 1906 May 12.
Library of Congress Prints and Photographs Division Washington, D.C. 20540 USA.
http://www.loc.gov/pictures/item/2006683399/
The prints of Alexander Hamilton and Aaron Burr have been downloaded from the relevant Wikipedia article on these men. Full attribution is given below.

Alexander Hamilton

Portrait of Alexander Hamilton by John Trumbull, 1806.
Washington University Law School
This is a faithful photographic reproduction of an original two-dimensional work of art. This work is in the public domain in the United States, and those countries with a copyright term of life of the author plus 100 years or fewer. PD-US.

Aaron Burr

Portrait of Aaron Burr, 1802 by John Vanderlyn (1775-1852)
http://www.alexanderhamiltonexhibition.org/about/pop_preview/downloads/A107_BurrPortrait_1931_58.jpg
This is a faithful photographic reproduction of an original two-dimensional work of art. The work of art itself is in the public domain because the copyright has expired. PD-US.

SOURCES

In this book, I have attempted to use sources which are accessible to any reader, so that anyone who is interested in finding out more about Lewis and Clark suffers no impediment in doing so. *The Journals of Lewis and Clark* and Stephen Ambrose's book, *Undaunted Courage*, both of which are detailed below in the source notes, are the obvious starting points.

These websites also provide a wealth of information, often with links to maps and other primary source material:

"Lewis and Clark Trail" at www.lewisandclarktrail.com is a mine of information and contains a first class, informative timeline of the expedition.

"Discovering Lewis and Clark" at http://lewis-clark.org is the website of the Lewis and Clark Fort Mandan Association of Washburn, North Dakota

"Lewis and Clark Expedition. A National Register of Historic Places Travel Itinerary" is part of the National Park Services Website, which as well as containing information about the expedition itself, has links to many other websites about it. www.nps.org/nr/travel.lewisandclark/learnmore.htm

"Lewis and Clark. Corps of Discovery" at www.history.army.mil/ls is the website of the US Army Center of Military History.

In obtaining information about the various small towns we cycled through on the way to the Pacific, I have used information on the website of each relevant town where possible, although there is often a dearth of historical information. I have also used the relevant pages from Wikipedia which, generally, has information about every American town in standard form, with links to the census and other official government statistics.

END NOTES

CHAPTER ONE

1   Unstead, R.J., *People in History*. (London: A. and C. Black. Ltd., 1957)

2   *Ibid.*, p.281.

3   *Ibid.*, p.502.

4   *Ibid.*, p.56.

5   *Ibid.*, p.201.

6   *Ibid.*, p.202.

7   *Ibid.*, p.60.

8   *Ibid.*, p.146.

9   *Ibid.*, p.291.

10 *Ibid.*, p.297.

11 *Ibid.*, p. 371.

12 Elton, G.R., *Reformation Europe 1517-1559*, (Glasgow: Fontana Books William Collins Sons & Co. September 1963) p.35.

13 *Ibid.*, pp. 36,37.

14 This information is from *U.S. News and World Report* and appears on Wellesley's own website *www.wellesley.edu*

15 On board the Arbella, John Winthrop began to write a diary which is now available in Google books. The edition is that published by the President and Fellows of Harvard College and Massachusetts Historical Society 1996.

16 A full account of the trial of Sacco and Vanzetti can be found in the Famous American Trials series published by the University of Missouri-Kansas City at www.umkc.edu/famoustrials

17 For a brief history of the life of William Penn see the entry at www.ushistory. org

CHAPTER TWO

18 My edition of the *The Journals of Lewis and Clark* is that in two volumes published by The Heritage Press, New York, edited by Nicholas Biddle with an introduction by John Bakeless. The special contents of this edition are copyright © 1962 by The George Macy Companies, Inc. There are numerous editions available in print and online, including a paperback in the National Geographic Adventure Classics series and one produced by Penguin in the Penguin Nature Classics series. The University of Nebraska at Lincoln has also put them online on an excellent website www.lewisandclarkjournals.unl.edu/index.htm

19 The best, easy to understand, visual description of the political geography of the United States that I have been able to find is on Wikipedia under '*Territorial Evolution of the United States*'. On this site, numerous maps illustrate the progression of the nation. The map in the text is a rough sketch map I drew myself after a friend told me she could not visualise the information in the text.

20 For a short biography of Thomas Jefferson and other American Presidents, see the official website of the White House: www.whitehouse.gov. See also www.monticello.org which has more extensive information about Jefferson and his times.

21 See the entry for Alexander Hamilton at www.pbs.org and numerous articles on the internet about the scandal involving Maria Reynolds. One of the most entertaining books about Aaron Burr, albeit classed as a novel is *Burr* by Gore Vidal (Vintage, First International Edition, February 2000)

22 The New York Historical Society has a website about Alexander Hamilton www.alexanderhamiltonexhibition.org and an article about the Reynolds affair by Robert C. Albert can be found at www.americanheritage.com

23 The website of the US Bureau of Engraving and printing www.moneyfactory.gov gives interesting information about US currency including the fact that there are two pictures of Alexander Hamilton on the $10 bill, one being a watermark which can be seen from both sides of the note.

24 For a list of states by date of admission to the Union, see www.americanhistory.about.com

25 Yale Law School has made available documents relating to the Louisiana Purchase online as part of *The Avalon Project, Documents in Law, History and Diplomacy*. These may be found at http://avalon.law.yale.edu

26 A picture of a model of the *Columbia Rediviva* may be found at www.lewis-clark.org

27 For the most entertaining and gripping account of the life of Meriwether Lewis and the Lewis and Clark Expedition, *Undaunted Courage* by Stephen Ambrose, first published in 1996, is a must. My edition was published by Pocket Books in 2003. It is also available from iTunes as an audio book.

28 See the brief biography of William Small on the website of the College of William and Mary www.wm.edu. Small Hall, named after him, now houses the physics department at the university.

29 www.monticello.org contains mountains of information about the house and its owner.

30 Hailman, John, *Thomas Jefferson on Wine*. University of Mississippi Press 2010

31 See the quotations section of the John F. Kennedy Presidential Library and Museum website at www.jfklibrary.org

32 A detailed but accessible account of the Whiskey Rebellion may be found at www.ttb.gov/public_info/whiskey_rebellion on the website of the US Department of Treasury, Alcohol and Tobacco Tax Trade Bureau

33 Hickman, Kennedy, *American Revolution: Major General Anthony Wayne* at www.militaryhistory.about.com

34 *The Journals of Lewis and Clark, op.cit.,*Vol.1, p.xxi.

CHAPTER THREE

35 The Wikipedia entry on Lewis and Clark refers to a collection of essays which, *inter alia*, discusses this point: Ronda, James P., (editor) *Voyages of Discovery: essays on the Lewis and Clark Expedition*. The University of Montana Press in 1998

36 Another book by Stephen Ambrose, *Nothing like it in the World: The Men Who Built the Railway that United America*, published by Pocket Books September 2005, is a gripping account of this enterprise.

37 The most recent history of the Alliance Trust is *Alliance Trust: A Short History 1888-2008* by Professor Charles W. Munn, OBE, FCIBS, University of Dundee

38 See the history of the ranch on the website of the Texas State Historical Association www.tshonline.org

39 Gray, Taylor Austin, *"Geothermal Resource Assessment of the Gueydan Salt Dome and the Adjacent Southeast Gueyden Field, Vermilion Parish, Louisiana"*. This is a thesis submitted to the Graduate Faculty of the Louisiana State University and the Agricultural and Mechanical College in partial fulfilment of the requirements for the degree of Master of Science in the Department of Geology and Geophysics. Texas A&M University 2007: August 2010

40 Information about Reid is taken from a document in the library of the Oregon Historical Society called *Biographical Sketch of William Reid's Career*, from a book by the same author, Hon. H.W. Scott, entitled *The History of Portland, Oregon, U.S.A.*. Syracuse, New York : D. Mason & Co. 1890

41 From *'The Feud between Lords Airlie and Argyle' in 'The Scottish Wars'* at www.electricscotland.com

42   This quotation appears in all the histories of the Alliance Trust including the most recent by Professor Charles W. Munn, *op. cit.*

43   Hilton, George Woodman, *American Narrow Gauge Railroads* Stanford University Press 1990. See also *History of the Narrow Gauge Railroad in the Willamette Valley* by Leslie M. Scott, published by The Quarterly of the Oregon Historical Society Volume XX June 1919 Number 2 which is available at www.gesswhoto.com .For date of death of the Earl of Airlie see www.thepeerage.com

CHAPTER FOUR

44   *The Journals of Lewis and Clark, op.cit.,* Vol. 1, p.2.

45   Waiting for the rain to stop at Fort Osage in Missouri, I attended a talk on the history of the flag of the United States. See also www.usa-flag-site.org

46   A replica may be seen at the Lewis and Clark Interpretive Centre in Nebraska City

47   "The Touring Cyclist" at 11816 St. Charles Rock Road, Bridgeton, MO 63044

48   The 14th Amendment to the Constitution was passed in 1868 to rectify the injustice of the Dred Scott decision. It provides in Section 1 that "All persons born or naturalised in the United States, and subject to the jurisdiction thereof, are citizens of the United States and of the state in which they reside". For details of the progression of the case see The Oyez Project by Chicago-Kent College of Law : *Dred Scott v. Sandford*, 60 U.S. 393 (1857) available at www.oyez.org/cases/1851-1900/1856/1856_0

49   In January 2011, the City of St. Louis announced that it would allow the homeless to continue to live at Hopeville and also gave permission for them to use propane heaters to keep warm in the winter. This was provided the homeless "don't bother themselves or others, and as long as public safety and public health are not put at jeopardy". However, in September 2011, the city announced its intention to close the camp by 1 December 2011. See reports at www.stltoday.com for 21 January and 22 September 2011

CHAPTER FIVE

50   Dillon, Richard , *Meriwether Lewis: A Biography.* July 2003 : Great West Books, 2nd Edition

51   "The Columbian" 19 January 2001. See www.columbian.com/history/lewis-and-clark

CHAPTER SIX

52   Information taken from the Wikipedia article on William Crush.

53   Date from www.weatherunderground.com

54 *Independent* newspaper 14 November 2002

55 www.lionsclubs.org

56 As told to the members of the Tour of Discovery by the Mayor of Lexington, MO. Wikipedia has lots of information about the Battles of Lexington.

57 *The Journals of Lewis and Clark*, op.cit.,Vol.1, p.8

58 www.fortosagenhs.org

59 Website of The Science and Mathematics Teaching Centre, University of Wyoming. www.wsgs.uwyo.edu

60 *The New York Times* : 13 June 2010

61 Historic Resource Study on the Pony Express www.nps.gov

62 Richard Burton, (1862) *The Look of the West 1860,* (Lincoln: Univ. Nebraska Press, reprint, n.d.,) p.23.

63 *Our History* section of the website of Plymouth Church of the Pilgrims in Brooklyn Heights. www.plymouthchurch.org

CHAPTER SEVEN

64 Information about the tribe may be found at www.winnebagotribe.com

65 *The Journals of Lewis and Clark, op.cit.*,Vol 1, p.29

66 *Ibid.*

67 www.citydata.com

68 www.waymarking.com

69 Further information may be found at www.stjo.org

70 See the article on John "Scotty" Philips on Wikipedia.

71 See the *Memorandum submitted by Glasgow City Council to the UK Parliamentary Select Committee on Culture, Media and Sport* which may be found at http://www.publications.parliament.uk/pa/cm199900/cmselect/cmcumeds/371/0051808.htm

72 See the document available from the House of Commons Information office called "House of Commons Green". It is available at www.parliament.uk/factsheets

73 The website of South Dakota Game, Fish and Parks www.gfp.sd.gov

74 Details of this carrot can be found in Fur Trade Stories which is a web-based presentation from the collections of Canada's National History Society, HBCA – Archives of Manitoba, The Manitoba Museum, Parks Canada and several First Nation communities. It can be found at www.furtradestories.ca

75 *The Journals of Lewis and Clark, op.cit.,* Vol 1.,p 53

CHAPTER EIGHT

76 See Wikipedia entry on Gettysburg, South Dakota

77 See Wikipedia entry on the WPA

78 For more information about Oscar Howe see the website of the Oscar Howe Memorial Association www.oscarhowe.org

79 See Wikipedia articles on Aberdeen, SD and L. Frank Baum

80 Norris, K., *Dakota: A Spiritual Biography (New York, Houghton Mifflin Company, 2003), p. 150*

81 Custer, Elizabeth B., *Boots and Saddles or Life in Dakota with General Custer.* Harper& Brothers: 1885 This is available on Amazon in an edition published by the University of Oklahoma in 1961 but a free edition is available for download in Kindle books. The quotes on this page are from this edition.

82 There is masses of information about Zip to Zap on the internet. I have relied on information in *Prairie Murders* by Robert Dodge, published by North Start Pr. of St. Cloud in 2009, which is an excellent read.

83 Website of the USGS www.usgs.gov

84 The Bakken Formation Information Resource http://thebakkenformation.com

85 *Bakken Watch. Keeping an eye on oil and natural gas development in North Dakota* at http://bakkenwatch.blogspot.com

86 An article in the *Guardian* newspaper on 1 March 2011 pointed out that the US energy firm carrying out the fracking tests would only be required to disclose the composition of the liquid in 2015. Operations at this site in Lancashire were suspended after indications that they may have resulted in two small earthquakes (see the report in the *Financial Times* 1 June 2011)

CHAPTER NINE

87 Norris, K., *op. cit.*, pp. 151,152

88 See the *Report to the Shareholders of Berkshire Hathaway Inc. 2010* which is available at www.berkshirehathaway.com/letters/2010ltr.pdf

89 See the Wikipedia entries for Malta and Saco

90 US Government National Weather Service : www.weather.gov

91 This story is from C.M. Russell's own account of the background to *Waiting for the Chinook*. It is on the website of the Cattlemen's Texas Longhorn Conservancy at http://www.ctlc.org/Last of the 5000.pdf

CHAPTER TEN

92 The lowest temperature in any of the states was recorded in Alaska in January 1971 as minus 80°F. See www.currentresults.com

93 See *Six ads that changed the way you think* by Kate Connelly. BBC News 3 January 2011

94 See www.davidsonlegacy.com

95 www.northwest-national.com. The original cabin is on display in Washington, D.C. See www.newseum.org

96 See www.ovandomontana.net

97 See *State v. Stanko No.97-486 Argued Oct.14,1998-December 23,1998* on www.FindLaw.com

98 *The Journals of Lewis and Clark, op.cit.*, Vol. 2, p. 272

99 This recipe is taken from *The Book of Household Management* by Mrs Isabella Mary Beeton 1836-1865. Kindle Edition.

100 Information from www.montanaplant-life.org

101 National Parks Service www.nps.gov

102 US Forest Service www.fs.fed.us

103 *The Journals of Lewis and Clark, op.cit.*, Vol. 2,p. 278.

104 See the article on Chief Joseph in *New Perspectives on the West* at www.pbs.org

105 The Kooskia Internment Camp Archaeological Project www.uidaho.edu

106 Information from *The Spokesman-Review* for 15 December 2011. www.spokesman.com

107 Nokes, R. Gregory, *Massacred for Gold, The Chinese in Hells Canyon* October 2009: Oregon State University Press. A shorter article by the same author is available in The Oregon Encyclopedia at www.oregonencyclopedia.org

CHAPTER ELEVEN

108 US Army Chemical Materials Agency www.cma.army.mil

109 Haberkorn v. Commissioner,75 T.C. 259 (Nov 12,1980 filed)

110 *The Journals of Lewis and Clark, op.cit.*, Vol. 2, p. 295.

111 More information about McLoughlin is available at www.bluebook.state.or.us

112 See the section on the history of the highway on www.columbiariverhighway.com

113   See the entry for Viento State Park at www.oregonstateparks.org

114   For more detail on this legend see www.portofcascadelocks.org

115   My editions of *The Journals of Lewis and Clark* do not actually record this. Instead, the entry for the day, in Vol.2, page 318, says " ... that ocean, the object of all our labour, the reward of all our anxieties", O! The Joy!, however, is what everyone refers to as Clark's words as they may appear in another edition of the journals.

116   Website of the National Park Service www.nps.gov

117   *The Journals of Lewis and Clark, op.cit.,* Vol. 2, p.350.

118   *Ibid.,*

119   *Ibid.,* Vol. 2,p. 351.

120   See the entry for Sacagawea on www.pbs.org/lewisandclark/inside/saca. html

121   See the entry for Jean Baptiste Charbonneau at www.pbs.org/lewisandclark/ inside/char.html

122   See www.seasidemuseum.org